跟雅思考官
Simon
学阅读 2.0

王辰雨　主编

北京理工大学出版社
BEIJING INSTITUTE OF TECHNOLOGY PRESS

图书在版编目（CIP）数据

跟雅思考官 Simon 学阅读 2.0 / 王辰雨主编 . -- 北京：
北京理工大学出版社 , 2022.10
ISBN 978-7-5763-1747-3

Ⅰ . ①跟… Ⅱ . ①王… Ⅲ . ① IELTS －阅读教学－自
学参考资料 Ⅳ . ① H319.4

中国版本图书馆 CIP 数据核字 (2022) 第 185696 号

出版发行 / 北京理工大学出版社有限责任公司
社　　　址 / 北京市海淀区中关村南大街 5 号
邮　　　编 / 100081
电　　　话 / （010）68914775（总编室）
　　　　　　（010）82562903（教材售后服务热线）
　　　　　　（010）68944723（其他图书服务热线）
印　　　刷 / 三河市京兰印务有限公司
开　　　本 / 889 毫米 ×1194 毫米　1/16
印　　　张 / 15.25
字　　　数 / 376 千字
版　　　次 / 2022 年 10 月第 1 版　2022 年 10 月第 1 次印刷
定　　　价 / 79.00 元

责任编辑 / 王梦春
文案编辑 / 把明宇
责任校对 / 周瑞红
责任印制 / 李志强

目录
contents

雅思阅读，通常是中国考生比较擅长的科目，因为无论是题型还是科目都是我们从小到大比较熟悉的。总结一下这几年来学生在阅读上所遇到的困难，主要有以下几点：

看不懂，即文章中大量生词影响对句意表达的理解。我想这个问题困扰了很多雅思分数在5.5分或以下的学生。在这本《跟雅思考官Simon学阅读2.0》中，Simon老师在不断重复一个简单的事实：阅读考试其实是词汇测试，题型只是外衣。无论何种雅思题型，本质上其实都是考察对原文的理解，笔者曾经将雅思阅读题目拿给从未了解过雅思考试的国内专八学生和海外学生，他们都能获得8分以上的分数，原因就是具备足够的词汇量。下面是Simon老师关于阅读考试词汇重要性介绍视频。

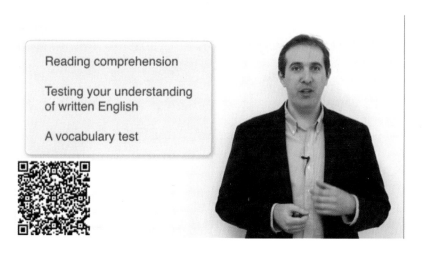

（扫描图片上的二维码收看视频）

当你解决了词汇的问题，进入到刷题的第二层境界，通常会遇到一个普遍的问题：读不完。单词都认识，但句子一长就摸不着头脑了，通常无法在有效的60分钟内完成三篇文章的阅读与答题。为什么英文句子一长就会跟丢？其实是对英文句法结构熟悉程度不够，说得通俗一点，汉语长难句从来不会难倒你是因为你一直沉浸在这样的语言环境中，习惯成自然。笔者亲身体会，如果在国外待五年以上再阅读中文，经常会出现跟丢的情况，但回国一段时间之后便能适应。在本书中，Simon老师一直建议大家除了雅思阅读真题之外，需要增加一些自己感兴趣的阅读素材，增加更多的语言输入。本书在部分题目后配有延伸阅读，就是为了达到这个目的。（如下。）

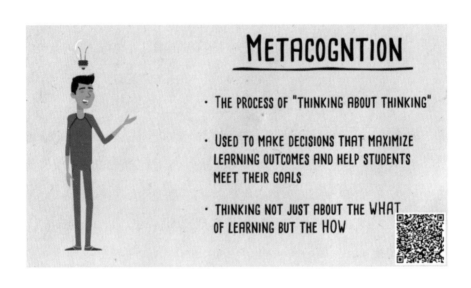

接着你会进入刷题的第三层境界，遇到另一个大BOSS：解不出。具体地说，对于标题配对题，即使读懂了全段也无法做出正确的匹配，而对于判断题，通常存在逻辑误区，导致无法做对。在本书中，我们将题型分类，将原文掐头去尾，尽量缩减理解部分，只考察方法。同时按照难度梯度排列，循序渐进，逐步提升正确率。每道题都有详尽的解析，不仅告诉你正确选项为什么对，也会解释错误选项为什么错。

完成了上述三个步骤，雅思阅读的能力就真正上了一层楼，笔者的另外一本书《雅思阅读真题还原2.0》比较适合作为检验工具。该书收集历年阅读考场真题，原文、原题都做了最大程度的还原。阅读一定是需要大量练习的一个科目，所有的错题也要进行归纳和整理。可以像这样制作一个表格：

题型：	错题来源：
□ 选择题	题干：
□ 总结 / 填空题	
□ 判断题	
□ 信息配对题	
□ 段落大意题	阅读原文：
□ 其他题型	
错因归类：	
□ 单词不认识	正确答案 & 解析：
□ 听力 / 原文不理解	
□ 题干读不懂	
□ 信号词没找到	
□ 同替没找对 / 识别	
□ 其他原因	

（该表格来自《雅思效率笔记本》）

及时对自己的错因进行归纳，我们需要刷题的数量，更需要刷题的质量。

本书从考生的几大弊病出发，侧重于方法的讲授，同学们先通过《鸭圈雅思真题词2.0》积累词汇，再通过《跟雅思考官Simon学阅读2.0》学习方法，最后用《雅思阅读真题还原2.0》刷题，这也是鸭圈雅思陪考营过去三年学生的学习方法，十分有效。最后，笔者能力有限，本书不足之处，还请读者通过鸭圈雅思公众账号与我们交流。

鸭圈雅思教研组 王辰雨

2022.6

关键词技巧

接下来要给大家讲解一下阅读考试中最重要的一个技巧：关键词技巧（**keyword technique**），这个技巧会贯穿所有阅读题型，是同学们必须掌握技能。这边结合一道例题给大家讲解一下。

当我们拿到一篇阅读题目时，首先不是阅读文章，而是看题干，划出题干中的关键词。

Pasteur is famous for .... a process to make milk and wine safe for consumption.

我划出了Pasteur，famous for...a process和milk and wine；Pasteur，这是一个人名，是一个专有名词，由于它无法替换，所以特别适合在原文中定位；接着是famous for...a process，最后是milk and wine。接着我们回到原文，按照正常速度去阅读，希冀找到关键词或关键词的同义词，如果找到，说明我们找到了出题点。

Louis Pasteur was a French chemist and microbiologist who is remembered for his remarkable breakthroughs in understanding and preventing diseases. He is best known to the general public for inventing a method to stop milk and wine from causing sickness. This method came to be called pasteurisation.

在这句话中我发现了Pasteur和milk and wine，说明答案就在其间。然后我们仔细阅读，发现原文的best known to the general public for和a method是题干中famous for和a process的同义词，这样就确定了答案就是inventing。

做完一整道题之后，我们还会列如下表格，将题干中的关键词和原文中的同义词（组）进行整理：

题干中的关键词	原文中的同义词
Pasteur	Pasteur
milk and wine	milk and wine

famous for	best known to the public for
a process	a method
make safe for consumption	stop from causing sickness

当然，咱们只是在练习时这么做，考试时是不需要的。如果你持续不断地这样练习，阅读分数会很快提升。其实这个方法并不是Simon老师的独创，它也是雅思官方建议大家使用的方法。

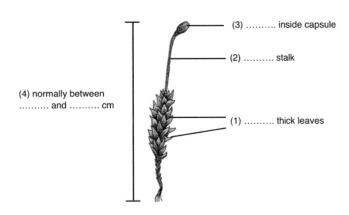

阅读是一场词汇游戏

我一直都说，阅读考试其实是词汇测验。如果文章中的大部分词你都不认识，你如何读得懂呢？我们举下面的例子说明：

Roman towns and garrisons in the United Kingdom between 46 BC and 400 AD had complex sewer networks sometimes constructed out of hollowed-out elm logs.

Is the following statement TRUE,FALSE or NOT GIVEN?

Some sewage networks built by the Romans in the UK were made of wood. ....

有三个问题需要你回答一下：

答案是T,F还是NG？

题干中的关键词你划的是哪几个？原文中的关键词你又划的是哪几个？

你觉得那个词你读不懂这题你没法做？

正确答案是： TRUE。

需要划出来的关键词是：

Roman towns and garrisons in the United Kingdom between 46 BC and 400 AD had complex sewer networks sometimes constructed out of hollowed-out elm logs.

Some sewage networks built by the Romans in the UK were made of wood.

如果你不认识"logs"或"elm"，那么这题你就很难做出来了。

有些同学可能会选NG，因为他们认为Roman towns可能不是由Romans建的，这就有点钻牛角尖了。Roman towns，在我看来，就是"a town that was originally built by the Romans"的意思，这没有歧义。此外，出题人并不想在这种地方给你"下套儿"。TA其实就是想问你，"同学，你到底知不知道logs和wood是同义词？"

While the same meaning could be conveyed through the roughly equivalent *powerful tea*,that fact is that English prefers to speak of tea in terms of being strong rather than in terms of being powerful.

It is possible, but not normal, to say "powerful tea". ....

首先我们先读题干，划出关键词。

It is possible, but not normal, to say "powerful tea".

特别是powerful tea这个名词，我猜在原文中应该很容易找到。接着我们用正常速度来阅读原文，试图找到关键词的同义词：

While the same meaning could be conveyed through the roughly equivalent *powerful tea*, that fact is that English prefers to speak of tea in terms of being strong rather than in terms of being powerful.

It is possible, but not normal, to say "powerful tea".

这里我们找到了几组同义词：

meaning...conveyed=to say；

could be=possible；

that fact is that=but；

prefers...rather than=not normal；

当把这些词组找到以后，很容易得出答案就是YES。题干只不过用一种简单的方式把原文又复述了一遍。从这道题大家不难看出，其实雅思阅读出题方式就是句子翻译，将原文的句子进行一定的同义词替换得到一个新的题干，而词汇是破题的关键。

题型练习

填空题

这种题型要求考生回答关于文章中具体的、事实性的信息的问题，考生需在问卷上填写多个单词或数字进行作答。这种题型要求考生能够有效地进行跳读（**skimming**），在文章中寻找相关的段落，并能够有效地进行扫读（**scanning**），寻找相关的句子并对详细信息进行仔细阅读。题目的顺序通常是经过了编排的，所以答案出现的顺序通常来说是与文章的顺序相同的。

——雅思考试官方

关于填空题，你需要理解句子细节，用原文中的信息完成笔记、表格或流程图（题目会告诉你可以填写多少个单词和数字），有时候你需要从选项中选择答案（选项多于空格数，且不重复），答案出现的顺序一般与原文顺序相同。

对于表格填空题，你需要用列表缩小范围，用那些没有空格的信息去定位原文中的内容，并按照词数要求填空。对于流程填空题，要理解细节描述（流程填空题一般都是描述细节的），记住流程图的信息出现是有顺序的。

咱们在做填空题的时候手里一定要拿着笔，空格的前后必定是你可以在原文中找到同义词（组）的关键词，这一点对于填空题来说至关重要。

最后，想提醒大家的是关于填空的字数问题。如果题目要求你写***TWO WORDS AND/OR A NUMBER***，这意味着你可以写：

一个单词 + 一个数字 或 两个单词 + 一个数字

记住，如果一个数字写成单词形式，它还是被算作一个数字。比如twenty five trees=one word and a number

如果题目要求***NO MORE THAN TWO WORDS*** *from the reading passage.* 答案是： black, white（而不是原文的 black and white）

再举一个例子。

如果题目要求***ONE WORD ONLY*** *from the passage*，你就千万不能把额外的信息加进去了，如 tools(而不是 bone tools)，shells (而不是 abalone shells), 总之，要严格按照题目要求来。

例题讲解

A Useful Plant

Mosses are small flowerless plants that usually grow in dense green clumps, in damp and shady locations. The individual plants are usually composed of simple, one-cell thick leaves, covering a thin stem that supports them. At certain times they produce thin stalks topped with capsules containing spores. They are typically 1–10 centimetres tall, though some species are much larger, like Dawsonia, the tallest moss in the world, which can grow to 50 cm in height.

Species of moss can be classed as growing on: rocks, exposed mineral soil,disturbed soils, acid soil, calcareous soil, cliff seeps and waterfall spray areas,stream sides, shaded humusy soil, downed logs, burnt stumps, tree trunk bases, upper tree trunks, and tree branches or in bogs. While mosses often grow on trees as epiphytes, they are never parasitic on the tree.

Moss is often considered a weed in grass lawns, but is deliberately encouraged to grow under aesthetic principles exemplified by Japanese gardening. In old temple gardens, for example, moss can be added to carpet a forest scene, as it is thought to add a sense of calm, age and stillness. Moss is also used in bonsai to cover the soil and enhance the impression of age.

There is a substantial market in mosses gathered from the wild. The uses for intact moss are principally in the florist trade and for home decoration. Decaying moss in the genus Sphagnum is also the major component of peat, which is "mined" for use as a fuel, as a horticultural soil additive, and in smoking malt in the production of Scotch whisky.

Some Sphagnum mosses can absorb up to 20 times their own weight in water. In World War I, Sphagnum mosses were used as first-aid dressings on soldiers' wounds, as these mosses were said to absorb liquids three times faster than cotton, to retain liquids better, and to distribute liquids uniformly throughout themselves, as well as being cooler, softer and less irritating than cotton. It was also claimed that they have mild antibacterial properties.

Questions 1 to 4

*Complete each label on the diagram below with **NO MORE THAN TWO WORDS** from the passage.*

Parts of the moss plant

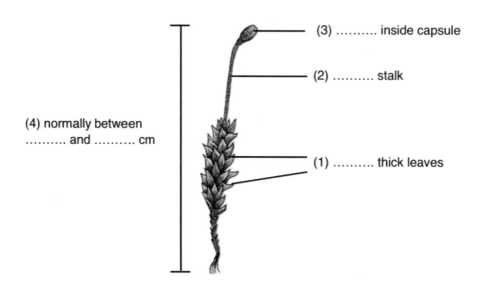

(3) .... inside capsule

(2) .... stalk

(4) normally between .... and .... cm

(1) .... thick leaves

Questions 5 to 9

Complete the following summary using words from the box below.

Mosses grow in **5**..................., shaded locations on rocks, soil, wood or in bogs. When mosses grow on trees, they are not classed as **6**..................., but when they grow on lawns, they are typically seen as **7**................... Japanese gardeners believe that moss has special **8**..................., and it is often used as a **9**................... in temple gardens.

dense	species	weeds	aesthetic	moist	sense	qualities	age
carpet	parasites						

Questions 10 to 13

*Complete the table below using **NO MORE THAN ONE WORD** from the passage to fill each gap.*

The Uses of Moss

Type of moss	Uses
Wild, must be **10**................	Florist trade and home decoration
Decaying Sphagnum	As a component of peat for: - fuel - horticultural **11**................ -**12**................ Production
Some Sphagnum species	To dress **13**................ During the First World War

填空题是顺序题型，无论是出题的顺序还是答案的顺序。第一题的题干非常短，所以我们只能画出这一个关键词。

1 .... thick leaves

带着这个关键词，我们回去读原文。非常容易地选出答案：**one-cell**。

Mosses are small flowerless plants that usually grow in dense green clumps, in damp and shady locations. The individual plants are usually composed of simple, **one-cell** thick leaves, covering a thin stem that supports them.

接着我们做第二题，第二题的答案必然位于第一题之后，我们接着读下面的文章。

2 .... stalk   **3** .... inside capsule

At certain times they produce **thin** stalks topped with capsules containing **spores**.

非常容易地选出答案**thin**和**spores**。

请注意这里有一个实战小经验，我是带着第二题和第三题的关键字一起回原文找的，这样做的好处是我不会遗漏。如果我发现第三题的答案，根据顺序原则，第二题的答案必定位于第三题之前。接着我们做第四题。

4 Normally between .... and .... cm

They are typically **1–10** centimetres tall, though some species are much larger, like Dawsonia, the tallest moss in the world, which can grow to 50 cm in height.

这几题的答案都非常邻近并且也没有做太多的同义词替换，因为类似这种有图片的填图题是填空题中最简单的一类。接着我们要尝试去做稍微难一点的，选词填空。我们所使用的方法跟所有题型一致。因为这是一个新的题型，所以我们回到文章开头重新阅读。

5 Mosses grow in ...., shaded locations on rocks, soil, wood or in bogs.

Mosses are small flowerless plants that usually grow in dense green clumps, in **damp** and **shady** locations.

在文章的第一句话中找到了关键词，所以空格处需要填damp或其同义词，即**moist**。

6 When mosses grow on trees, they are **not** classed as ....

第六题的关键词是grow on trees和classed as，带着关键词回去读原文，第二段定位到了关键词，接下来就要仔细阅读。

Species of moss can be classed as growing on: rocks, exposed mineral soil, disturbed soils, acid soil, calcareous soil, cliff seeps and waterfall spray areas, stream sides, shaded humusy soil, downed logs, burnt stumps, tree trunk bases, upper tree trunks, and tree branches or in bogs. While mosses often grow on trees as epiphytes, they are **never parasitic** on the tree.

不难得出答案是**parasitic**。

7 but when they grow on lawns, they are typically seen as ....

Moss is often considered a **weed** in grass lawns,

第7题比较简单，通过lawns可以定位，同时又找到了typically seen as的同义词often considered，答案是**weeds**。

8-9 Japanese gardeners believe that moss has special ...., and it is often used as a .... in temple gardens.

but is deliberately encouraged to grow under aesthetic principles exemplified by Japanese gardening. In old temple gardens, for example, moss can be added to carpet a forest scene, as it is thought to add a sense of calm, age and stillness. Moss is also used in bonsai to cover the soil and enhance the impression of age.

通过Japanese gardeners可以定位到第8题出题点，仔细阅读，原文中的a sense of calm, age and stillness是一种**qualities**。这道题有同学可能会选sense。第9题通过temple gardens定位，填**carpet**。接下来我们做表格填空题。还是带着题干中的关键词，回到原文继续读。

Types of moss	Uses
10 Wild, must be	...Florist trade and home decoration

There is a substantial market in mosses gathered from the wild. The **uses for** intact moss are principally in the florist trade and for home decoration.

当我们定位到了两个关键词之后，仔细阅读题干，唯一可以填的单词就只有**intact**。

- fuel

11 - horticultural ....

12 - .... production

13 To dress .... during the First World War

表格填空的题干都非常短，往往只有一两个单词，其实这对我们定位是有帮助的，因为需要检索的信息非常少。

Decaying moss in the genus Sphagnum is also the major component of peat, which is "mined" for use as a fuel, as a horticultural soil additive, and in smoking malt in the production of Scotch whisky.

Some Sphagnum mosses can absorb up to 20 times their own weight in water. In World War I, Sphagnum mosses were used as first-aid dressings on soldiers' wounds, ...

第11到13题都不难，主要是要根据题目要求：*NO MORE THAN ONE WORD*，只能填写一个单词。到这里我们就几个类型的填空题都做完了。同样的顺序题型，同样的关键词解题方法，最后我们来总结一下这道题的同义词（组）：

同义词替换	题干中的关键词	原文中的同义词
第 3 题	inside	containing
第 4 题	between...and...	-
	normally	typically
第 5 题	shaded	shady
	moist	damp
第 6 题	not classed as parasites	never parasitic
第 7 题	typically seen as	often considered as
第 8 题	special qualities	sense of calm, age and stillness
第 13 题	to dress wounds	as dressings on soldiers' wounds

IELTS Reading

Lesson 2

Basic exam techniques, Gap-fill questions

（手机淘宝扫码收看本节配套付费视频课）

题型练习

第1题

There are even more insects that are masters of exploiting filthy habitats, such as faeces and carcasses, where they are regularly challenged by thousands of microorganisms. These insects have many antimicrobial compounds for dealing with pathogenic bacteria and fungi, suggesting that there is certainly potential to find many compounds that can serve as or inspire new antibiotics.

Choose ONE WORD from the passage to fill each gap below.

They are also interested in compounds which insects use to protect themselves from pathogenic bacteria and fungi found in their **1**.................... . Piper hopes that these substances will be useful in the development of drugs such as **2**.................... .

第2题

Many collectors collect to develop their social life, attending meetings of a group of collectors and exchanging information on items. This is a variant on joining a bridge club or gym, and similarly brings them into contact with like-minded people.

Another motive for collecting is the desire to find something special, or a particular example of a collected item, such as a rare early recording by a particular singer. Some may spend their whole lives in a hunt for this. Psychologically, this can give a purpose to a life that otherwise feels aimless.

Complete each sentence below with ONE WORD ONLY from the passage.

1 Collectors' clubs provide opportunities to share ....

2 Collectors' clubs offer .... with people who have similar interests.

3 Collecting sometimes involves a life-long .... for a special item.

4 Searching for something particular may prevent people from feeling their life is completely ....

 **第3题**

Religion was central to the curriculum of early European universities. However, its role became less significant during the 19th century, and by the end of the 1800s, the German university model, based on more liberal values, had spread around the world. Universities concentrated on science in the 19th and 20th centuries, and became increasingly accessible to the masses. In Britain, the move from industrial revolution to modernity saw the arrival of new civic universities with an emphasis on science and engineering.

The funding and organisation of universities vary widely between different countries around the world. In some countries, universities are predominantly funded by the state, while in others, funding may come from donors or from fees which students attending the university must pay.

Complete the sentences below with NO MORE THAN THREE WORDS from the passage.

1 The German university model, which became popular in the 19th century, promoted ....

2 Over the last 200 years, a university education has become .... the general public.

3 Depending on the country, universities may be funded by the state, by donors, or by fee-paying ....

 第4题

A very close positive relationship was found when children's IQ scores were compared with their home educational provision (Freeman, 2010). The higher the children's IQ scores, especially over IQ 130, the better the quality of their educational backup, measured in terms of reported verbal interactions with parents, number of books and activities in their home etc.

To be at their most effective in their self-regulation, all children can be helped to identify their own ways of learning - metacognition - which will include strategies of planning, monitoring, evaluation, and choice of what to learn. Emotional awareness is also part of metacognition, so children should be helped to be aware of their feelings around the area to be learned, feelings of curiosity or confidence, for example.

Fill the gaps below with NO MORE THAN TWO WORDS from the passage.

1 One study found a strong connection between children's IQ and the availability of .... and .... at home.

2 Metacognition involves children understanding their own learning strategies, as well as developing ....

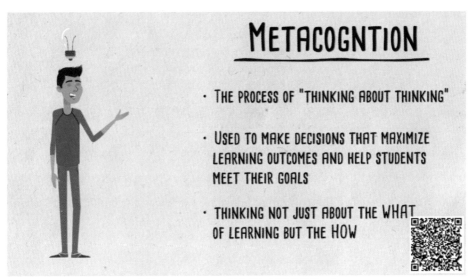

（所以Metacognition到底是如何学习的呢？）

 第5题

The discovery of penicillin is attributed to Scottish scientist *Alexander Fleming*. *Fleming* recounted that the date of his breakthrough was on the morning of September 28, 1928. It was a lucky accident: in his laboratory in the basement of St.Mary's Hospital in London, *Fleming* noticed a petri dish containing Staphylococcus culture that he had mistakenly left open. The culture had become contaminated by blue-green mould, and there was a halo of inhibited bacterial growth around the mould. *Fleming* concluded that the mould was releasing a substance that was repressing the growth of the bacteria. He grew a pure culture and discovered that it was a Penicillium mould, now known to be Penicillium notatum. *Fleming* coined the term "penicillin" to describe the filtrate of a broth culture of the Penicillium mould.

Fill the gaps in the summary below using words from the passage.

Alexander Fleming discovered penicillin by **1**.................. on September 28,1928. He found that the growth of bacteria on a petri dish was **2**.................. by a blue-green mould that had contaminated the culture. He realised that the mould was producing a substance that was responsible for **3**.................. bacterial growth.

词 汇

attributed to 归因于   breakthrough 突破   contaminated 被污染   inhibited 抑制

substance 物质   filtrate 过滤   broth culture 培养物

第6题

New research, prompted by the relatively high number of literary families, shows that there may be an inherited element to writing good fiction. Researchers from Yale in the US and Moscow State University in Russia launched the study to see whether there was a scientific reason why well-known writers have produced other writers.

The study analysed the creative writing of 511 children aged eight to 17 and 489 of their mothers and 326 fathers. All the participants wrote stories on particular themes. The stories were then scored and rated for originality and novelty, plot development and quality, and sophistication and creative use of prior knowledge. The researchers also carried out detailed intelligence tests and analysed how families functioned in the Russian households.

Taking into account intelligence and family background, the researchers then calculated the inherited and the environmental elements of creative writing. They found what they describe as a modest heritability element to creative writing.

Fill each gap in the summary below using a maximum of TWO WORDS.

Creative writing ability may be **1**.................. from parents, according to a new study. Researchers compared **2**.................. written by children and their parents, looking at elements such as originality and use of **3**.................. . After conducting intelligence tests and allowing for **4**.................., they concluded that there is a **5**.................. link between genetics and creative writing.

Nocturnality is an animal behaviour characterised by activity during the night and sleep during the day. The common adjective is "nocturnal", versus its opposite "diurnal".

Nocturnal creatures generally have highly developed senses of hearing and smell, and specially adapted eyesight. Such traits can help animals such as the Helicoverpa zea moth to avoid predators. Some animals, such as cats and ferrets, have eyes that can adapt to both low-level and bright day levels of illumination. Others, such as bushbabies and some bats, can function only at night. Many nocturnal creatures, including most owls, have large eyes in comparison with their body size to compensate for the lower light levels at night.

Being active at night is a form of niche differentiation, where a species' niche is partitioned not by the amount of resources but by time (i.e. temporal division of the ecological niche). For example, hawks and owls can hunt the same field or meadow for the same rodents without conflict because hawks are diurnal and owls are nocturnal.

Fill the gaps in the summary using words from the list below it.

most   sensitive   asleep   conflict   diurnal   exceptional   sleep

Nocturnal animals sleep during the daytime, whereas **1**................... animals are awake during the day and they **2**................... at night. Animals that are active at night tend to have **3**................... hearing and smell, and they may have **4**................... eyesight. Nocturnality allows animals to hunt for prey without having to **5**................... with predators that are active during daylight hours.

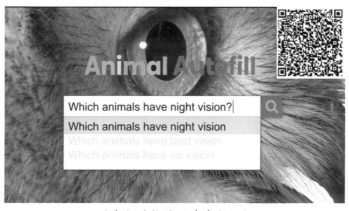

（夜行动物的眼睛真大！）

In the 1960s, researchers tried firing rockets trailing wires into thunderclouds to set up an easy discharge path for the huge electric charges that these clouds generate. But while rockets are fine for research, they cannot provide the protection from lightning strikes that everyone is looking for. And anyway, who would want to fire streams of rockets in a populated area? What goes up must come down.

Another project is trying to use lasers to discharge lightning safely. The idea began some 20 years ago, when high-powered lasers were revealing their ability to extract electrons out of atoms and create ions. If a laser could generate a line of ionisation in the air all the way up to a storm cloud, this conducting path could be used to guide lightning to Earth. To stop the laser itself being struck, it would not be pointed straight at the clouds. Instead it would be directed at a mirror, and from there into the sky. Ideally, the cloud-zapper (gun) would be cheap enough to be installed around all key power installations.

Complete the following summary using words from the box below it.

A cloud-zappers   **B** atoms   **C** storm clouds   **D** mirrors   **E** technique   **F** ions

G rockets   **H** conductors   **I** thunder

In this method, a laser is used to create a line of ionisation by removing electrons from **1**................... . This laser is then directed at **2**................... in order to control electrical charges, a method which is less dangerous than using **3**................... As a protection for the lasers, the beams are aimed firstly at **4**................... .

A large number of European towns and cities have made part of their centres car-free since the early 1960s. These are often accompanied by car parks on the edge of the pedestrianised zone, and, in the larger cases, park and ride schemes. Central Copenhagen is one of the largest and oldest examples: the auto-free zone is centred on Strget, a pedestrian shopping street, which is in fact not a single street but a series of interconnected avenues which create a very large auto-free zone, although it is crossed in places by streets with vehicular traffic. Most of these zones allow delivery trucks to service the businesses located there during the early morning, and street- cleaning vehicles will usually go through these streets after most shops have closed for the night.

In North America, where a more commonly used term is pedestrian mall, such areas are still in their infancy. Few cities have pedestrian zones, but some have pedestrianised single streets. Many pedestrian streets are surfaced with cobblestones, or pavement bricks, which discourage any kind of wheeled traffic, including wheelchairs. They are rarely completely free of motor vehicles.

Fill the gaps below with *NO MORE THAN THREE WORDS* from the text.

1 In some cases,people are encouraged to park .... of the town or city centre.

2 The only vehicles permitted in most pedestrian zones are those used for .... or .... cleaning.

3 Certain types of road surface can be used to .... traffic.

 第10题

Humans are driving mammals including deer, tigers and bears to hide under the cover of darkness, jeopardising the health of the creatures that are only supposed to be active by day, new research his found. The presence of people can instil strong feelings of fear in animals and as human activities now cover 75 per cent of the land, we are becoming increasingly harder to avoid. Unable to escape during the day, mammals are forced to emerge during the night.

A team led by *Kaitlyn Gaynor* at the University of California, Berkeley arrived at this conclusion after analysing nearly 80 studies from six continents that monitored the activity of various mammals using GPS trackers and motion-activated cameras. The scientists used this data to assess the night time antics of the animals during periods of low and high human disturbance.

Such disturbances ranged from relatively harmless activities like hiking to overtly destructive ones like hunting, as well as larger scale problems like farming and road construction. Overall, the researchers concluded that from beavers to lions, there was an increase in nocturnal behaviour when humans were in the vicinity.

Fill the gaps in the summary using words from the list below it.

hunt   tracking   emerge   construction   nocturnal   agriculture

monitor   disturbance   active

A recent study has shown that many mammals are being forced to become **1**.................... due to the presence of humans. Scientists reached these findings by **2**.................... and analysing the movements of mammals in areas with different levels of **3**.................... They showed that human activities, ranging from hiking to **4**.................... to road building, made it more likely that mammals would **5**.................... at night.

（一起来逛一下这条步行街）

第11题

The Wright brothers, Orville and Wilbur, were two American brothers, inventors, and aviation pioneers who were credited with inventing and building the world's first successful airplane and making the first controlled, powered and sustained heavier-than-air human flight, on December 17,1903. In the two years afterward, the brothers developed their flying machine into the first practical fixed-wing aircraft.

The brothers' fundamental breakthrough was their invention of three-axis control, which enabled the pilot to steer the aircraft effectively and to maintain its equilibrium. This method became standard and remains standard on fixed-wing aircraft of all kinds. From the beginning of their aeronautical work, the Wright brothers focused on developing a reliable method of pilot control as the key to solving "the flying problem". This approach differed significantly from other experimenters of the time who put more emphasis on developing powerful engines. Using a small homebuilt wind tunnel, the Wrights also collected more accurate data than anyone had before, enabling them to design and build wings and propellers that were more efficient than rival models.

They gained the mechanical skills essential for their success by working for years in their shop with printing presses, bicycles, motors, and other machinery. Their work with bicycles in particular influenced their belief that an unstable vehicle like a flying machine could be controlled and balanced with practice.

Fill each gap in the summary below with a maximum of TWO WORDS.

In 1903, the Wright brothers completed development of the first airplane that was capable of sustaining controlled **1**.................. . The key to their success was a system that gave the pilot the means to control and **2**.................. the airplane. This set them apart from other inventors who had focused on building **3**.................. .The brothers had previous experience with a wide variety of **4**..................,but it was their work with **5**.................. that had the greatest influence on their ideas.

（来看一下莱特兄弟的试飞实况）

The Major Oak is a large English oak tree in Sherwood Forest, Nottingham shire. According to local folklore, Robin Hood and his Merry Men used the Major Oak as their hideout. The size of the tree and its mythical status have led it to become a popular tourist attraction.

The Major Oak weighs an estimated 23 tons, has a girth of 10 metres, a canopy of 28 metres, and is about 800 to 1,000 years old. In a 2002 survey, it was voted 'Britain's favourite tree', and in 2014 it was voted 'England's Tree of the Year' in a public poll by the Woodland Trust.

There are several theories concerning why the Major Oak became so huge and oddly shaped. One theory is that the Major Oak may be several trees that fused together as saplings. An alternative explanation is that the tree may have been pollarded. Pollarding is a pruning system that can cause a tree's trunk and branches to grow large and thick. Due to their size and weight, the tree's massive limbs require the partial support of an elaborate system of scaffolding, which was first put in place during the Victorian era.

Interestingly, in 2002, someone attempted to illegally sell acorns from the Major Oak on an internet-based auction website.

Fill the gaps using words from the box.

weight   height   circumference   branches   put in   joined

den   put up   were   myth

1 Legend has it that the Major Oak was Robin Hood's ....

2 The .... of the tree's trunk is 10 metres.

3 The tree may actually be more than one tree that .... together.

4 Some of the tree's .... have to be held up by props.

5 Acorns from the oak were once .... for auction on the Internet.

（一起来看看这棵树有多大）

🔍 第13题

Large migrations are some of nature's greatest spectacles. Wildebeest and zebra chase the rains through the Mara ecosystem every year, monarch butterflies trace a path from Mexico to Canada and back, and tiny songbirds fly nonstop for days at a time. And now scientists are starting to figure out how they know where to go, and when.

Some of these animals, they've found, have their migration pathways written into their genes. A songbird hatched in a laboratory, having seen nothing of the natural world, still attempts to begin migration at the right time of year and in the right cardinal direction.

But large mammals like bighorn sheep and moose are a different story. Wildlife researchers have long suspected that they require experience to migrate effectively, that their annual journeys are the result of learning from one another, not of genetic inheritance. A new study, published Thursday in the journal Science, suggests that those hunches may be correct - some animals must learn how to migrate.

The existence of collective information and knowledge, that can be passed from older animals to younger ones, is a form of "culture", researchers explain. And when animals learn as a result of social interaction and the transfer of this information, that's a type of cultural exchange - as opposed to genetic.

Fill each gap in the summary below with ONE WORD ONLY from the passage.

Scientists believe that **1**................... are responsible for some animal migrations. Songbirds, for example, do not need to learn when and in which **2**................... to migrate. On the other hand, bighorn sheep appear to **3**................... migration habits from the herd. They, and other mammals, seem to have a **4**................... that is passed from one generation to the next through interaction and exchange of **5**...................

第14题

By the beginning of the 15th century, after a hundred years of construction, Florence Cathedral was still missing its dome. The building required an octagonal dome which would be higher and wider than any that had ever been built, with no external buttresses to keep it from spreading and falling under its own weight.

The building of such a masonry dome posed many technical problems. Filippo Brunelleschi, who is now seen as a key figure in architecture and perhaps the first modern engineer, looked to the great dome of the Pantheon in Rome for solutions. The dome of the Pantheon is a single shell of concrete, the formula for which had long since been forgotten. Soil filled with silver coins had held the Pantheon dome aloft while its concrete set. This could not be the solution in the case of the Florence Cathedral dome, due to its size. Another possible solution, the use of scaffolding, was also impractical because there was not enough timber in the whole of the region of Tuscany.

Brunelleschi would have to build the dome out of brick, due to its light weight compared to stone and being easier to form, and with nothing under it during construction. His eventual success can be attributed, in no small degree, to his technical and mathematical genius. Brunelleschi used more than four million bricks to create what is still the largest masonry dome in the world.

Fill each gap in the summary with a letter A-I.

A brick   **B** width   **C** materials   **D** earth   **E** wood   **F** succeeded

G concrete   **H** height   **I** achieved

Due to the **1**.................. and **2**.................. of the required structure, the construction of a dome for the cathedral in Florence had challenged architects for many years. A method employed by the Romans, using **3**.................. to support a dome while it was being built, was not suitable, and an insufficient supply of **4**.................. meant that scaffolding could not be used either. The architect Brunelleschi finally **5**.................. in building the largest **6**.................. dome in the world.

（一起来了解一下穹顶的建造过程吧）

选择题

题目可能已经给出句子的前半部分，考生需在选项中选择一个最佳的答案完成这个句子。题目也可能是一个完整的问题，考生需在选项中选择一个最佳的答案。考生需从四个可供选择的答案A、B、C或D中选择一个最佳的答案。题目的顺序与相对应的信息在文章中出现的顺序是相同的。这种题型可能出现的形式有：有时考生需从多于四个可供选择的选项中进行选择，也有可能需选择不止一个作为正确答案。另外，也有可能在一组问题的末尾再提出一个总括性的问题，如为文章选择一个最适合的标题。

——雅思考试官方

选择题是雅思阅读中的一种常见题型，我们对它也并不陌生。它的难点主要体现在所需阅读的内容较多，因为你不仅要读题干还要阅读四个选项，我建议大家按照下面的顺序来做选择题：

首先，不要读原文，只浏览一下文章标题和副标题（如有）即可。接着读题干，把关键词画出来，你大概率会在原文中发现这些关键词的同义词。接着读选项，把选项中的关键词也画出来。（就是那些最能代表整个选项的词，或者说把该选项和其他选项区分开来的词）然后回到原文，去找题干关键词或它的同义词，找对位置后，仔细阅读原文，不要放过任何一个字，看看跟哪个选项最接近。最后，当选定之后，你要能说出来其他几个选项为什么是错的，这才算完。

例题讲解

The Brain Drain

Human capital flight, sometimes called "brain drain",refers to the emigration of intelligent, well-educated individuals to another country for better pay or conditions, causing the home country to lose those skilled people, or "brains".

The term "brain drain" was coined by the Royal Society in the 1950s to describe the emigration of scientists and technologists to North America from post-war Europe. Albert Einstein was an earlier,and perhaps the most famous,example of this form of emigration. Einstein was visiting the United States when Adolf Hitler came to power in 1933 and, being Jewish, did not go back to Germany, where he had been a professor at the Berlin Academy of Sciences.He settled in the U.S., becoming an American citizen in 1940. Although the term originally referred to science and technology workers leaving a nation,the meaning has broadened to describe "the departure of educated or professional people from one country, economic sector, or field for another, usually for better pay or living conditions".

As with other human migration, the social environment is considered to be a key reason for this population shift. In source countries, lack of opportunities, political instability or oppression, economic depression, and health risks contribute to brain drain.Host countries,on the other hand, may offer employment opportunities,political stability and freedom, a developed economy, and better living conditions.At the individual level, family influences (relatives living overseas, for example), as well as personal preferences, career ambitions and other motivating factors can be considered.

In spite of its negative connotation, "brain drain" migration can be seen in a positive light. There is obviously a benefit to the migrating individuals, in terms of career progression, quality of life and earning power. These professionals often send remittances home to family members, and they may at some point return to their home countries with enhanced knowledge and skills. The home country may also experience an increase in demand for higher level education as people see the opportunities for educated workers overseas.

On the other hand, it is almost certainly more beneficial for a country to gain educated professionals than to lose them. It can be argued that the brain drain leads to an uneven distribution of knowledge, promoting innovation and development in destination countries, while stripping 'source' countries of their best workers, and therefore hindering their progress.

Some governments have policies to retain skilled workers. In Germany, Switzerland, Austria and France, for example, government-funded initiatives have been established to assist professionals working abroad to return to their home countries. By contrast, the Indian government has not adopted such policies, believing that the lost talent will eventually contribute to the nation in the future.

Questions 1 to 4

*Choose the best answer for each of the questions. Write **A**, **B**, **C**, or **D** as your answer.*

1 People first used the term "brain drain"

A during the Second World War

B when Albert Einstein decided to settle in the USA

C to refer to the emigration of skilled Europeans after the Second World War

D to describe immigration in North America

2 "Brain drain" migration is thought to be the result of

A social and environmental factors in developing countries

B the problems people face in source countries, and the allure of a better life

C families living in different parts of the world

D workers becoming more ambitious

3 When people emigrate to work abroad

A they may help their families by sending money home

B they usually return home to visit family members

C they benefit from better education systems in the destination countries

D their home countries receive money for higher education

4 To curb the negative effects of a "brain drain"

A most countries promote innovation

B all governments have policies to stop skilled workers leaving

C Indian migrants are expected to send financial contributions home

D schemes have been implemented in some countries to bring migrants home

因为选择题是有顺序的，所以我们先来做第一道题，画出关键词：

1 People first used the term "<u>brain drain</u>"

A <u>during</u> the <u>Second World War</u>

B <u>when Albert Einstein</u> decided to <u>settle in the USA</u>

C to refer to the <u>emigration of skilled Europeans after</u> the Second World <u>War</u>

D to describe <u>immigration in North America</u>

带着first used the term "brain drain"这个关键词回到原文去搜索：

Human capital flight, sometimes called "brain drain", refers to the emigration of intelligent, well-educated individuals to another country for better pay or conditions, causing the home country to lose those skilled people, or "brains".

在第一段我们找到了"brain drain"，但是并没有找到first used，我们继续往下读。在下一段我又看到了brain drain，这里的was coined是first used的同义词，所以应该离答案很近了。继续仔细阅读并对比题干。

The term "brain drain" <u>was coined</u> by the Royal Society in the <u>1950s</u> to describe the <u>emigration of scientists and technologists</u> to North America from <u>post-war</u> Europe. Albert <u>Einstein</u> was <u>earlier</u>, and perhaps the most famous, <u>example</u> of this form of emigration.

1 People first used the term "<u>brain drain</u>"

A <u>during</u> the <u>Second World War</u> 根据原文，这个词是post-war产生的，不是during；

B <u>when Albert Einstein</u> decided to <u>settle in the USA</u> 这个词是在Einstein settle in the USA之前产生的，他是最好的例子但并不是因为他而创造的；

C to refer to the <u>emigration of skilled Europeans</u> after the Second World War 题干中的

emigration of skilled Europeans和post-war对应原文中的scientists and technologists和after the Second World War；

D to describe <u>immigration in North America</u> 这个答案太笼统了；

正确答案是C；

接着我们做第二道题，先画出关键词：the result of。

2 "Brain drain" migration is thought to be <u>the result of</u>
A <u>social and environmental</u> factors in <u>developing countries</u>
B <u>the problems</u> people face in <u>source countries</u>, and the <u>allure of a better life</u>
C <u>families</u> living in <u>different parts of the world</u>
D <u>workers</u> becoming more <u>ambitious</u>

因为选择题是顺序题型，所以第二题的答案一定位于第一题之后，我们接着读第三段。

As with other human migration, the <u>social environment</u> is considered to be <u>a key reason</u> for this <u>population shift</u>. In source countries, <u>lack of opportunities, political instability or oppression, economic depression, and health risks</u> contribute to brain drain.

读完前两句话，我们可以找到the result of的同义词a key reason；而population shift也是migration的同义词；但需要注意的是，原文中的social environment（社会环境）和题干中的social and environmental（社会与环境）并不是组同义词（虽然它们长得很像），而原文中的source countries也并不代表题干中的developing countries。所以A选项是错误的。我们接着往下读。

In source countries, <u>lack of opportunities, political instability or oppression</u>, economic <u>depression, and health risks</u> contribute to brain drain. Host countries, on the other hand, may offer employment opportunities, political stability and freedom, a developed economy, and <u>better living conditions</u>.

首先我们可以找到一个关键词source countries，而lack of opportunities...health risks指代的就是原文中的the problems，题干中的allure of a better life对应原文中的better living conditions。

所以B选项似乎是正确选项，但我们还需要把剩下两个选项看一下，继续读下去。

At the individual level, family influences (relatives living overseas, for example), as well as personal preferences, career ambitions and other motivating factors can be considered.

C选项和D选项的关键词都有提及，但只是...can be considered，所以不是正确选项。

正确答案是B。

接着我们做第三道题。

3 When people emigrate to work abroad
A they may help their families by sending money home
B they usually return home to visit family members、
C they benefit from better education systems in the destination countries
D their home countries receive money for higher education

In spite of its negative connotation, "brain drain" migration can be seen in a positive light. There is obviously a benefit to the migrating individuals, in terms of career progression, quality of life and earning power. These professionals often send remittances home to family members, and they may at some point return to their home countries with enhanced knowledge and skills. The home country may also experience an increase in demand for higher level education as people see the opportunities for educated workers overseas.

题干中的When people emigrate对应原文中的These professionals often，而help their families by sending money home对应原文中的send remittances home to family members，基本可以确定选项A就是正确答案，不过还是继续读下去。B选项的return home to visit和原文中的return to their home countries是对应的，但原文说的是may at some point而不是题干的usually。很多粗心的同学会选C选项，但实际上题干的better education system（更好的教育）和原文的demand higher level education（接受高等教育）不是一个意思；D选项我们可以找到关键词home countries，但是题干中说的是receive而原文中是反义词demand。

正确选项是A。

接着做最后一道题，我们画出题干关键词curb the negative effects。

4 To curb the negative effects of a "brain drain"

A most countries promote innovation

B all governments have policies to stop skilled workers leaving

C Indian migrants are expected to send financial contributions home

D schemes have been implemented in some countries to bring migrants home

On the other hand, it is almost certainly more beneficial for a country to gain educated professionals than to lose them. It can be argued that the brain drain leads to an uneven distribution of knowledge, promoting innovation and development in destination countries, while stripping 'source' countries of their best workers, and therefore hindering their progress.

Some governments have policies to retain skilled workers. In Germany, Switzerland, Austria and France, for example, government-funded initiatives have been established to assist professionals working abroad to return to their home countries. By contrast, the Indian government has not adopted such policies, believing that the lost talent will eventually contribute to the nation in the future.

原文中说的是...promoting innovation...in destination countries，而选项A说的是most countries，不符；B选项中的stop对应原文中的retain，但原文中说的是some governments不是B选项说的all government；通过Indian可以找到C选项对应的原文信息，expected to 对应原文中的believing that，不过选项中的send financial contributions home只是原文中eventually contribute to the nation的一种形式，并不是全部。D选项中schemes，implemented和bring migrants home分别对应原文中的initiatives，established和assist professionals working abroad to return their home countries，所以正确答案是D。

让我们来梳理一下四道题的同义词（组）替换：

同义词替换	题干中的关键词	原文中的同义词
第一题	first used	coined
	to describe	to refer to
	after the war	post-war
第二题	allure of a better life	offer better living conditions
	brain drain the result of	...contribute to the brain drain
	problem people face	lack of opportunities, political instability etc.
	source countries	countries that people are leaving
	host countries	countries where migrants are going
第三题	a remittance	money sent as payment or as gift
	when people emigrate	migrating individuals
第四题	initiatives	schemes
	established	implemented
	to curb negative effects of brain drain	to retain skilled workers
	some countries	some governments
	to bring migrants home	assist professionals to return to their home countries

你可以很清晰地看到，表面上我们是在做阅读选择题，但实际它是四道词汇题，特别是加粗字体部分，如果你不认识这几个词，理解起来就会吃力一些。

Multiple choice questions:

You can normally find the answers in order in the passage.

（手机淘宝扫码收看本节配套付费视频课）

题型练习

 第1题

A third source of confusion is the attitude of the media. People are clearly more curious about bad news than good. Newspapers and broadcasters are there to provide what the public wants. That, however, can lead to significant distortions of perception. （《剑桥雅思真题5》）

1 The writer suggests that newspapers print items that are intended to

A educate readers

B meet their readers' expectations

C encourage feedback from readers

D mislead readers

 第2题

There is one stubborn question for which archaeology has yet to provide any answers: how did the Lapita* accomplish the ancient equivalent of a moon landing, many times over? No-one has found one of their canoes or any rigging, which could reveal how the canoes were sailed. Nor do the oral histories and traditions of later Polynesians offer any insights, for they turn into myths long before they reach as far back in time as the Lapita.

*The Lapita were an ancient tribe/people

1 According to the writer, there are difficulties explaining how the Lapita* accomplished their journeys because

A the canoes that have been discovered offer relatively few clues.

B archaeologists have shown limited interest in this area of research.

C little information relating to this period can be relied upon for accuracy.

D technological advances have altered the way such achievements are viewed.

A placebo is a sham or simulated medical intervention. Sometimes patients given a placebo treatment will have a perceived or actual improvement in a medical condition, a phenomenon commonly called the placebo effect.

A study of Danish general practitioners found that 48% had prescribed a placebo at least 10 times in the past year. The most frequently prescribed placebos were antibiotics for viral infections, and vitamins for fatigue. Specialists and hospital-based physicians reported much lower rates of placebo use.

1 The placebo effect refers to

A a simulated medical treatment

B an improvement in a patient's health as a result of a simulated medical treatment

C a common medical phenomenon

2 According to a study, placebos were prescribed in Denmark

A mainly by doctors working in hospitals

B instead of antibiotics

C for fatigued patients or those suffering with viruses

Then, if the new drug showed a significant benefit compared to the placebo,

（一起来了解一下"假药"的疗效）

第4题

The ethos of the aristocracy, as exemplified in the English public schools, greatly influenced *Pierre de Coubertin*. The public schools subscribed to the belief that sport formed an important part of education, an attitude summed up in the saying 'mens sana in corpore sano', a sound mind in a sound body. In this ethos, a gentleman was one who became an all-rounder, not the best at one specific thing. There was also a prevailing concept of fairness, in which practising or training was considered tantamount to cheating.

1 *De Coubertin* agreed with the idea that:

A sport is an activity for gentlemen.

B schooling should promote both physical and mental health.

C sport is the most important part of a child's education.

2 In *De Coubertin*'s view:

A it is easier to be good at many sports, rather than the best at one sport.

B training is necessary if you want to be an all-rounder.

C training gives the athlete an unfair advantage.

第5题

In linguistics, a corpus (plural corpora) is a large and structured set of texts (now usually electronically stored and processed). A corpus may be used to help linguists to analyse a language, or for the purpose of dictionary writing or language teaching. The British National Corpus (BNC) is a 100-million-word text corpus of samples of written and spoken English from a wide range of sources. The corpus covers British English of the late twentieth century from a wide variety of genres with the intention that it be a representative sample of spoken and written British English of that time.

1 What is a corpus?

A A type of large dictionary.

B A single written text.

C A tool for language analysis.

2 Why was the BNC compiled?

A For the purpose of language teaching.

B To document written and spoken English from a particular period in time.

C To document the history of the English language.

 第6题

The Eiger is a mountain in the Bernese Alps in Switzerland. Since 1935, at least sixty-four climbers have died attempting the Eiger's north face, earning it the German nickname Mordwand, literally "murder wall" - a pun on its correct title of Nordwand (North Wall). Before it was successfully climbed, in 1938, most of the attempts on the face ended tragically and the Bernese authorities even banned climbing it and threatened to fine any party that should attempt it again. Since the first successful attempt, the north face has been climbed many times, but even today it is regarded as a formidable challenge.

1 Which **TWO** of the following statements are true according to the text?

A The Eiger is the most dangerous mountain in the Bernese Alps.

B The north face of the mountain has an infamous history.

C The Nordwand was finally conquered in 1938.

D The Bernese authorities fined climbers who attempted the north face.

E Climbers consider the north face to be the world's most challenging climb.

（为什么登山者都想征服"她"？）

The term "IQ" comes from German "Intelligenz-Quotient", coined by the German psychologist William Stern in 1912, who proposed a method of scoring children's intelligence tests. Since the early 20th century, scores on IQ tests have increased in most parts of the world. The phenomenon of rising score performance means that if test-takers are scored by a constant standard scoring rule, IQ test scores have been rising at an average rate of around three IQ points per decade. This phenomenon was named the Flynn effect in the book *The Bell Curve* after James R.Flynn, the author who did the most to bring this phenomenon to the attention of psychologists.

1 "IQ" refers to

A a type of intelligence test for children

B a means of rating intelligence tests

C an area of psychology

2 Flynn noticed that

A IQ scores were constant around the world

B IQ was a global phenomenon

C intelligence scores had gradually risen over several decades

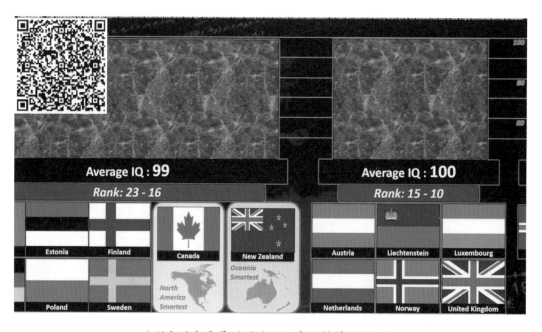

（哪个国家是最聪明的呢？中国排第几呢？）

第8题

Ecotourism is a form of tourism where tourists visit fragile, pristine, and relatively undisturbed natural areas. Its purpose may be to educate the traveller, to provide funds for ecological conservation, to directly benefit the economic development and political empowerment of local communities, or to foster respect for different cultures and for human rights.

However, ecotourism operations occasionally fail to live up to conservation ideals. Even a modest increase in population puts extra pressure on the local environment and necessitates the development of additional infrastructure. The construction of water treatment plants, sanitation facilities, and lodges come with the exploitation of non-renewable energy sources and the utilisation of already limited local resources. The environment may suffer because local communities are unable to meet these infrastructure demands.

1 One aim of ecotourism is to

A allow people to visit areas that were previously restricted.

B educate local communities in fragile areas.

C raise money for environmental projects in natural areas.

2 However, ecotourism can cause problems when

A the local population does not welcome visitors.

B extra facilities and amenities are required to cope with a population increase.

C communities do not have the funds to improve local facilities.

 第9题

Ethnography, from the Greek ethnos (folk, people, nation) and grapho (I write), is the systematic study of people and cultures. It is designed to explore cultural phenomena where the researcher observes society from the point of view of the subject of the study.

According to the leading social scientist, John Brewer, ethnographic data collection methods are meant to capture the "social meanings and ordinary activities" of people (known as "informants") in "naturally occurring settings" that are commonly referred to as "the field". The goal is to collect data in such a way that the researcher imposes a minimal amount of personal bias. Methods of data collection can include participant observation, field notes, interviews, and surveys.

1 According to the passage,which **TWO** of the statements below are true?

A Ethnography is a field of study that began in Greece.

B Ethnographic research is concerned with ancient cultures and societies.

C The subjects of ethnographic research are referred to as "informants".

D Ethnographers try to make their research as objective as possible.

E Observation is the most effective form of data collection.

 第10题

The world's largest collection of maps resides in the basement of the Library of Congress in Washington,D.C. The collection, consisting of up to 4.6 million map sheets and 63,000 atlases, includes magnificent bound collections of elaborate maps - the pride of the golden age of Dutch cartography. In the reading room scholars, wearing thin cotton gloves to protect the fragile sheets, examine ancient maps with magnifying glasses. Across the room people sit at their computer screens, studying the latest maps. With their prodigious memories, computers are able to store data about people, places and environments - the stuff of maps - and almost instantly information is displayed on the screen in the desired geographic context, and at the click of a button, a print-out of the map appears.

1 The Library of Congress offers and opportunity to

A borrow from their collection of Dutch maps

B learn how to restore ancient and fragile maps

C enjoy the atmosphere of the reading room

D create individual computer maps to order

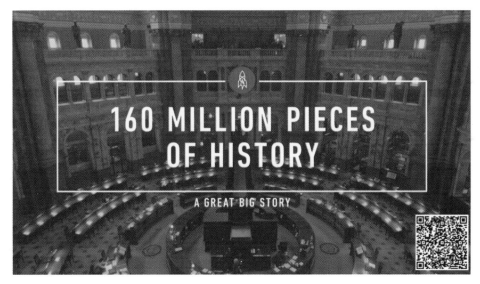

（一起来参观世界上最大的图书馆）

第11题

Etymology is the study of the history of words, their origins, and how their form and meaning have changed over time. For a language with a long written history, etymologists make use of texts in these languages, and texts about the languages, to gather knowledge about how words were used during earlier periods of their history and when they entered the languages in question.

Etymologists also apply the methods of comparative linguistics to reconstruct information about languages that are too old for any direct information to be available. By analysing related languages with a technique known as the comparative method, linguists can make inferences about their shared parent language and its vocabulary. In this way, word roots have been found that can be traced all the way back to the origin of, for instance, the Indo-European language family.

The word etymology is derived from the Greek word etymologia, itself from etymon, meaning "true sense", and the suffix -logia, denoting "the study of".

1 Which **TWO** of the following statements agree with the information above?

A Etymology involves the study of historical texts.

B Some languages are too old for linguists to understand.

C The ancient Greeks were the first to study the origins of words.

D Most words have their origins in Indo-European languages.

E The word "etymology" derives from a word meaning "the study of true sense".

 第12题

The term 'learning styles' refers to a variety of ways of learning. The 'learning styles' theory is based on the observation that most people prefer an identifiable method of interacting with, taking in, and processing stimuli or information. The idea of individualised 'learning styles' originated in the 1970s, and acquired enormous popularity. Proponents say that teachers should assess the learning styles of their students and adapt their classroom methods to best fit each student's preference.

The basis and efficacy of these proposals are extensively criticised. Although children and adults express personal preferences, there is no evidence that identifying a student's learning style produces better outcomes, and there is significant evidence that the hypothesis (that a student will learn best if taught in a method deemed appropriate for his or her learning style) may be invalid.

1 The idea that people should learn according to their preferred learning style

A has influenced all teachers.

B became popular around 40 years ago.

C has never been disputed.

2 There is no evidence that

A people have learning preferences.

B the hypothesis might be wrong.

C it is beneficial to identify students' preferred learning styles.

 第13题

Secondly, environmental groups need to be noticed by the mass media. They also need to keep the money rolling in. Understandably, perhaps, they sometimes overstate their arguments. In 1997, for example, the Worldwide Fund for Nature issued a press release entitled: 'Two thirds of the world's forests lost forever'. The truth turns out to be nearer 20%.

Though these groups are run overwhelmingly by selfless folk, they nevertheless share many of the characteristics of other lobby groups. That would matter less if people applied the same degree of scepticism to environmental lobbying as they do to lobby groups in other fields. A trade organisation arguing for, say, weaker pollution controls is instantly seen as self-interested. Yet a green organisation opposing such a weakening is seen as altruistic, even if an impartial view of the controls in question might suggest they are doing more harm than good.

1 The writer quotes from the Worldwide Fund for Nature to illustrate how

A influential the mass media can be.

B effective environmental groups can be.

C the mass media can help groups raise funds.

D environmental groups can exaggerate their claims.

2 What is the writer's main point about lobby groups?

A Some are more active than others.

B Some are better organised than others.

C Some receive more criticism than others.

D Some support more important issues than others.

 第14题

The researchers who publish the annual *World Happiness Report* found that about three-quarters of human happiness is driven by six factors: strong economic growth, healthy life expectancy, quality social relationships, generosity, trust, and freedom to live the life that's right for you. These factors don't materialize by chance; they are intimately related to a country's government and its cultural values. In other words the happiest places incubate happiness for their people.

To illustrate the power of place, John Helliwell, one of the report's editors, analyzed 500,000 surveys completed by immigrants who'd moved to Canada from 100 countries over the previous 40 years, many from countries considerably less happy. Remarkably Helliwell and his colleagues discovered that, within a few years of arriving, immigrants who came from unhappy places began to report the increased happiness level of their adoptive home. Seemingly their environment alone accounted for their increased happiness.

1 Which **TWO** of the following statements are true according to the passage?

A Personal autonomy was identified as one of the factors that lead to happiness.

B No relationship between happiness and culture was found.

C Canada is one of the world's happiest countries.

D Moving to live in a different country made some people happier.

E Immigrants were found to be less happy than other individuals.

 第15题

The Thames Tunnel is an underwater tunnel that was built beneath the River Thames in London between 1825 and 1843. It is 396 metres long, and runs at a depth of 23 metres below the river surface. It was the first tunnel known to have been constructed successfully underneath a navigable river.

Although it was a triumph of civil engineering, the Thames Tunnel was not a financial success, with building costs far exceeding initial estimates. Proposals to extend the entrance to accommodate wheeled vehicles failed, and it was used only by pedestrians. However, the tunnel did become a major tourist destination, attracting about two million people a year, each of whom paid a penny to pass under the river.

The construction of the Thames Tunnel showed that it was indeed possible to build underwater tunnels, despite the previous scepticism of many engineers. Its historic importance was recognised on 24th March 1995, when the structure was listed Grade II* in recognition of its architectural importance.

1 Which **THREE** of the following statements are correct?

A The Thames Tunnel was the world's first ever tunnel.

B Construction of the tunnel was more expensive than predicted.

C There were plans to allow vehicles to use the tunnel.

D Tourism eventually made the tunnel profitable.

E Many engineers had already tried to build underwater tunnels.

F The Thames Tunnel is now considered to be a significant work of architecture.

now 52 meters below ground at this
end you'll notice cast iron reinforced

 第16题

The Painting Fool is one of a growing number of computer programs which, so their makers claim, possess creative talents. Classical music by an artificial composer has had audiences enraptured, and even tricked them into believing a human was behind the score. Artworks painted by a robot have sold for thousands of dollars and been hung in prestigious galleries. And software has been built which creates art that could not have been imagined by the programmer.

Human beings are the only species to perform sophisticated creative acts regularly. If we can break this process down into computer code, where does that leave human creativity? 'This is a question at the very core of humanity,' says *Geraint Wiggins*, a computational creativity researcher at Goldsmiths, University of London. 'It scares a lot of people. They are worried that it is taking something special away from what it means to be human.'

1 What is the writer suggesting about computer-produced works in the first paragraph?

A People's acceptance of them can vary considerably.

B A great deal of progress has already been attained in this field.

C They have had more success in some artistic genres than in others.

D The advances are not as significant as the public believes them to be.

2 According to Geraint Wiggins, why are many people worried by computer art?

A It is aesthetically inferior to human art.

B It may ultimately supersede human art.

C It undermines a fundamental human quality.

D It will lead to a deterioration in human ability.

 第17题

Old English, or Anglo-Saxon, is the earliest historical form of the English language, spoken in England and southern and eastern Scotland in the early Middle Ages. It was brought to Great Britain by Anglo-Saxon settlers probably in the mid-5th century, and the first Old English literary works date from the mid-7th century.

After the Norman conquest of 1066, English was replaced, for a time, as the language of the upper classes by Anglo-Norman, a relative of French. This is regarded as marking the end of the Old English era, as during this period the English language was heavily influenced by Anglo- Norman, developing into a phase known now as Middle English.

Like other old Germanic languages, Old English is very different from Modern English and difficult for Modern English speakers to understand without study. Old English grammar is quite similar to that of modern German: nouns, adjectives, pronouns and verbs have many inflectional endings and forms, and word order is much freer.

1 What happened in the 7th century?

A The English language was first established in Britain.

B The first oral stories in Old English were told.

C The earliest examples of creative writing in Old English come from that time.

2 Old English is...

A related to the French language.

B more easily understood by German speakers than English speakers.

C largely indecipherable to English speakers nowadays.

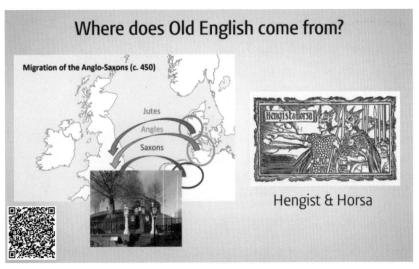

Where does Old English come from?

（了解一下Old English的发展史）

 第18题

The Suzuki method is an internationally known music curriculum and teaching philosophy dating from the mid-20th century, created by Japanese violinist and pedagogue *Shinichi Suzuki* (1898-1998). The method aims to create an environment for learning music which parallels the linguistic environment of acquiring a native language. Suzuki believed that this environment would also help to foster good moral character.

As a skilled violinist but a beginner at the German language who struggled to learn it, Suzuki noticed that children pick up their native language quickly, and even dialects adults consider "difficult" to learn are spoken with ease by children at age five or six. He reasoned that if children have the skill to acquire their native language, they have the necessary ability to become proficient on a musical instrument.

Suzuki believed that every child, if properly taught, was capable of a high level of musical achievement. He also made it clear that the goal of such musical education was to raise generations of children with "noble hearts", as opposed to creating famous musical prodigies.

1 Which **THREE** of the following statements are correct?

A Suzuki saw similarities between learning languages and music.

B He learnt German using his own method.

C He found it easy to learn German.

D He believed that all children have musical potential.

E His aims went deeper than simply teaching music.

F He hoped to create the next generation of famous musicians.

 第19题

Cultivation theory examines the long-term effects of television. Its primary proposition is that the more time people spend 'living' in the television world, the more likely they are to believe social reality aligns with reality portrayed on television.

Cultivation theory suggests that exposure to television, over time, subtly "cultivates" viewers' perceptions of reality. Researchers George Gerbner and Larry Gross, the originators of this idea, assert: "Television is a medium of the socialisation of most people into standardised roles and behaviours. Its function is in a word, enculturation".

Initial research on the theory establishes that concern regarding the effects of television on audiences stem from the unprecedented centrality of television in American culture. Gerbner posited that television as a mass medium of communication had formed into a common symbolic environment that bound diverse communities together, socialising people into standardised roles and behaviours. He thus compared the power of television to that of religion, stating that television was to modern society what religion once was in earlier times.

1 Which **THREE** of the following statements correctly describe cultivation theory?

A It looks at the physical impact of watching too much television.

B It proposes that television influences the way we see the world.

C It suggests that the effects of television occur gradually.

D It is an established theory that is widely accepted by researchers.

E It refers to a uniquely American phenomenon.

F It looks at the role of television in society.

（一起来了解更多关于Cultivation Theory的背景知识）

According to Carol Dweck, individuals can be placed on a continuum according to their implicit views of where ability comes from. Some believe their success is based on innate ability; these are said to have a "fixed" theory of intelligence (fixed mindset). Others, who believe their success is based on having opposite mindset, which involves hard work, learning, training and doggedness are said to have a "growth" or an "incremental" theory of intelligence (growth mindset).

Individuals may not necessarily be aware of their own mindset, but their mindset can still be discerned based on their behaviour. It is especially evident in their reaction to failure. Fixed- mindset individuals dread failure because it is a negative statement on their basic abilities, while growth mindset individuals do not mind or fear failure as much because they realise their performance can be improved and learning comes from failure. These two mindsets play an important role in all aspects of a person's life. Dweck argues that the growth mindset will allow a person to live a less stressful and more successful life.

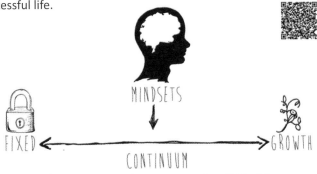

（Fixed mindset和growth mindset的区别）

The Nobel Peace Prize is one of the five Nobel Prizes established by the will of Swedish industrialist, inventor, and armaments manufacturer Alfred Nobel, along with the prizes in Chemistry, Physics, Physiology or Medicine, and Literature. Since March 1901, it has been awarded annually (with some exceptions) to those who have "done the most or the best work for fraternity between nations, for the abolition or reduction of standing armies and for the holding and promotion of peace congresses".

Nobel died in 1896 and he did not leave an explanation for choosing peace as a prize category. As he was a trained chemical engineer, the categories for chemistry and physics were obvious choices. The reasoning behind the peace prize is less clear. According to the Norwegian Nobel Committee, his friendship with *Bertha von Suttner*, a peace activist and later recipient of the prize, profoundly influenced his decision to include peace as a category. Some Nobel scholars suggest it was Nobel's way to compensate for developing destructive forces. His inventions included dynamite and ballistite, both of which were used violently during his lifetime.

1 Which **TWO** of the statements below are correct?

A The creator of the Nobel Peace Prize was himself a producer of weapons.

B The Nobel Peace Prize is a controversial award.

C Nobel was a peace activist during his lifetime.

D The 'peace' prize category was suggested by one of Nobel's friends.

E Nobel saw the destructive application of some of his inventions.

A new 'super-Earth' has been discovered that could have a life-supporting climate and water. The planet, given the catchy name HD 40307g, was discovered in a multi-world solar system 42 light years from the Sun and lies at exactly the right distance from its star to allow liquid surface water. It orbits well within the star's "habitable" or "Goldilocks" zone - the region where temperatures are neither too hot nor too cold to sustain life.

Professor *Hugh Jones*, from the University of Hertfordshire said: "The longer orbit of the new planet means that its climate and atmosphere may be just right to support life. Just as Goldilocks liked her porridge to be neither too hot nor too cold but just right, this planet or indeed any moons that is has lie in an orbit comparable to Earth, increasing the probability of it being habitable." The 'super earth' is one of six planets believed to circle the dwarf star HD 40307 in the constellation Pictor. All the others are located outside the habitable zone, too close to their parent star to support liquid water.

1 Why is it thought that the planet may be able to support life?

A It has been shown to have water.

B It is 42 light years from the Sun.

C It orbits its own star at the perfect distance.

D It has several moons.

2 Which statement is true of the "Goldilocks" zone?

A It is the region of a planet which has a habitable climate.

B It refers to a zone which is too close to the parent star.

C It refers to a planet with several moons and a long orbit.

D It is an orbit region which is comparable to the Earth's.

 第23题

Physicist *Richard Feynman* returned over and over to an idea that drove his groundbreaking discoveries. His approach was documented by his Caltech colleague David Goodstein in the book *Feynman's Lost Lecture about physics classes* Feynman taught in the 1960s:

Once, I said to him, "Dick, explain to me, so that I can understand it, why spin one-half particles obey Fermi-Dirac statistics." Sizing up his audience perfectly, Feynman said, "I'll prepare a freshman lecture on it." But he came back a few days later to say, "I couldn't do it. I couldn't reduce it to the freshman level. That means we don't really understand it."

Feynman didn't mean all human knowledge must be distilled into an introductory college course. His point was that we need to build our grasp of science and technology from the ground up if we are to master it, not to mention reimagine how it works. Feynman was famous as a student for redoing many of physics' early experiments himself to build a foundational understanding of the field. By mastering these first principles, Feynman often saw things that others did not in quantum mechanics, computing, and nuclear physics, earning him the Nobel Prize in 1965.

1 When asked to explain a difficult concept, physicist Richard Feynman

A immediately replied that he could not

B replied that he had already prepared a lecture on it

C said that he did not understand the concept either

D promised to give his answer in an introductory lesson

2 Feynman believed that

A scientists should master basic scientific principles first

B early physics experiments need to be redone

C most science students do not have a good foundation in physics

D his knowledge of first principles earned him a Nobel Prize

 第24题

All these activities may have damaging environmental impacts. For example, land clearing for agriculture is the largest single cause of deforestation; chemical fertilisers and pesticides may contaminate water supplies; more intensive farming and the abandonment of fallow periods tend to exacerbate soil erosion; and the spread of monoculture and use of highyielding varieties of crops have been accompanied by the disappearance of old varieties of food plants which might have provided some insurance against pests or diseases in future. Soil erosion threatens the productivity of land in both rich and poor countries. The United States, where the most careful measurements have been done, discovered in 1982 that about one-fifth of its farmland was losing topsoil at a rate likely to diminish the soil's productivity. The country subsequently embarked upon a program to convert 11 per cent of its cropped land to meadow or forest. Topsoil in India and China is vanishing much faster than in America.

Government policies have frequently compounded the environmental damage that farming can cause. In the rich countries, subsidies for growing crops and price supports for farm output drive up the price of land. The annual value of these subsidies is immense: about $250 billion, or more than all World Bank lending in the 1980s. To increase the output of crops per acre, a farmer's easiest option is to use more of the most readily available inputs: fertilisers and pesticides. Fertiliser use doubled in Denmark in the period 1960-1985 and increased in The Netherlands by 150 per cent. The quantity of pesticides applied has risen too: by 69 per cent in 1975-1984 in Denmark, for example, with a rise of 115 per cent in the frequency of application in the three years from 1981.

In the late 1980s and early 1990s some efforts were made to reduce farm subsidies. The most dramatic example was that of New Zealand, which scrapped most farm support in 1984. A study of the environmental effects, conducted in 1993, found that the end of fertiliser subsidies had been followed by a fall in fertiliser use (a fall compounded by the decline in world commodity prices, which cut farm incomes). The removal of subsidies also stopped land-clearing and over- stocking, which in the past had been the principal causes of erosion. Farms began to diversify. The one kind of subsidy whose removal appeared to have been bad for the environment was the subsidy to manage soil erosion.

In less enlightened countries, and in the European Union, the trend has been to reduce rather than eliminate subsidies, and to introduce new payments to encourage farmers to treat their land in environmentally friendlier ways, or to leave it fallow. It may sound strange but such payments need to be higher than the existing incentives for farmers to grow food crops. Farmers, however, dislike being paid to do nothing. In several countries they have become interested in the possibility of using fuel produced from crop residues either as a replacement for petrol (as ethanol) or as fuel for power stations (as biomass). Such fuels produce far less carbon dioxide than coal or oil, and absorb carbon dioxide as they grow. They are therefore less likely to contribute to the greenhouse effect. But they are rarely competitive with fossil fuels unless subsidised - and growing them does no less environmental harm than other crops.

1 Research completed in 1982 found that in the United States soil erosion

A reduced the productivity of farmland by 20 per cent.

B was almost as severe as in India and China.

C was causing significant damage to 20 per cent of farmland.

D could be reduced by converting cultivated land to meadow or forest.

2 By the mid-1980s, farmers in Denmark

A used 50 per cent less fertiliser than Dutch farmers.

B used twice as much fertiliser as they had in 1960.

C applied fertiliser much more frequently than in 1960.

D more than doubled the amount of pesticide they used in just 3 years.

3 Which one of the following increased in New Zealand after 1984?

A farm incomes

B use of fertiliser

C over-stocking

D farm diversification

判断题

题目会提供一组表示意见/看法，或是事实性信息的陈述。这种题型考查考生进行跳读、扫读和对细节进行阅读理解的能力。

- 针对意见或看法，考生需回答这些陈述是否符合或反映了作者的观点或看法。答案的形式有"是"(YES/Y)、"否"(NO/N)、或"无从判断"(NOT GIVEN/NG)。
- 针对事实性信息，考生需回答这些陈述是否与文章中的信息一致。答案的形式有"一致"(TRUE/T)、"不一致"(FALSE/F)、或"无从判断"(NOT GIVEN/NG)。

——雅思考试官方

有同学会问，TFNG 和 YNNG 题型是一样的吗？它们的确有点区别。一般情况下，如果问题是关于某一个事实(facts) 的，通常会让你在"True/False/Not given"中间去选；如果问题是关于某一个观点(opinion)而不是事实，或是问题所列的陈述是否跟作者的观点相一致时，一般会要你在"Yes/No/Not given"中间去选。不过从应试的角度来说，这种区别可以不用去管。反正你做题的方法还是一样的：定位关键词，然后决定该信息是否正确，或没有相关信息。

"烤鸭"们在判断题上栽跟头，主要是在该选 FALSE 还是NOT GIVEN上傻傻分不清楚。其实很简单。之所以选FALSE，是因为题干中的信息与原文相悖（相反），换句话说，原文中存在与之相反的观点。之所以选NOT GIVEN，仅仅只是因为文中没有包含题干中的信息（未提及）而已。

我们来看几个小题。

Tourism has a profound impact both on the world economy, and because of the educative effect of travel and the effects on employment, on society itself. （《剑桥雅思真题10》，page67）

Tourism has a social impact because it promotes recreation. ....

很多同学会选**FALSE**，因为原文中说旅游业有着很大的社会影响。但正确的答案是**NOT**

GIVEN。这句话前半句是对的，但后半句并没有提及。原文中完全没有提到"it promotes recreation"。如果原文中有"recreation is not part of the social impact of tourism"，我们才可以选 **FALSE**。大家要注意，只有当题干信息与原文信息相反时，我们才可以选**FALSE**，如果题干中有信息（或者部分信息）原文中未提及，我们就只能选**NOT GIVEN**。

People who speak two languages have a clear learning advantage over their monolingual schoolmates. This depends on how much of each language they can speak, not on which language is used.

Some languages develop your intelligence more than others. ....

这道题的答案是**FALSE**。这篇文章确实提到了语言对智力有帮助，但原文中明确说了"...not on which language is used"，这与题干信息相反，所以是**FALSE**，而不能选**NOT GIVEN**。

但我也需要提醒同学们，不要钻牛角尖，比如像下面这道题：

原文：
The two week planned study into the psychological impact of prison life...

判断题：
The study aimed to investigate the mental and behavioural effects of life in prison. ....

答案是**TRUE**，很多同学会选**NOT GIVEN**，因为他们在 "psychological" 上想多了。他们认为，psychological 的定义应该比 "mental and behavioural"更加复杂。mental and behavioural 的确不是 psychological 的精确定义，但大体上来说是相同的。

例题讲解

The Development of Sanitation Systems

The first sanitation systems were built in the prehistoric Middle East, in the south-east of the modern country of Iran near Zabol. An inverted siphon system, along with glass covered clay pipes, was used for the first time in the palaces of Crete, Greece. It is still in working condition, after about 3000 years.

Higher population densities required more complex sewer collection and conveyance systems to maintain sanitary conditions in crowded cities. The ancient cities of Harappa and Mohenjo-daro of the Indus Valley civilisation constructed complex networks of bricklined sewage drains from around 2600 BC and also had outdoor flush toilets connected to this network. The urban areas of the Indus Valley civilisation provided public and private baths, sewage was disposed through underground drains built with precisely laid bricks, and a sophisticated water management system with numerous reservoirs was established.

Roman towns and garrisons in the United Kingdom between 46 BC and 400 AD had complex sewer networks sometimes constructed out of hollowed-out elm logs, which were shaped so that they butted together with the down-stream pipe providing a socket for the upstream pipe.

In some cities, including Rome, Istanbul (Constantinople) and Fustat, networked ancient sewer systems continue to function today as collection systems for those cities' modernised sewer systems. Instead of flowing to a river or the sea, the pipes have been re-routed to modern sewer treatment facilities.

This basic system remained in place with little positive change, until the 16th century, when Sir John Harington invented the first flush toilet as a device for Queen Elizabeth I (his godmother) that released wastes into cesspools. Despite this innovation, most cities did not have a functioning sewer system before the Industrial era, relying instead on nearby rivers or occasional rain showers to wash away the sewage from the streets.

The prevailing system was sufficient for the needs of early cities with few occupants, but the tremendous growth of cities during the Industrial Revolution quickly led to terribly overpolluted streets, which acted as a constant source for the outbreak of disease. As recently as the late 19th century sewerage systems in some parts of the highly industrialised United Kingdom were so inadequate that water-borne diseases such as cholera and typhoid remained a risk.

The first comprehensive sewer system was built in Hamburg, Germany in the mid-19th century, and the first such systems in the United States were built in the late 1850s in Chicago and Brooklyn. Initially these systems discharged sewage directly to surface waters without treatment. But as pollution of water bodies became a concern, cities attempted to treat the sewage before discharge. During the half-century around 1900,these public health interventions succeeded in drastically reducing the incidence of waterborne diseases among the urban population, and were an important cause in the increases of life expectancy experienced at the time.

*Are the following statements are **TRUE, FALSE** or **NOT GIVEN**?*

1 Early sanitation systems became more intricate as city populations grew. ....

2 The ancient water management systems of the Indus Valley are still in use today. ....

3 Some sewage networks built by the Romans in the UK were made out of wood. ....

4 Rome had the most developed of all ancient sanitation systems. ....

5 By the time of Queen Elizabeth 1, the majority of cities had built sewers for waste water. ....

6 Poor sanitation systems during the Industrial era posed a significant health risk. ....

7 The world's first complete sewage network was constructed in the USA. ....

我们先来做第一题，画出题干中的关键词。

1 Early sanitation systems became more intricate as city populations grew.

带着这几个关键词回到原文用正常速度阅读。

The first sanitation systems were built in the prehistoric Middle East, in the south-east of the modern country of Iran near Zabol. An inverted siphon system, along with glass covered clay pipes, was used for the first time in the palaces of Crete, Greece. It is still in working condition, after about

3,000 years.

首先我们找到了first(early) sanitation systems，但是并没有more intricate和city populations grew的相关信息，继续往下读。

Higher population densities required more complex sewer collection and conveyance systems to maintain sanitary conditions in crowded cities.

在上面这句话里，我们找到了关键词对应的同义词，原文信息与题干相符，第一题的答案是**TRUE**。这道题其实是在考intricate这个词，如果你知道intricate就是complex的意思，那就简单多了。

在第二题的题干中，我们有了一个专属名词，一个地名，这对我们定位信息非常有帮助。

2 The ancient water management systems of the Indus Valley are still in use today.

由于判断题是有顺序的，所以我们接着第一题的原文往下读。

The ancient cities of Harappa and Mohenjo-daro of the Indus Valley civilisation constructed complex networks of bricklined sewage drains from around 2600 BC and also had outdoor flush toilets connected to this network. The urban areas of the Indus Valley civilisation provided public and private baths, sewage was disposed through underground drains built with precisely laid bricks, and a sophisticated water management system with numerous reservoirs was established.

我们找到了Indus Valley，说明这是第二题的出题点，也找到了water management systems的同义词，但是并没有找到still in use today的相关信息，所以第二题只能选**NOT GIVEN**。

接着我们做第三题，画出题干关键词。

3 Some sewage networks built by the Romans in the UK were made out of wood.

Roman towns and garrisons in the United Kingdom between 46 BC and 400 AD had complex sewer networks sometimes constructed out of hollowed-out elm logs, which were shaped so that they butted together with the down-stream pipe providing a socket for the upstream pipe.

我们找到了好几组关键词的同义词，第三题的答案是TRUE。这道题其实就在考elm logs这个单词，如果你知道它的同义词是wood的话，这题就简单了。

4 Rome had the most developed of all ancient sanitation systems.

In some cities, including Rome, Istanbul (Constantinople) and Fustat, networked ancient sewer systems continue to function today as collection systems for those cities' modernised sewer systems. Instead of flowing to a river or the sea, the pipes have been re-routed to modern sewer treatment facilities.

在原文中我们并没有找到第四题题干中关于Rome有most developed的信息，或者Rome与其他城市比较的信息，所以这道题的答案是**NOT GIVEN**。

在第五题中，我们又发现了一个专属名词：Queen Elizabeth 罗（伊丽莎白一世在位期间），这对我们快速定位原文信息是非常有帮助的。

5 By the time of Queen ElizabethI 罗, the majority of cities had built sewers for waste water.

This basic system remained in place with little positive change, until the 16th century, when Sir John Harington invented the first flush toilet as a device for Queen ElizabethI (his godmother) that released wastes into cesspools. Despite this innovation, most cities did not have a functioning sewer system before the Industrial era, relying instead on nearby rivers or occasional rain showers to wash away the sewage from the streets.

根据原文，我们发现了the majority of cities的同义词，继续仔细阅读，发现原文信息与题干是相反的，这道题选**FALSE**。

在第六题，我们同样找到了一个专属名词：Industrial era（工业时代）。

6 Poor sanitation systems during the Industrial era posed a significant health risk.

The prevailing system was sufficient for the needs of early cities with few occupants, but the tremendous growth of cities during the Industrial Revolution quickly led to terribly overpolluted streets, which acted as a constant source for the outbreak of disease. As recently as the late 19th century sewerage systems in some parts of the highly industrialised United Kingdom were so inadequate that water-borne diseases such as cholera and typhoid remained a risk.

阅读原文，我们发现了Industrial era的同义词Industrial Revolution，题干中的a significant health risk对应原文中的the outbreak disease和water-borne diseases...remained at risk，sanitation 的同义词sewerage system。而解题的关键词就是inadequate，如果你知道它的同义词就是poor 的话，这道题就简单了。本题答案：**TRUE**。

接着我们做最后一题，在这个题干中我们也有一个专有名词，USA，这对我们定位非常有帮助。

7 The world's first complete sewage network was constructed in the USA.

The first comprehensive sewer system was built in Hamburg, Germany in the mid-19th century, and the first such systems in the United States were built in the late 1850s in Chicago and Brooklyn.

首先我们找到了world's first complete sewage network的同义词the first comprehensive sewer system，接着仔细阅读原文，原文说到United States(USA)类似的系统要1850年才出现，所以很 显然，题干是错误的，这道题选**FALSE**。世界上第一个下水系统出现在Hamburg,Germany。

到这里我们就算做完这道例题了，接下来整理一下本题的同义词替换。

同义词替换	题干中的关键词	原文中的同义词
第一题	**more intricate**	**more complex**
	early	the first
	city populations grew	higher population densities...in crowded cities
第二题	water management systems	networks of bricklined sewage
第三题	UK	United Kingdom
	made out of wood	constructed out of hollowed-out elm logs
第五题	the majority of cities	most cities
	sewers for waste water	sewer system

同义词替换	题干中的关键词	原文中的同义词
第六题	**poor** sanitation	sewerage systems...**so inadequate**
	Industrial era	during the Industrial Revolution
	pose a significant health risk	source for the outbreak of disease
第七题	the world`s first complete sewage network	the first comprehensive sewer system
	USA	United States

特别是加粗红字，这些单词直接决定了这道题是否能够解出，与其说是在考判断，不如说是在考词汇。

Is there a difference between the following?

- True, False, Not given
  when the passage is about facts
  (Are the statements true according to the
  information in the passage?)

- Yes, No, Not given
  when the passage is about the writer's views
  (Do the statements agree with the views
  expressed by the writer?)

题型练习

 第1题

Many diaries of notable figures have been published and form an important element of autobiographical literature. *Samuel Pepys* (1633-1703) is the earliest diarist who is well-known today; his diaries, preserved in Magdalene College, Cambridge, were first transcribed and published in 1825. Pepys was amongst the first who took the diary beyond mere business transaction notation, into the realm of the personal.

1 Samuel Pepys is more famous today than he was during his own lifetime. ....

2 Pepys kept a diary for purely business reasons. ....

 第2题

In the year 1971, *Zimbardo* accepted a tenured position as professor of psychology at Stanford University. There he conducted the Stanford prison study, in which 21 normal college students were randomly assigned to be "prisoners" or "guards" in a mock prison located in the basement of the psychology building at Stanford. The two week planned study into the psychological impact of prison life ended only after 6 days due to emotional trauma being experienced by the participants.

1 The participants in the study were all psychology students. ....

2 They were given the choice of playing the role of prisoner or guard. ....

3 A real prison was used in the experiment. ....

4 The study aimed to investigate the mental and behavioural effects of life in prison. ....

 第3题

On the website, visitors can search for activities not solely by geographical location, but also by the particular nature of the activity. This is important as research shows that activities are the key driver of visitor satisfaction, contributing 74% to visitor satisfaction, while transport and accommodation account for the remaining 26%. The more activities that visitors undertake, the more satisfied they will be. It has also been found that visitors enjoy cultural activities most when they are interactive, such as visiting a marae (meeting ground) to learn about traditional Maori life.

1 It was found that most visitors started searching on the website by geographical location. ....

2 According to research, 26% of visitor satisfaction is related to their accommodation. ....

3 Visitors to New Zealand like to become involved in the local culture. ....

 第4题

Minority languages are occasionally marginalised within nations for a number of reasons. These include the small number of speakers, the decline in the number of speakers, and their occasional consideration as uncultured, primitive, or simple dialects when compared to the dominant language. Support for minority languages is sometimes viewed as supporting separatism. Immigrant minority languages are often also seen as a threat and as indicative of the non-integration of these communities. Both of these perceived threats are based on the notion of the exclusion of the majority language speakers. Often this is added to by political systems which do not provide support (such as education and policing) in these languages.

1 Minority languages sometimes disappear. ....

2 Minority languages are simpler to learn than majority languages. ....

3 Minority languages are sometimes considered to be harmful. ....

 第5题

The Stanford marshmallow experiment was a study on deferred gratification. The experiment was conducted in 1972 by psychologist *Walter Mischel* of Stanford University. It has been repeated many times since, and the original study at Stanford is regarded as one of the most successful experiments in the study of human behaviour. In the study, a marshmallow was offered to each child. If the child could resist eating the marshmallow, he was promised two instead of one. The scientists analysed how long each child resisted the temptation of eating the marshmallow, and whether or not doing so had an effect on their future success. The results provided researchers with great insight on the psychology of self control.

1 When repeated by other researchers, the experiment was less successful. ....

2 Children were offered a second marshmallow if they managed not to eat the first one. ....

3 Scientists found a correlation between resisting temptation and future success. ....

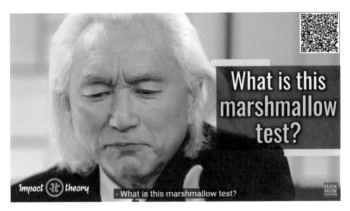

（延迟满足和成功到底有关系吗？）

 第6题

'Biometrics' refers to the identification of humans by their characteristics or traits. Biometric identifiers are often categorised as physiological versus behavioural characteristics. Physiological characteristics are related to the shape of the body. Examples include fingerprint, face recognition, DNA, Palm print, hand geometry and iris recognition. Behavioural characteristics are related to the behaviour of a person, including typing rhythm, gait, and voice.

More traditional means of identification include token-based systems, such as a driver's license or passport, and knowledge-based systems, such as a password or personal identification number. Since biometric identifiers are unique to individuals, they are more reliable in verifying identity than token and knowledge-based methods; however, the collection of biometric identifiers raises privacy concerns about the ultimate use of this information.

1 There are two main types of biometric identifier. ....

2 Fingerprinting is the best known biometric identification system. ....

3 The use of a password is another example of biometric identification. ....

4 Some people may worry about how biometric data is used. ....

第7题

The travel industry includes:hotels, motels and other types of accommodation; restaurants and other food services; transportation services and facilities; amusements, attractions and other leisure facilities; gift shops and a large number of other enterprises. Since many of these businesses also serve local residents, the impact of spending by visitors can easily be overlooked or underestimated. In addition, Meis (1992) points out that the tourism industry involves concepts that have remained amorphous to both analysts and decision makers. Moreover, in all nations this problem has made it difficult for the industry to develop any type of reliable or credible tourism information base in order to estimate the contribution it makes to regional, national and global economies.

1 Visitor spending is always greater than the spending of residents in tourist areas. ....

2 It is easy to show statistically how tourism affects individual economies. ....

 第8题

According to *the Early Office Museum*, the first patent for a bent wire paper clip was awarded in the United States to *Samuel B.Fay*, in 1867. This clip was originally intended primarily for attaching tickets to fabric, although the patent recognized that it could be used to attach papers together. Although functional and practical, *Fay*'s design along with the 50 other designs patented prior to 1899 are not considered reminiscent of the modern paper clip design known today.

The most common type of wire paper clip still in use, the Gem paper clip, was never patented, but it was most likely in production in Britain in the early 1870s by "*The Gem Manufacturing Company*", according to the American expert on technological innovations, Professor *Henry J.Petroski*.

1 *Samuel B.Fay*'s paper clip was only patented for one specific use. ....

2 *Fay*'s paper clip was not as practical as those we use today. ....

3 Nobody has a patent on the paper clip that most people use today. ....

 第9题

Coffee consumption has been shown to have minimal or no impact, positive or negative, on cancer development. However, researchers involved in an ongoing 22-year study by *the Harvard School of Public Health* state that "the overall balance of risks and benefits [of coffee consumption] are on the side of benefits."

Other studies suggest coffee consumption reduces the risk of being affected by Alzheimer's disease, Parkinson's disease, heart disease, diabetes mellitus type 2, cirrhosis of the liver, and gout. A longitudinal study in 2009 showed that those who consumed a moderate amount of coffee or tea (3–5 cups per day) at midlife were less likely to develop dementia and Alzheimer's disease in late-life compared with those who drank little coffee or avoided it altogether.

1 Scientists have linked coffee consumption to accelerated cancer development. ....

2 Some scientists believe that the benefits of drinking coffee outweigh the drawbacks. ....

3 Recent research links coffee consumption with a reduced risk of some illnesses. ....

 ## 第10题

Sir *Isaac Newton* was an English physicist, mathematician, astronomer, natural philosopher, alchemist, and theologian. His Philosophiae Naturalis *Principia Mathematica* (Latin for "Mathematical Principles of Natural Philosophy"; usually called the *Principia*), published in 1687, is one of the most important scientific books ever written. It lays the groundwork for most of classical mechanics.

Newton is considered by many scholars and members of the general public to be one of the most influential people in human history. French mathematician Joseph-Louis Lagrange often said that Newton was the greatest genius who ever lived. Newton himself had been rather more modest of his own achievements, famously writing in a letter to Robert Hooke in February 1676: "If I have seen further, it is by standing on the shoulders of giants."

1 Newton's *Principia* is recognised as a groundbreaking text in its field. ....

2 Many experts regard Newton as the greatest genius the world has seen. ....

3 Newton wrote that he had achieved everything without the help of others. ....

Contrary to the common wisdom that sharks are instinct-driven "eating machines", recent studies have indicated that many species possess powerful problem-solving skills, social skills and curiosity. The brain-to body-mass ratios of sharks are similar to those of mammals and birds, and migration patterns in sharks may be even more complex than in birds, with many sharks covering entire ocean basins. However, shark behaviour has only begun to be formally studied, so there is much more to learn.

A popular myth is that sharks are immune to disease and cancer; however, this remains to be proven. The evidence that sharks are at least resistant to cancer and disease is mostly anecdotal and there have been few, if any, scientific or statistical studies that show sharks to have heightened immunity to disease.

1 Research shows that sharks are more intelligent than most people think. ....

2 Relative to their body size, sharks have bigger brains than birds. ....

3 There is no real evidence proving that sharks are resistant to diseases. ....

 第12题

"All our life, so far as it has definite form, is but a mass of habits," *William James* wrote in 1892. Most of the choices we make each day may feel like the products of well-considered decision making, but they're not. They're habits. And though each habit means relatively little on its own, over time, the meals we order, what we say to our kids each night, whether we save or spend, how often we exercise, and the way we organize our thoughts and work routines have enormous impacts on our health, productivity, financial security, and happiness. One paper published by a Duke University researcher in 2006 found that 40 percent or more of the actions people performed each day weren't actual decisions, but habits.

1 The majority of choices we make on a daily basis are conscious decisions. ....

2 Saving money is the key to financial security. ....

3 Habits account for at least 40 percent of the things we do each day. ....

NASA has released stunning photos of something like "Niagara falls" on Mars – except even more stunning than the one on Earth. The flows are made of flowing molten lava that once moved over the Red Planet's surface, and have been pictured in stunning new 3D images. The photos were sent back by the *Mars Reconnaissance Orbiter (MRO)*, which was launched in 2005 and has been sending images back of the planet's surface since soon after that.

NASA notes that a lot of time is spent wondering about and searching for proof of liquid water on Mars, which would be a signal of life. But the new pictures show that the planet itself was once far more alive than it is today – made up of flowing molten lava that spread across its surface.

1 Lava flows on Mars are more beautiful than one of Earth's most famous waterfalls. ....

2 NASA has just released the first ever 3D images of Mars. ....

3 The new photographs prove that liquid may be present on Mars. ....

4 The photos show that the surface of Mars is more active than ever. ....

In a recent study published in the journal *Medicine & Science in Sports & Exercise*, researchers looked at 10 pairs of male identical twins in their 30s. Each twin was similar to his brother in most ways, right down to their eating habits - except that one in each pair had stopped exercising regularly in adulthood.

Despite the fact that the less active twins had the exact same DNA as their fit brothers, after just three sedentary years, they had begun to develop insulin resistance (a precursor to diabetes), had more body fat and lower endurance - and, perhaps most notably, had less grey matter in the brain regions responsible for motor control and coordination. While the study was small, it is evidence that exercise may have as large an effect on your health as your genes do.

1 The twins in the study were very similar, but they had different diets. ....

2 The fitter twins had less body fat than their brothers. ....

3 The less active twins performed badly in tests of coordination. ....

4 The size of the study means that no conclusions can be drawn. ....

The evidence is crystal clear: Physical activity is great for children. Researchers around the world agree that young people who are active have better brain function, higher self-esteem, more motivation and better school performance.

During the school day, children do not need to exercise for long periods of time. A review of studies published in 2011 found that short bursts of physical activity - 10 minutes or less - increased pupils' attention in the classroom. Children who took short breaks for physical activity also performed better in school and displayed lower stress levels and better moods.

What about linking physical activity with teaching? A review published in 2015 found that when children learn while moving their bodies, they perform significantly better on standardised tests. There are all sorts of examples of how to make this happen, such as doing jumping jacks while spelling words.

1 Physical exercise can make children feel better about themselves. ....

2 The optimal amount of physical activity for children is 10 minutes. ....

3 Children can benefit when tasks provide both mental and physical stimulation. ....

 第16题

The killer whale, commonly referred to as the orca, and less commonly as the blackfish, is a toothed whale belonging to the oceanic dolphin family. Killer whales are found in all oceans, from the frigid Arctic and Antarctic regions to tropical seas. As a species they have a diverse diet, although individual populations often specialize in particular types of prey. Some feed exclusively on fish, while others hunt marine mammals such as sea lions, seals, walruses and even large whales. Killer whales are regarded as apex predators, lacking natural predators and preying on even large sharks.

Killer whales are highly social; some populations are composed of family groups which are the most stable of any animal species. Their sophisticated hunting techniques and vocal behaviors, which are often specific to a particular group and passed across generations, have been described as manifestations of culture.

1 Killer whales are predominantly found in cold water areas. ....

2 Some killer whale groups only eat fish. ....

3 They may even eat large sharks. ....

4 Killer whales are able to pass on skills to their young. ....

第17题

From a single point of origin, Mainz, Germany, printing spread within several decades to over two hundred cities in a dozen European countries. By 1500, printing presses in operation throughout Western Europe had already produced more than twenty million volumes. In the 16th century, with presses spreading further afield, their output rose tenfold to an estimated 150 to 200 million copies. The operation of a press became so synonymous with the enterprise of printing that it lent its name to an entire new branch of media, the press.

In Renaissance Europe, the arrival of mechanical movable type printing introduced the era of mass communication which permanently altered the structure of society. The relatively unrestricted circulation of information and ideas transcended borders and threatened the power of political and religious authorities. The sharp increase in literacy broke the monopoly of the literate elite on education and learning and bolstered the emerging middle class.

1 By the beginning of the 16th century, the printing press was in use in several different countries. ....

2 The printing press was popular because it was so easy to operate. ....

3 Movable type printing can be linked to a rise in the number of people who could read and write. ....

4 Printing had a negative effect on the middle classes. ....

第18题

In the late 20th century, mass media could be classified into eight mass media industries: books, the Internet, magazines, movies, newspapers, radio, recordings, and television. The explosion of digital communication technology in the late 20th and early 21st centuries gave rise to the question: what forms of media should be classified as "mass media"? For example, it is controversial whether to include cell phones and video games in the definition.

Each mass medium has its own content types, creative artists, technicians, and business models. For example, the Internet includes blogs, podcasts, web sites, and various other technologies built atop the general distribution network. Internet and mobile phones are often referred to collectively as digital media, and radio and TV as broadcast media. Some argue that video games have developed into a distinct mass form of media, in the sense that they provide a common experience to millions of people across the globe and convey the same messages and ideologies to all their users.

1 In the 21st century, it is widely accepted that there are now more than eight mass media industries. ....

2 Digital media can be subdivided into various content types. ....

3 Video games are the newest mass media platform. ....

 第19题

The Beaufort scale is an empirical measure that relates wind speed to observed conditions at sea or on land. Its full name is the Beaufort wind force scale, although it is a measure of wind speed and not of force in the scientific sense.

The scale was devised in 1805 by Francis Beaufort, an Irish Royal Navy officer. In the early 19th century, naval officers made regular weather observations, but there was no standard scale and so they could be very subjective. The initial scale of thirteen classes (zero to twelve) did not reference wind speed numbers but related qualitative wind conditions to effects on the sails of a frigate, then the main ship of the Royal Navy.

In 1916, to accommodate the growth of steam power, the descriptions were changed to how the sea, not the sails, behaved. The Beaufort scale was extended in 1946, when forces 13 to 17 were added. Today, hurricane force winds are sometimes described as Beaufort scale 12 to 16.

1 The Beaufort scale is a scientific measure of wind force. ....

2 In the early 1800s, naval officers demanded a more accurate way to measure weather conditions. ....

3 The original scale measured the effect of wind on a ship's sails. ....

4 Today, the Beaufort scale is still the predominant scale for wind description. ....

（蒲福风级的具体表现是什么样的呢？）

 第20题

Iceland has a high concentration of active volcanoes due to unique geological conditions. The island has about 130 volcanic mountains, of which 18 have erupted since the settlement of Iceland, circa 900 CE. Over the past 500 years, Iceland's volcanoes have erupted a third of the total global lava output.

Geologists explain this high concentration of volcanic activity as being due to a combination of the island's position on the Mid-Atlantic Ridge and a volcanic hotspot underneath the island. The island sits astride the boundary between the Eurasian and North American Plates, and most volcanic activity is concentrated along the plate boundary, which runs across the island from the south-west to the north-east of the island. Some volcanic activity occurs offshore, especially off the southern coast. This includes wholly submerged submarine volcanoes and even newly formed volcanic islands such as Surtsey and jolnir.

The most recent volcanic eruption in Iceland was that of Eyjafjallajokull, which started on April 14, 2010. The Eyjafjallajokull eruption closely followed an eruption in Eyjafjallajokull, which had erupted on March 20.

1 People first settled in Iceland around the beginning of the 10th century. ....

2 The island is situated at the point where two of the earth's plates meet. ....

3 Volcanic activity also takes place in the ocean near Iceland. ....

第21题

The Deepwater Horizon oil spill is making Americans think more about a clean energy future — but not yet to the extent of having to pay for it, or to tackle climate change, one of the leading US thinkers on global warming policy said yesterday.

US citizens are "horrified" by the pollution in the Gulf of Mexico, and are starting to think more about cleaner energy sources such as wind and wave power, said *Eileen Clausen*, president of America's foremost climate think-tank, the Washington-based *Pew Center on Global Climate Change*.

However, she said, when consumers are asked by pollsters if they would be willing to pay more for such a future, they say no, and say the government should pay. Furthermore, Ms *Clausen* said, the Gulf disaster was giving US energy policy "a nudge rather than a shift" in the direction of clean energy, but it would probably not be enough to bring forward legislation to curb carbon emissions, at least for the present.

1 The oil spill in the Gulf of Mexico was the result of a human error. ....

2 US citizens accept that they will need to pay for a clean energy future. ....

3 In spite of the disaster, the government is unlikely to introduce laws to reduce carbon emissions. ....

第22题

Watching television makes toddlers fatter and stupider at primary school, according to new research. Scientists who tracked the progress of pre-school children found that the more television they watched the worse they were at mathematics, the more junk food they ate, and the more they were bullied by other pupils.

The findings, which support earlier evidence indicating television harms cognitive development, prompted calls for the Government to set limits on how much children should watch. American paediatricians advise that under-twos should not watch any television and that older children should view one to two hours a day at most. France has banned shows aimed at under-threes, and Australia recommends that three to five year-olds watch no more than an hour a day. Britain has no official advice.

Researchers said that pre-school is a critical time for brain development and that TV watching displaced time that could be spent engaging in "developmentally enriching tasks". Even incremental exposure to TV delayed development, said the lead author Dr *Linda Pagani*, of Montreal University.

1 Scientists believe that there is a link between the amount of television young children watch and their mental ability. ....

2 Shows aimed at under-twos are banned in the USA. ....

3 Children's television programming is more strictly controlled in France than in Britain. ....

第23题

Thousands of experiments have been performed to study the preferences of hungry and thirsty animals. The results are universal: all animals are highly sensitive to subtle differences in amount of food or water.

Consider experiments using hungry pigeons. A pigeon is trained to peck at an illuminated button on the wall of its cage, and the experimenter follows each peck with delivery to the pigeon of a small amount of mixed grain. The pigeon soon learns to peck the button. Then the experimenter puts two illuminated buttons, a red one and a green one, side by side on the wall. If the pigeon pecks the red button, it gets 2 ounces of food; if it pecks the green button, it gets 1 ounce of food. Almost all pigeons soon learn to peck the red one and ignore the green one.

However, the results are completely different when a time delay is introduced after the red button is pecked. Virtually all pigeons strongly prefer 1 ounce of food delivered immediately to 2 ounces delayed by only 4 seconds.

1 Experiments using hungry and thirsty animals give inconsistent results. ....

2 Pigeons can be taught to do simple actions in order to get a reward. ....

3 Hungry pigeons choose the larger reward, regardless of whether they have to wait for it. ....

第24题

For 27 years the philosopher *Arthur Schopenhauer* followed an identical routine. He rose every morning at seven and had a bath but no breakfast; he drank a cup of strong coffee before sitting down at his desk and writing until noon. At noon he ceased work for the day and spent half an hour practicing the flute, on which he became quite a skilled performer. Then he went out for lunch at his favourite restaurant. After lunch he returned home and read until four, when he left for his daily walk; he walked for two hours no matter what the weather. At six o'clock he visited the reading room of the library and read *The Times*. In the evening he attended the theatre or a concert, after which he had dinner at a hotel or restaurant. He got back home between nine and ten and went early to bed. He was willing to deviate from this routine in order to receive visitors.

1 Schopenhauer got up at the same time every day. ....

2 He dedicated the whole day to his work. ....

3 He ate the same meal every evening. ....

4 Schopenhauer allowed nothing to interrupt his daily routine. ....

第25题

Although some of the steps in photosynthesis are still not completely understood, the overall photosynthetic equation has been known since the 1800s.

Jan van Helmont began the research of the process in the mid-1600s when he carefully measured the mass of the soil used by a plant and the mass of the plant as it grew. After noticing that the soil mass changed very little, he hypothesised that the mass of the growing plant must come from the water, the only substance he added to the potted plant. His hypothesis was partially accurate - much of the gained mass also comes from carbon dioxide as well as water.

In 1796, *Jean Senebier*, a Swiss pastor, botanist, and naturalist, demonstrated that green plants consume carbon dioxide and release oxygen under the influence of light. Soon afterwards, *Nicolas-Théodore de Saussure* showed that the increase in mass of the plant as it grows could not be due only to uptake of CO2, but also to the incorporation of water.

1 We now fully understand the process of photosynthesis. ....

2 Van Helmont's hypothesis did not take into account that plants consume carbon dioxide. ....

3 *De Saussure* demonstrated that both carbon dioxide and water contribute to an increase in mass in plants as they grow. ....

 第26题

The Suzuki method is a method of teaching music conceived and executed by Japanese violinist Shin'ichi Suzuki (born 1898, died 1998), dating from the mid-20th century. The central belief of Suzuki is that all people are capable of learning from their environment. The essential components of his method spring from the desire to create the "right environment" for learning music. He also believed that this positive environment would also help to foster character in students.

As a skilled violinist but a beginner at the German language who struggled to learn it, Suzuki noticed that children pick up their native language quickly, and even dialects adults consider "difficult" to learn are spoken with ease by 5-year-olds. He reasoned that if children have the skill to acquire their mother tongue, then they have the necessary ability to become proficient on a musical instrument. He pioneered the idea that pre-school age children could learn to play the violin if learning steps were small enough and if the instrument was scaled down to fit their body.

1 Suzuki believed that environment is crucial for anyone learning a musical instrument. ....

2 His method helped him to learn German. ....

3 Suzuki compared language learning with learning to play an instrument. ....

4 He introduced new ideas about teaching music to infants. ....

 第27题

What constitutes the good life? What is the true value of money? Why do we work such long hours merely to acquire greater wealth? These are some of the questions that many asked themselves when the financial system crashed in 2008. This book tackles such questions head-on. The authors begin with the great economist *John Maynard Keynes*. In 1930, *Keynes* predicted that within a century people's basic needs would be met, and no one would have to work more than fifteen hours a week.

Clearly, he was wrong: though income has increased as he envisioned, our wants have seemingly gone unsatisfied, and we continue to work long hours. The authors explain why Keynes was mistaken. Then, arguing from the premise that economics is a moral science, they trace the concept of the good life from *Aristotle* to the present and show how our lives over the last half century have strayed from that ideal. Finally, they issue a call to think anew about what really matters in our lives and how to attain it.

1 Before 2008, people were less concerned about economics. ....

2 Keynes' prediction about working hours was wide of the mark. ....

3 The book asks us to consider what is important in life. ....

 第28题

Learning a second language can boost thinking skills, improve mental agility and delay the ageing of the brain, according to scientists who believe that speaking minority languages should be positively encouraged in schools and universities. Studies have found that children and adults who learn or speak another language benefit from the extra effort it takes to handle two sets of vocabularies and rules of grammar.

"Fewer parents speak minority languages to their children because of the perceived lack of usefulness. Many people still think that a minority language makes children confused and puts them at a disadvantage at school," said *Antonella Sorace* of *the University of Edinburgh*. "These feelings clash with much research on bilingualism, which shows instead that when there are differences between monolingual and bilingual children, these are almost invariably in favour of bilinguals," Dr *Sorace* said.

"Bilingual children tend to have enhanced language abilities, a better understanding of others' points of view, and more mental flexibility in dealing with complex situations," she told the *American Association for the Advancement of Science* in Washington.

1 Some scientists believe that the teaching of minority languages should be promoted. ....

2 Research into bilingualism supports the idea that learning two languages can be detrimental to children. ....

3 Bilingual children tend to get high scores in intelligence tests. ....

 第29题

Collocation is defined as a sequence of words or terms which co-occur more often than would be expected by chance. Collocation comprises the restrictions on how words can be used together, for example which prepositions are used with particular verbs, or which verbs and nouns are used together. An example of this (from *Michael Halliday*) is the collocation *strong tea*. While the same meaning could be conveyed through the roughly equivalent *powerful tea*, the fact is that English prefers to speak of tea in terms of being *strong* rather than in terms of being *powerful*. A similar observation holds for *powerful computers* which is preferred over *strong computers*.

If the expression is heard often, the words become 'glued' together in our minds. 'Crystal clear', 'middle management', 'nuclear family', and 'cosmetic surgery' are examples of collocated pairs of words. Some words are often found together because they make up a compound noun, for example 'text message' or 'motor cyclist'.

1 It is possible, but not normal, to say 'powerful tea'. ....

2 It is equally acceptable in English to say 'powerful computers' or 'strong computers'. ....

3 Our brains remember some pairs of words better than others. ....

 第30题

It's easy to see why economists would embrace cities, warts and all, as engines of prosperity. It has taken a bit longer for environmentalists. By increasing income, cities increase consumption and pollution too. If what you value most is nature, cities look like concentrated piles of damage - until you consider the alternative, which is spreading the damage. From an ecological standpoint, says *Stewart Brand*, founder of *the Whole Earth Catalog*, a back-to-the-land ethic would be disastrous. Cities allow half of humanity to live on around 4 percent of the arable land, leaving more space for open country.

Per capita, city dwellers tread more lightly in other ways as well, as *David Owen* explains in *Green Metropolis*. Their roads, sewers, and power lines are shorter and so use fewer resources. Their apartments take less energy to heat, cool, and light than do houses. Most important, people in dense cities drive less. Their destinations are close enough to walk to, and enough people are going to the same places to make public transit practical. In cities like New York, per capita energy use and carbon emissions are much lower than the national average.

1 Both economists and environmentalists may now see the benefits of cities. ....

2 A return to rural living would be a bad idea ecologically speaking. ....

3 City dwellers are more environmentally aware than the average person. ....

 第31题

Before the twentieth century, the term "philology" was commonly used to refer to the science of language, which was then predominantly historical in focus. However, this focus has shifted and the term "philology" is now generally used for the "study of a language's grammar, history and literary tradition", especially in the United States. The term "linguistics" is now the usual academic term in English for the scientific study of language.

Linguistics concerns itself with describing and explaining the nature of human language. Relevant to this are the questions of what is universal to language, how language can vary, and how human beings come to know languages. Humans achieve competence in whatever language is spoken around them when growing up, with apparently little need for explicit conscious instruction.

Linguists assume that the ability to acquire and use language is an innate, biologically-based potential of human beings, similar to the ability to walk. It is generally agreed that there are no strong genetic differences underlying the differences between languages: an individual will acquire whatever language(s) he or she is exposed to as a child, regardless of parentage or ethnic origin.

1 Up until the 1900s, the science of language was usually referred to as 'philology'. ....

2 In order to learn a language, children need a significant amount of instruction. ....

3 Research has shown that humans have an inbuilt capacity for language learning. ....

Michael Faraday, (1791 - 1867) was an English scientist who contributed to the fields of electromagnetism and electrochemistry. Although Faraday received little formal education he was one of the most influential scientists in history, and historians of science refer to him as having been the best experimentalist in the history of science.

The young *Michael Faraday*, who was the third of four children, having only the most basic school education, had to educate himself. At fourteen he became the apprentice to *George Riebau*, a local bookbinder and bookseller. During his seven-year apprenticeship he read many books, including *Isaac Watts' The Improvement of the Mind*, and he enthusiastically implemented the principles and suggestions contained therein.

In 1812, at the age of twenty, and at the end of his apprenticeship, *Faraday* attended lectures by the eminent English chemist *Humphry Davy*. Faraday subsequently sent *Davy* a three-hundred-page book based on notes that he had taken during these lectures. Davy's reply was immediate, kind, and favourable. When one of the Royal Institution's assistants was sacked, *Davy* was asked to find a replacement, and appointed *Faraday* as Chemical Assistant at the Royal Institution.

1 Many experts regard Faraday as the foremost experimentalist of all time. ....

2 Faraday educated himself by reading books that were recommended to him by *George Riebau*. ....

3 Faraday came to the attention of a famous chemist after he wrote a book based on the chemist's lectures. ....

but also unraveled one of science's all-time greatest mysteries.

（法拉第有哪些重大的发现？）

第33题

The human brain evolved to focus on one thing at a time. This enabled our ancestors to hunt animals, to create tools, and to protect their clan from predators or invading neighbours. In parallel, an attentional filter evolved to help us to stay on task, letting through only information that was important enough to deserve disrupting our train of thought.

But a funny thing happened on the way to the twenty-first century: The plethora of information and the technologies that serve our brain changed the way we use it. Increasingly, we demand that our attentional system try to focus on several things at once. Uni-tasking is getting harder and harder to do. The information age now buries us in data coming at us from every which way. We are bombarded with more information than at any time in history - the equivalent of 175 newspapers a day, five times as much information as we took in thirty years ago.

If we want to be more productive and creative, and to have more energy, the science suggests that we should tame the multi-tasking and immerse ourselves in a single task for sustained periods, say 30 to 50 minutes.

第34题

The word 'talent' comes from the Latin word 'talentum', meaning a sum of money, and from the Greek 'talanton', meaning a unit of money or weight. An ancient Greek talent was 26 kilograms, which was approximately the mass of water required to fill an amphora - an ancient jar or jug.

When used as a measure of money, the word 'talent' typically referred to a weight of gold or silver. A Roman talent was around 33 kilograms of gold, while an Egyptian talent was 27 kilograms and a Babylonian talent was 30.3 kilograms. At the current price of around 38 US dollars per gram, a Roman talent of gold would cost roughly 1.25 million dollars.

Another way to calculate the modern equivalent to a talent is from its use in estimating military pay. During the Peloponnesian war in Ancient Greece, a talent was the amount of silver needed to pay the crew of a trireme (a warship requiring about 170 oarsmen) for one month. Alternatively, a talent of silver was said to be equivalent to the value of nine years of one man's skilled work.

1 For the ancient Greeks, a talent was the weight of water in a particular container. ....

2 In modern terms, the Roman talent would be equivalent to a considerable amount of money. ....

3 A 'trireme' was the name of a group of ancient Greek warriors. ....

4 The Greeks were the first people to use the word talent in its modern sense. ....

 第35题

Hell Creek is heaven for paleontologists. The Montanan wildlife refuge is rife with clay and stones that hold clues to our prehistoric past. It was in *Hell Creek* that researchers from the University of Kansas recently stumbled on the remains of a young *Tyrannosaurus rex* - they think.

Fossils from various periods have been found there, and this isn't the first T. rex fossil to be found, but *University of Kansas* scientists think it could be one of the most intact. The entire fossil remains of the upper part of the dinosaur's jaw, with all its teeth, was found. Paleontologists dug up parts of a skull, foot, hips, and backbones. If the remains do in fact belong to a T. rex, that would make them around 66 million years old. Adding to the rarity of the find is the fact that the fossils may belong to a juvenile.

Further work will determine whether the team actually has a T. rex on their hands, or possibly a Nanotyrannus, a tiny genus of tyrannosaur that's a matter of scientific debate. Many paleontologists think that so-called Nanotyrannus fossils are actually juvenile T. rex specimens.

（看看科学家们在Hell Creek是如何挖恐龙化石的）

1 Researchers have discovered a new fossil in Hell Creek, Montana. ....

2 It is thought that the unearthed bones belong to a mature Tyrannosaurus rex. ....

3 Some paleontologists doubt whether the Nanotyrannus actually existed. ....

 第36题

According to a survey, most Britons believe "green" taxes on 4×4s, plastic bags and other consumer goods have been imposed to raise cash rather than change our behaviour, while two-thirds of Britons think the entire green agenda has been hijacked as a ploy to increase taxes.

The UK is committed to reducing carbon emissions by 60 per cent by 2050, a target that most experts believe will be difficult to reach. The results of the poll by *Opinium*, a leading research company, indicate that maintaining popular support for green policies may be a difficult act to pull off and attempts in the future to curb car use and publicly fund investment in renewable resources will prove deeply unpopular.

The findings were released as the *Prince of Wales* yesterday called on Britain's business leaders to take "essential action" to make their firms more sustainable. Speaking in central London to some of the country's leading chief executives, *Prince Charles* said: "What more can I do but urge you, this country's business leaders, to take the essential action now to make your businesses more sustainable. I'm exhausted with repeating that there really is no time to lose."

1 Most Britons think that the Government wants to change people's behaviour. ....

2 By the year 2050 the Government will have imposed higher green taxes. ....

3 The survey predicts that it will be difficult to change people's dependence on cars. ....

4 The Prince of Wales believes that most businesses are not sustainable. ....

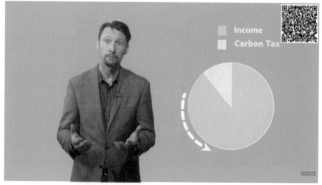

（碳减排对人们意味着什么？）

Most contemporary ethologists view the elephant as one of the world's most intelligent animals. With a mass of just over 5 kg, an elephant's brain has more mass than that of any other land animal, and although the largest whales have body masses twenty times those of a typical elephant, a whale's brain is barely twice the mass of an elephant's brain. In addition, elephants have a total of 300 billion neurons. Elephant brains are similar to humans' and many other mammals' in terms of general connectivity and functional areas.

Elephants manifest a wide variety of behaviours, including those associated with grief, learning, mimicry, play, altruism, use of tools, compassion, cooperation, self-awareness, memory, and communication. Further, evidence suggests elephants may understand pointing: the ability to nonverbally communicate an object by extending a finger, or equivalent.

Elephants are thought to be highly altruistic animals that even aid other species, including humans, in distress. In India, an elephant was helping locals lift logs by following a truck and placing the logs in pre-dug holes upon instruction from the mahout (elephant trainer). At a certain hole, the elephant refused to lower the log. The mahout came to investigate the hold-up and noticed a dog sleeping in the hole. The elephant only lowered the log when the dog was gone.

1 An elephant's brain is larger than that of a whale. ....

2 In some respects, an elephant's brain resembles the human brain. ....

3 Elephants can copy the behaviour of humans. ....

4 Elephants may understand a certain type of body language. ....

5 The story about an elephant in India is an example of altruism. ....

（大象到底能有多聪明？）

A 'megacity' is usually defined as a metropolitan area with a total population in excess of ten million people. A megacity can be a single metropolitan area or two or more metropolitan areas that converge. The terms conurbation, metropolis and metroplex are also applied to the latter. As of 2017, there are 37 megacities in existence. The largest of these are the metropolitan areas of Tokyo and Shanghai, each of these having a population of over 30 million inhabitants, with 38.8 million and 35.5 million respectively. Tokyo is the world's largest metropolitan area, while Shanghai has the world's largest city proper population. The UN predicts there will be 41 megacities by 2030.

By contrast, a 'global city', also called 'world city' or sometimes 'alpha city' or 'world center', is a city generally considered to be an important node in the global economic system. *The Institute for Urban Strategies at The Mori Memorial Foundation* in Tokyo issued a comprehensive study of global cities in 2016. The ranking is based on six overall categories: Economy, Research & Development, Cultural Interaction, Livability, Environment, and Accessibility. According to this particular ranking system, the top three 'global cities' at present are London, New York and Tokyo.

1 The term 'megacity' refers to population size, whereas the term 'global city' is primarily used to denote economic importance. ....

2 Currently there are 37 cities with a population of over 10 million people. ....

3 London is classified as being both a megacity and a global city. ....

A Stradivarius is one of the violins, cellos, and other stringed instruments built by members of the Stradivari (Stradivarius) family, particularly Antonio Stradivari, during the 17th and 18th centuries. According to their reputation, the quality of their sound has defied attempts to explain or equal it, though this belief is disputed. The name "Stradivarius" has become a superlative often associated with excellence, and the fame of Stradivarius instruments is widespread, appearing in numerous works of fiction.

Depending on condition, instruments made during Stradivari's "golden period" from 1'700 to about 1,725 can be worth millions of dollars. In 2011, his "*Lady Blunt*" violin from 1'721, which is in pristine condition, was sold at Tarisio auctions for £9.8 million.

These instruments are famous for the quality of sound they produce. However, the many blind tests from 1817 to the present have never found any difference in sound between Stradivari's violins and high-quality violins in comparable style of other makers and periods, nor has acoustic analysis. In a particularly famous test on a BBC Radio programme in 1977, the violinists *Isaac Stern* and *Pinchas Zukerman* and the violin expert and dealer *Charles Beare* tried to distinguish between the "*Chaconne*" Stradivarius and three other violins, including one made in 1976, played behind a screen by a professional soloist. None of the listeners identified more than two of the four instruments. Two of the listeners identified the 20th-century violin as the Stradivarius.

1 The superior reputation of Stradivarius instruments has never been questioned. ....

2 The "Lady Blunt" Stradivarius is the most expensive violin every sold. ....

3 Tests have shown that experts are able to distinguish the famous Stradivarius sound. ....

第40题

The ease of our modern workday could come at the expense of our longevity. A new study of older women in the *American Journal of Preventive Medicine* finds that sitting for long stretches of time increases the odds of an untimely death. The more hours women in the study spent sitting at work, driving, lying on the couch watching TV, or engaged in other leisurely pursuits, the greater their odds of dying early from all causes, including heart disease and cancer.

Even women who exercised regularly risked shortening their lifespan if most of their daily hours were sedentary ones. "Even if you are doing the recommended amount of moderate to vigorous exercise, you will still have a higher risk of mortality if you're spending too many hours sitting," says Dr. *JoAnn Manson*, one of the study's authors.

How much sitting can you safely do in a day? In the study, women who were inactive for 11 or more hours a day fared the worst, facing a 12% increase in premature death, but even lesser amounts of inactive time can cause problems. "Once you're sitting for more than 6 to 8 hours a day, that's not likely to be good for you," Dr. *Manson* says. You want to avoid prolonged sitting and increase the amount of moderate or vigorous exercise you do each day, she adds.

1 The study looked at the effects of sitting on elderly women only. ....

2 A link was found between hours spent sitting and serious health problems. ....

3 The warnings about sitting do not apply to people who exercise regularly. ....

4 Less than 6 hours a day is a safe amount of sitting. ....

 第41题

Microplastics are small pieces of plastic less than five millimetres in size. Some microplastics are manufactured, such as the microbeads added to health and beauty products, while others result from larger plastics gradually breaking down. These plastics are pervasive in marine environments, and they are known to harbour toxic substances such as heavy metals and phthalates.

Since many animals are known to eat microplastics, scientists are concerned about the toxic substances contained within them, as well as their capacity to accumulate within the animals and stop them from absorbing nutrients correctly.

Even the largest marine creatures are vulnerable to tiny fragments of plastic littering the world's oceans. A new study has found whales and whale sharks – the largest fish in the world – are ingesting microplastics in alarming quantities. These creatures are filter feeders, meaning they consume large quantities of small prey by straining them out of the ocean water. In the process, they swallow hundreds to thousands of cubic meters of water daily, meaning there is the potential for them to take in substantial amounts of microplastic floating in the water.

Recently, plastic pollution has received a lot of attention for its effects on marine animals. In the UK, microbeads have been banned, and other plastic items such as water bottles and disposable coffee cups have also been in the firing line. However, while scientists agree that plastic pollution is a problem for marine animals, there is still a lot they do not know about the magnitude of its impact.

1 Harmful microplastics are widespread in the world's oceans and seas. ....

2 Larger fish are the most likely to be harmed by these toxic plastics. ....

3 The only fish that ingest microplastics are those that swallow water. ....

4 Water bottles and disposable cups have been banned in the UK. ....

5 Scientists are yet to discover how serious the microplastic problem is. ....

this plastic pollution for ourselves.

（我们吃的海鲜中含有大量的微塑料）

第42题

Parentese, the exaggerated, drawn-out form of speech that people use to communicate with babies, apparently is universal and plays a vital role in helping infants to analyse and absorb the phonetic elements of their parents' language. An international study shows that infants are so good at analysing this speech that by the age of 20 weeks they are beginning to produce the three vowel sounds common to all human languages — "ee," "ah" and "uu."

"Parentese has a melody to it. And inside this melody is a tutorial for the baby that contains exceptionally well-formed versions of the building blocks of language," explains Patricia Kuhl, a University of Washington neuroscientist.

The new study examined differences in how American, Russian and Swedish mothers speak to their infants and to other adults. The study shows that parentese is characterised by over-articulation that exaggerates the sounds contained in words. Mothers in the study were, in effect, sounding out "super-vowels" to help their infants learn the phonetic elements of language.

"In normal, everyday speech adults generally race along at a very fast pace," Kuhl says. "But we know it is easier to understand a speaker when they stretch out sounds. That's why we tend to speak more slowly and carefully to increase understanding when we teach in the classroom or talk to strangers. We also do this unconsciously with babies, giving them an improved verbal signal they can capitalise on by slowing down and over articulating."

1 'Parentese' is not common to all cultures. ....

2 Parents tend to lengthen and over-emphasise certain sounds when speaking to infants. ....

3 Adults are aware that they need to use parentese when speaking to babies. ....

（父母语对婴儿到底有何影响？）

 第43题

A Interested in making your holiday greener and more sustainable, ensuring that local people get a fair cut of the money you've handed over, and that no rivers are being dried up or forests felled to accommodate your trip? Congratulations – for being in a well-meaning minority.

B A recent survey by the travel trade body, ABTA, found that just 20 per cent of travel agents have ever been asked for such holidays or asked questions about sustainability, though they did report a "feeling" that interest in sustainability was growing. Despite apocalyptic warnings about climate change, water scarcity, pollution, and peak oil, there isn't exactly a stampede to the travel industry's door demanding it play its part.

C "The industry feels there isn't a huge demand out there," says Sue Hurdle, chief executive of the independent charity The Travel Foundation. "They don't have a lot of people banging on the door asking for greener holidays."

D Others are more specific, such as Professor Harold Goodwin, of the International Centre for Responsible Tourism (ICRT), an independent academic research centre. "There is a big shift in values and approach – it's not just travel, it's a general consumer trend," he says. "If you're worried about where your pork comes from at home, why wouldn't you worry about that when on holiday?"

E For those of us who are bothered, working out when the travel industry is doing its bit, and when it isn't, and separating good operators from charlatans peddling greenwash, is a bewildering and frustrating experience. England alone usually has around 20 certification schemes or logos on the go at any one time, split into two categories: awards, where hotels and operators are judged independently; and certification schemes, where they generally pay to be included. It also helps to know what the industry is aiming for. We're not talking about genuine eco-tourism – which remains a niche and narrow market – but on what the industry prefers to call "sustainable", or "responsible" tourism.

F "Many people make the mistake of thinking that when anyone describes a business or activity as being 'green' that they are environmentally friendly," says Jason Freezer, destinations manager for Visit England. "Being green, sustainable, or responsible is about ensuring economic viability, social inclusion and contributing to the natural environment. A sustainable business is doing its most to enhance its own success financially, while contributing to the local economy and minimising or negating the damage it might do to its environment or community."

(from *The Independent*, 9th October 2011)

1 Travel agents report that few people express an interest in sustainability. ....

2 In England, certification schemes make it easy for consumers to judge whether or not hotels and operators are 'green'. ....

3 Sustainable businesses are more successful financially than businesses that are not environmentally friendly. ....

标题配对题

题目会给出一组小标题，这些小标题对应文章中的部分段落。考生需将这些小标题与具体的段落进行配对。通常考生需要对7~8个小标题进行配对，而文章可能有不止7~8个段落，有一些小标题可能已经作为示范进行了配对。小标题的数量总是比段落的数量要多，而且每个小标题只能使用一次，所以考生需要进行仔细思考再选择。这种题型考察的是考生区分要点和补充性细节信息的能力。

——雅思考试官方

关于标题配对题型，我有四个小建议：

第一，最后做。

标题配对题型是所有题型中比较难的一类，因为它必须建立在对整段话大意的理解之上，并且它的答案还没有顺序。我建议考生先做其他题型，最后再做Heading题。因为当你在做其他顺序类题型时，你会对某几段有大致的了解，这对解题是十分有帮助的。

第二，从最短的段落开始。

我建议考生从最短的一段开始配对，而不是第一段。最短的一段信息量最少，相对来说难度最低，最容易理解段落大意。同时，从最简单的题入手，可以帮助你排除剩余选项。

第三，找同义词。

跟大多数题一样，你在小标题中画出的关键词也可能在某段中有同义词。

第四，实在做不出就跳过。

由于标题配对题比较难，考生在每道题上所花的时间也较多，有时候需要学会有舍有得，毕竟阅读40道题的分数权重是一样的，我们也不是每个人都要拿满分。

同学们经常告诉我，把每段话的第一句当成主旨句这招很好用。是否应该把每段话的第一句话都读完然后再做题？这招儿对标题配对题来说真的有用吗？我们先来看这道题：

It was once assumed that improvements in telecommunications would lead to more dispersal in the population as people were no longer forced into cities. However, the ISTP team's research demonstrates that the population and job density of cities rose or remained constant in the 1980s after decades of decline. The explanation for this seems to be that it is valuable to place people working in related fields together. 'The new world will largely depend on human creativity, and creativity flourishes where people come together face-to-face.'

Choose the best heading for the paragraph below.

A The impact of telecommunications on population distribution

B The benefits of working together in cities

A选项其实是段首句的同意替换，但段首句是否能够指代全段大意呢？答案是不行。因为However后面的内容都是在讲the benefits of working together，所以正确答案应该是B。

所以，如果你做题时只读开头句或结尾句，你很可能会做错题。对于绝大多数正常情况，我的方法还是跟处理其他题目一样：读题干，画关键词，带着它们回到原文，按照正常速度去阅读，找到出题点。

Techniques

1. Do 'paragraph headings' questions last .
   - Do all other questions for that passage first .
   - You will then be more familiar with the passage .
   - You might get some of the answers from memory .

2. Underline 'keywords' in each heading on the list .

3. Then read the shortest or easiest paragraph .
   - Read at normal speed .
   - Underline the main ideas in the paragraph .
   - Compare with <u>all</u> of the headings .
   - Choose the best one .

(《剑桥雅思真题6》Test2)

例题讲解

下面结合一道例题给同学们讲解一下段落大意题型的解题步骤。

List of Headings

i. Poor sanitation a cause of health problems

ii. The first flush toilets

iii. Wooden sewage pipes

iv. The birth of sanitation

v. A new invention not widely implemented

vi. Americans use German technology

vii. The impact of waste water treatment

viii. The need for increasingly sophisticated systems

ix. Why populations grew

x. Ancient sewers updated for modern use

Example	Answer
Paragraph **A**	iv

1. Paragraph **B**
2. Paragraph **C**
3. Paragraph **D**
4. Paragraph **E**
5. Paragraph **F**
6. Paragraph **G**

The Development of Sanitation Systems

(A) The first sanitation systems were built in the prehistoric Middle East, in the south-east of the modern country of Iran near Zabol.An inverted siphon system, along with glass covered clay pipes, was used for the first time in the palaces of Crete,Greece.It is still in working condition, after about 3000 years.

(**B**) Higher population densities required more complex sewer collection and conveyance systems to maintain sanitary conditions in crowded cities.The ancient cities of Harappa and Mohenjo-daro of the Indus Valley civilisation constructed complex networks of bricklined sewage drains from around 2600 BC and also had outdoor flush toilets connected to this network. The urban areas of the Indus Valley civilisation provided public and private baths, sewage was disposed through underground drains built with precisely laid bricks,and a sophisticated water management system with numerous reservoirs was established.

(**C**) Roman towns and garrisons in the United Kingdom between 46 BC and 400 AD had complex sewer networks sometimes constructed out of hollowed-out elm logs, which were shaped so that they butted together with the down-stream pipe providing a socket for the upstream pipe.

(**D**) In some cities, including Rome,Istanbul (Constantinople) and Fustat, networked ancient sewer systems continue to function today as collection systems for those cities' modernised sewer systems.Instead of flowing to a river or the sea, the pipes have been re-routed to modern sewer treatment facilities.

(**E**) Basic sewage systems remained in place with little positive change, until the 16th century, when Sir John Harington invented the first flush toilet as a device for Queen Elizabeth I (his godmother) that released wastes into cesspools.Despite this innovation,most cities did not have a functioning sewer system before the Industrial era, relying instead on nearby rivers or occasional rain showers to wash away the sewage from the streets.

(**F**) The prevailing system was sufficient for the needs of early cities with few occupants,but the tremendous growth of cities during the Industrial Revolution quickly led to terribly over-polluted streets, which acted as a constant source for the outbreak of disease. As recently as the late 19th century sewerage systems in some parts of the highly industrialised United Kingdom were so inadequate that water-borne diseases such as cholera and typhoid remained a risk.

(**G**) The first comprehensive sewer system was built in Hamburg, Germany in the mid-19th century, and the first such systems in the United States were built in the late 1850s in Chicago and Brooklyn.Initially these systems discharged sewage directly to surface waters without treatment. But as pollution of water bodies became a concern, cities attempted to treat the sewage before discharge.During the half-century around 1900,these public health interventions succeeded in drastically reducing the incidence of waterborne diseases among the urban population,and were an important cause in the increases of life expectancy experienced at the time.

拿到题我们首先要读的就是文章标题，了解全文大概是要讲什么。然后再读headings，也就是小标题，画出关键词。

The Development of Sanitation Systems

i. Poor sanitation a cause of health problems

ii. The first flush toilets

iii. Wooden sewage pipes

~~**iv**. The birth of sanitation~~（这个选项是题目示例，我已删除）

v. A new invention not widely implemented

vi. Americans use German technology

vii. The impact of waste water treatment

viii. The need for increasingly sophisticated systems

ix. Why populations grew

x. Ancient sewers updated for modern use

以上是我画出的关键词。很多同学可能有疑问，画这么多关键词看得过来吗？但实际上很多小标题整句话都是关键词，多画几个关键词能加深你对题干的印象，这样在阅读原文的时候能很快记起题干内容。

画完关键词以后，原文实际有A-G共7段，从哪一段读起呢？是第一段吗？答案是最短的一段，因为它的阅读内容最短。于是我们找到C段，用正常的速度从第一句开始阅读。

C Roman towns and garrisons in the United Kingdom between 46 BC and 400 AD had complex sewer networks sometimes constructed out of hollowed-out elm logs, which were shaped so that they butted together with the down-stream pipe providing a socket for the upstream pipe.

i. Poor sanitation a cause of health problems

ii. The first flush toilets

iii. Wooden sewage pipes

v. A new invention not widely implemented

vi. Americans use German technology

vii. The impact of waste water treatment

viii. The need for increasingly sophisticated systems

ix. Why populations grew

x. Ancient sewers updated for modern use

整个C段的大意是在讲罗马人是如何建造下水道的。这里有两组同义词：

sewer=sewage

elm logs=wooden

如果你认识**elm logs**这个词，基本上选出**iii**不是太难。所以这道题看似是在考段落大意，其实本质上还是在考词汇，不认识elm logs，解题难度就非常大。当然，我们也可以使用排除法，把除了**iii**的小标题都读一遍，如果发现与该段不相关，也可以排除。

接着我们做倒数第二长的段落**D**：

D In some cities, including Rome, Istanbul(Constantinople) and Fustat, networked ancient sewer systems continue to function today as collection systems for those cities` modernised sewer systems. Instead of flowing to a river or the sea, the pipes have been re-routed to modern sewer treatment facilities.

整个**D**段的大意是：一些城市的下水道系统至今仍在使用。

i. Poor sanitation a cause of health problems

ii. The first flush toilets

v. A new invention not widely implemented

vi. Americans use German technology

vii. The impact of waste water treatment

viii. The need for increasingly sophisticated systems

ix. Why populations grew

x. Ancient sewers updated for modern use

这里我们可以找到两组同义词组：

ancient sewers updated=ancient sewer systems continue to function today
for those cities` modernised=for modern use

可以确定x就是D段的标题了。接着我们找E段的标题。

E Basic sewage systems remained in place with little positive change, until the 16th century, when *Sir John Harington* invented the first flush toilet as a device for *Queen Elizabeth I* (his godmother) that released wastes into cesspools. Despite this innovation, most cities did not have a functioning sewer system before the *Industrial era*, relying instead on nearby rivers or occasional rain showers to wash away the sewage from the streets.

E段主要讲了第一个抽水马桶的发明，另外也提到了在工业革命之前，抽水马桶并未普及。很多同学可能会选**ii**，因为我们很容易找到the first flush toilet，但它只能代表前半段。

i. Poor sanitation a cause of health problems

ii. The first flush toilets

v. A new invention not widely implemented

vi. Americans use German technology

vii. The impact of waste water treatment

viii. The need for increasingly sophisticated systems

ix. Why populations grew

仔细阅读后半段，可以发现**v**标题和原文有一个同义词组：

not widely implemented=most cities did not have

其实这道题就是考你认不认识implement，如果认识的话，应该不会选错，**E**段的标题是**v**。接着我们找F段的标题。

F The prevailing system was sufficient for the needs of early cities with few occupants, but the tremendous growth of cities during the *Industrial Revolution* quickly led to terribly over-polluted streets, which acted as a constant source for the outbreak of disease. As recently as the late 19th century sewerage systems in some parts of the highly industrialised United Kingdom were so inadequate that water-borne diseases such as cholera and typhoid remained a risk.

F段的主要内容是随着城市的发展导致污水横流，导致一些基于水传播的疾病发生。

i. Poor sanitation a cause of health problems

ii. The first flush toilets

vi. Americans use German technology

vii. The impact of waste water treatment

viii. The need for increasingly sophisticated systems

ix. Why populations grew

我们可以看到，标题i里和F段最后一句有两组同义词组：

poor=inadequate

health problems=water-borne disease

有些同学可能会选ix，因为找到了populations grew和原文中the tremendous growth of cities是同义词，但仔细阅读上下文，发现这里只是提到了人口增长，并不能代表整段话的大意，同时也没有解释Why populations grew。接着我们来找一下B段的标题。

B Higher population densities required more complex sewer collection and conveyance systems to maintain sanitary conditions in crowded cities.The ancient cities of Harappa and Mohenjo-daro of the Indus Valley civilisation constructed complex networks of bricklined sewage drains from around 2600 BC and also had outdoor flush toilets connected to this network. The urban areas of the Indus Valley civilisation provided public and private baths, sewage was disposed through underground drains built with precisely laid bricks,and a sophisticated water management system with numerous reservoirs was established.

B段的第一句话其实就统领了全段大意：更多的城市人口对排污系统的需求更大了。

ii. The first flush toilets

vi. Americans use German technology

vii. The impact of waste water treatment

viii. The need for increasingly sophisticated systems

ix. Why populations grew

我们可以找到两组同义词：

need for=required   sophisticated systems=complex sewer collection

这道题其实就是在考你认不认识sophisticated这个词。需要提醒大家的是，像这样段首第一句统领全段大意的情况并不是每次都会出现。接着我们来找**G**段的标题。

G The first comprehensive sewer system was built in Hamburg, Germany in the mid-19th century, and the first such systems in the United States were built in the late 1850s in Chicago and Brooklyn.Initially these systems discharged sewage directly to surface waters without treatment. But as pollution of water bodies became a concern, cities attempted to treat the sewage before discharge.During the half-century around 1900,these public health interventions succeeded in drastically reducing the incidence of waterborne diseases among the urban population,and were an important cause in the increases of life expectancy experienced at the time.

ii. The first flush toilets

vi. Americans use German technology

vii. The impact of waste water treatment

ix. Why populations grew

List of Headings

i.   Poor sanitation a cause of health problems
ii. The first flush toilets
iii. Wooden sewage pipes Elm logs
iv. ~~The birth of sanitation~~
v.   A new invention not widely implemented
vi. Americans use German technology
vii. The impact of waste water treatment
viii. The need for increasingly sophisticated systems
ix. Why populations grew
x.   Ancient sewers updated for modern use

（本书配套课程：阅读-段落大意题型，手机淘宝扫码付费学习）

题型练习

第1题

It would have been easy to criticise the MIRTP for using in the early phases a 'top-down' approach, in which decisions were made by experts and officials before being handed down to communities, but it was necessary to start the process from the level of the governmental authorities of the district. It would have been difficult to respond to the requests of villagers and other rural inhabitants without the support and understanding of district authorities. (《剑桥雅思真题7》Page48-50)

Choose the correct heading for the paragraph below.

A Co-operation of district officials.

B Government authorities' instructions.

第2题

An estuary is a partly enclosed coastal body of water with one or more rivers or streams flowing into it, and with a free connection to the open sea. Estuaries are amongst the most heavily populated areas throughout the world, with about 60% of the world's population living along estuaries and the coast. As a result, estuaries are suffering degradation by many factors, including overgrazing and other poor farming practices; overfishing; drainage and filling of wetlands; pollutants from sewage inputs; and diking or damming for flood control or water diversion.

Choose the correct heading for the paragraph from the list below.

A The environmental impact of estuaries

B The human impact on certain coastal areas

C Why estuaries will disappear

第3题

Reading underwent serious changes in the 18th century. Until 1750, reading was done "intensively": people tended to own a small number of books and read them repeatedly, often to a small audience. After 1750, people began to read "extensively", finding as many books as they could, and increasingly reading them alone. Libraries that lent out their material for a small price started to appear, and occasionally bookstores would offer a small lending library to their patrons. Coffee houses commonly offered books, journals and sometimes even popular novels to their customers.

A The appearance of the first public libraries.

B Intensive and extensive reading habits.

C The reading revolution.

 第4题

For the first time, dictionary publishers are incorporating real, spoken English into their data. It gives lexicographers (people who write dictionaries) access to a more vibrant, up-to-date vernacular language which has never really been studied before. In one project, 150 volunteers each agreed to discreetly tie a Walkman recorder to their waist and leave it running for anything up to two weeks. Every conversation they had was recorded. When the data was collected, the length of tapes was 35 times the depth of the Atlantic Ocean. Teams of audio typists transcribed the tapes to produce a computerised database of ten million words. （《剑桥雅思真题1》）

Which paragraph heading would you chose, and why?

A New method of research

B The first study of spoken language

 第5题

Read the following paragraph and choose the best heading.

A A new method for language learning

B How phonics benefits children in the UK

C Children learn to link sounds with spellings

D Children learn the rules of spelling

'Phonics' refers to a method for teaching speakers of English to read and write that language. Young learners are taught to associate the sounds of spoken English with letters or groups of letters.

For example, they might be taught that the sound /k/ can be represented by the spellings c, k, ck, ch, or q. Using phonics, the teacher shows the learners how to blend the sounds of letters together to produce approximate pronunciations of unknown words. Phonics is a widely used method of teaching children to read and decode words. Children begin learning to read using phonics usually around the age of 5 or 6.

第6题

Read the following passage, and choose the best title from the list.

A 3D printing a historical structure.

B The benefits of 3D printing.

C Computer modelling or hands-on experience?

D A damaged cathedral is rebuilt.

Using a laser scan of Bourges cathedral in France, a team led by John Ochsendorf of the Massachusetts Institute of Technology have 3D-printed thousands of bricks and are building an exact 1:50 replica. The researchers hope to use the mock-up to devise a way to gauge the stability, and thus safety, of historical buildings built of brick and stone.

Building the replica is painstaking work, but Ochsendorf thinks the process itself may be as valuable as the mechanics uncovered. For students of architecture and structural engineering, hands-on experience has largely given way to computer modelling. Techniques like 3D printing could be a way of reconnecting them with the craft behind the science, he says.

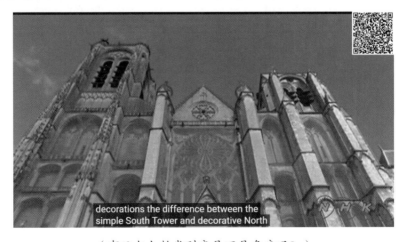

decorations the difference between the simple South Tower and decorative North

（布日尔大教堂到底是不是危房呢？）

第7题

Choose the best heading for the paragraph from the list below.

A The creator of the first industrial research laboratory.

B A pioneering and prolific inventor.

C Edison's contribution to mass communication.

Thomas Edison was an American inventor and businessman. He developed many devices that greatly influenced life around the world, including the phonograph, he motion picture camera, and a long-lasting, practical electric light bulb. He was one of the first inventors to apply the principles of mass production and large-scale teamwork to the process of invention, and because of that, he is often credited with the creation of the first industrial research laboratory. Edison is the fourth most prolific inventor in history, holding 1,093 US patents in his name, as well as many patents in the United Kingdom, France, and Germany. He is credited with numerous inventions that contributed to mass communication and, in particular, telecommunications.

（你还记得小学课本上的爱迪生吗？）

 第8题

Choose one title from the following list:

A Behaviour management in US schools may do more harm than good.

B How to improve behaviour in schools.

C The US education system in crisis.

D The long-term goals of discipline in schools.

How we deal with the most challenging children remains rooted in B.F.Skinner's mid-20th-century philosophy that human behaviour is determined by consequences, and that bad behaviour must be punished. During the 2011-12 school year, the US Department of Education counted 130,000 expulsions and roughly 7 million suspensions among 49 million primary and secondary students - one for every seven children. Furthermore, it is estimated that there are a quarter of a million instances of corporal punishment in US schools every year.

But contemporary psychological studies suggest that, far from resolving children's behaviour problems, these standard disciplinary methods often exacerbate them. They sacrifice long-term goals (student behaviour improving definitively) for the short-term gain of momentary peace in the classroom.

 第9题

"Big data" is a term being used more and more by politicians. It refers to the concept that any problem – from underperforming pupils to failing hospitals – can be solved by collecting some tightly focused data, crunching it and making tweaks, such as moving pupils or changing nurses' shifts, rather than dealing with bigger issues, such as poverty or spending cuts. This is an approach that focuses narrowly on "what works" without ever troubling to ask: "works for whom?" Its watchword is "smart", which can easily be appreciated, rather than "right", which can't. Putting trust in highly educated technocrats, it is naturally less interested in public debate.

A How data can be used to improve society.

B Big data: a smart approach to politics that works for everyone.

C A sceptical perspective on "big data".

D Why the public trusts technocrats more than politicians.

 第10题

The environmental challenges posed by agriculture are huge, and they'll only become more pressing as we try to meet the growing need for food worldwide. We'll likely have two billion more mouths to feed by mid-century - more than nine billion people. But sheer population growth isn't the only reason we'll need more food. The spread of prosperity across the world, especially in India and

China, is driving an increased demand for meat, eggs and dairy, boosting pressure to grow more corn and soybeans to feed more cattle, pigs and chickens. If these trends continue, the double whammy of population growth and richer diets will require us to roughly double the amount of crops we grow by 2050. （来源：《National Geographic》）

A Two key trends driving the demand for food worldwide.

B The impact of agriculture on the natural world.

C Growing populations and their need for food.

 第11题

A A fundamental question in ageing research is whether humans and other species possess an immutable lifespan limit. A theoretical study suggested the maximum human lifespan to be around 125 years. The longest-living person whose dates of birth and death were verified to the modern norms of Guinness World Records and the Gerontology Research Group was Jeanne Calment, a French lady who lived to 122.

B Reduction of infant mortality has accounted for most of the increased average life span longevity, but since the 1960s, mortality rates among those over 80 years have decreased by about 1.5% per year. The progress being made in lengthening lifespans and postponing senescence is entirely due to medical and public-health efforts, rising standards of living, better education, healthier nutrition and more salubrious lifestyles.

Choose the best heading for paragraphs A and B from the list below.

i. Why the elderly are living longer

ii. The impossibility of living beyond a certain age

iii. Medical and healthcare developments since the 1960s

iv. Is there a maximum age for humans?

Max Age Is 122?

（人类能活过122岁吗？）

 第12题

Match the correct headings with the paragraphs below.

1 The causes of stress among employers and employees

2 The increase in work-related stress

3 The increase in visits to physicians

4 Stress has wide-ranging effects on the body and on behaviour

A The number of stress-related disability claims by American employees has doubled according to the Employee Assistance Professionals Association in Arlington, Virginia. Seventy-five to ninety percent of physician visits are related to stress and, according to the American Institute of Stress, the cost to industry has been estimated at $200 billion-$300 billion a year. ....

B It is clear that problems caused by stress have become a major concern to both employers and employees. Symptoms of stress are manifested both physiologically and psychologically. Persistent stress can result in cardiovascular disease, a weaker immune system and frequent headaches, stiff muscles, or backache. It can also result in poor coping skills, irritability, jumpiness, insecurity, exhaustion, and difficulty concentrating. Stress may also perpetuate or lead to binge eating, smoking, and alcohol consumption. ....

One simple, but highly effective, lesson from the Olympics comes from the visionary British cycling coach, Dave Brailsford. Brailsford believes that by breaking down and identifying every tiny aspect of an athlete's performance and then making just a 1% improvement in each area, the athlete's overall performance can be significantly enhanced. His concept of 'the aggregation of marginal gains' has been making transformative ripples in classrooms and schools ever since the cycling team came to prominence a few years ago.

What is so brilliant about Brailsford's marginal gains concept is that it is so flexible. It provides an accessible, precise and useful language for achieving success in a school context in various ways: from students improving their learning, to teachers looking to enhance their pedagogy, and, more broadly, school leaders looking to make small, but highly significant improvements. (本文来自于《The Guardian》)

Choose the best title for the passage below.

A The story of a visionary cycling coach.

B Cycling's 'marginal gains' theory and its application in schools.

C The man behind Britain's Olympic cycling success.

D How cyclists implement the 'marginal gains' concept.

E Schools have improved since the Olympic Games.

The cinematograph is a motion picture film camera which also serves as a film projector and developer. It was invented in the 1890s, but there is much dispute as to the identity of its inventor.

Some argue that the device was first invented and patented as "Cinématographe Léon Bouly" by French inventor Léon Bouly on February 12, 1892. Bouly coined the term "cinematograph", which translates in Greek to "writing in movement". It is said that Bouly was not able to pay the rent for his patent the following year, and that the brothers Auguste and Louis Lumière bought the licence.

A more popular version of events is that Louis Lumière was the first to conceptualise the idea. The Lumière brothers shared the patent, and they made their first film, *Sortie de l'usine Lumière de Lyon*, in 1894.

Choose the best title for the whole passage from the list below.

A How the cinematograph was invented

B The first film projector

C Who invented the cinematograph?

D What is a cinematograph?

 第15题

Future Shock is a book written by the futurist Alvin Toffler in 1970.In the book, Toffler defines the term "future shock" as a certain psychological state of individuals and entire societies. His shortest definition for the term is a personal perception of "too much change in too short a period of time". The book became an international bestseller, selling over 6 million copies, and has been widely translated.

Toffler argued that society is undergoing an enormous structural change, a revolution from an industrial society to a "super-industrial society". This change overwhelms people, he believed, the accelerated rate of technological and social change leaving people disconnected and suffering from "shattering stress and disorientation" - future shocked. Toffler stated that the majority of social problems are symptoms of future shock. In his discussion of the components of such shock he popularized the term "information overload."

Choose the best heading for paragraphs from the list below.

A A shocking vision of the future.

B What is *"future shock"*?

C The career of the futurist Alvin Toffler.

D A changing society.

第16题

Read the following passage and choose the best title from the list below.

A Scientists present new findings about the unconscious mind

B Our growing understanding of the role of the unconscious

C How humans solve problems

D What is a "eureka moment"?

The attitude of the scientific community towards the unconscious mind has shifted dramatically in recent years. While once viewed as a lazy reservoir of memories and non-task oriented behaviour, the unconscious is now regarded as an active and essential component in the processes of decision making.

Historically, the unconscious mind was considered to be the source of dreams and implicit memory (which allows people to walk or ride a bicycle without consciously thinking about the activity), as well as the storing place for memories of past experiences. But recent research reveals that the unconscious brain might also be an active player in decision making, problem solving, creativity and critical thinking. One familiar example of the operation of the unconscious in problem solving is the well-known phenomenon of the "eureka moment", when a solution to a problem presents itself without the involvement of active thinking.

第17题

According to a new review of studies related to running and health, jogging for as few as five or six miles per week could substantially improve someone's health. "It seems like the maximum benefits of running occur at quite low doses," said *Dr.Carl J.Lavie*, medical director of cardiac rehabilitation and prevention at the Ochsner Medical Center in New Orleans. As little as "one to two runs per week, or three to six miles per week, and well less than an hour per week" can be quite beneficial, he said.

However, there may be an upper limit to the desirable mileage if your primary goal is improved health. Some evidence, he said, suggested that running strenuously for more than about an hour every day could slightly increase someone's risks for heart problems, as well as for running- related injuries and disabilities.

Choose title A, B,C or D.

A The health benefits of jogging

B How much running is best?

C Surprising findings about running

D The benefits and drawbacks of regular jogging

 第18题

Melbourne has topped the list of the best cities in the world to live in, according to a new report by *The Economist Intelligence Unit*. Vienna in Austria and Vancouver in Canada came in second and third place respectively on the *Global Livability Ranking*. Cities across the world are awarded scores depending on lifestyle challenges faced by the people living there. Each city is scored on its stability, healthcare, culture and environment, education and infrastructure. This is the third time that the Australian city has topped the list. Unfortunately, UK cities fared worse on the list with London coming 55 out of 140 cities while Manchester was ranked 51. The report also shows that livability across the world has fallen by 0.6 per cent.

A Livability survey produces some surprising results.

B How cities are ranked.

C Results of the latest "Most Livable Cities Index".

D Melbourne is top city for tourists.

These are the 10 most liveable cities in the world, according to monocle.com

（一起来看看最新的世界最宜居城市排名）

 第19题

Match two of the following headings with the paragraphs below.

1 Rapid sales of printing presses.

2 The revolutionary impact of the printing press.

3 New information and ideas.

4 The printing boom.

A From a single point of origin, Mainz, Germany, printing spread within several decades to over two hundred cities in a dozen European countries. By 1500, printing presses in operation throughout Western Europe had already produced more than twenty million volumes. In the 16th century, with presses spreading further afield, their output rose tenfold to an estimated 150 to 200 million copies. The operation of a press became so synonymous with the enterprise of printing that it lent its name to an entire new branch of media, the press.

B In Renaissance Europe, the arrival of mechanical movable type printing introduced the era of mass communication which permanently altered the structure of society. The relatively unrestricted circulation of information and ideas transcended borders and threatened the power of political and religious authorities. The sharp increase in literacy broke the monopoly of the literate elite on education and learning and bolstered the emerging middle class.

 第20题

Read the following article and choose the best title from the list below.

A Children's happiness

B Why teenagers use alcohol, cigarettes and drugs

C What teenagers really want

D Why families should dine together

A new survey reveals that a family sit-down at dinnertime may reduce a teenager's risk of trying or using alcohol, cigarettes and drugs. The study surveyed more than 1,000 teens and found that those who dined with their families five to seven times a week were four times less likely to use alcohol, tobacco or marijuana than those who ate with their families fewer than three times a week.

A recent UK survey also found that dining together as a family is a key ingredient in ensuring a child's happiness. Children in the survey reported higher levels of happiness when they dined together with their families at least three times a week. "Contrary to the popular belief that children only want to spend time playing video games or watching TV," said researcher Dr. Maris Iacovou of the University of Essex, "we found that they were most happy when interacting with their parents or siblings."(文章节选自《The Independent》)

 第21题

The Brazilian pepper tree, an invasive plant in the southern United States, is showing great potential in the fight against antibiotic-resistant bacterial infections. A team of scientists studied historical accounts of its use in traditional South American medicine from as early as 1648. Focusing their experiments on its fruits, which reportedly were used to treat wounds, they then produced an extract that's able to disarm a virulent type of Staphylococcus bacterium.

Modern antibiotics are designed to kill bacteria. But some bacterial cells survive and pass on their resistance to their offspring, making it increasingly difficult for physicians to fight tenacious infections that threaten their patients' lives. The Brazilian pepper tree extract deploys an unconventional tactic against infections. It prevents bacterial cells from communicating, which keeps them from ganging up to create tissue-destroying toxins. That, in turn, gives the body's immune system a change to mount it's own defence against the bacteria. (本文截取自《National Geographic》)

One of the four titles below is the real title of the article. Which do you think it is? Try to explain why.

A A weed that busts bacteria

B Traditional medicines make a comeback

C The problem of resistant bacteria

D New plant-based medicines are on the way

 第22题

Read the following passage, and choose the best title from the list below.

A A giant leap for tourism in the 21st century.

B The first space tourist.

C The pros and cons of space tourism.

Dennis Tito, an American engineer and multimillionaire, was the first space tourist to fund his own trip into space. In 2001, he spent nearly eight days in orbit as a crew member of ISS EP-1, a visiting mission to the International Space Station, after being accepted by the Russian Federal Space Agency as a candidate for a commercial spaceflight. Tito met criticism from NASA before the launch, primarily from *Daniel Goldin*, at that time the Administrator of NASA, who considered it inappropriate for a tourist to take a ride into space.

In the decade since Dennis Tito journeyed to the International Space Station, eight private citizens have paid the $20 million fee to travel to space, but it is believed that this number could increase fifteen-fold by 2020. A web-based survey suggested that over 70% of those surveyed were interested in travelling to space, 88% wanted to spacewalk, and 21% liked the idea of staying in a space hotel.

（为什么人们想尝试太空旅游？）

 第23题

Across the world, universities are more numerous than they have ever been, yet at the same time there is unprecedented confusion about their purpose and scepticism about their value. What Are Universities For? Offers a spirited and compelling argument for completely rethinking the way we see our universities, and why we need them.

Stefan Collini challenges the common claim that universities need to show that they help to make money in order to justify getting more money. Instead, he argues that we must reflect on the different types of institution and the distinctive roles they play. In particular we must recognise that attempting to extend human understanding, which is at the heart of disciplined intellectual enquiry, can never be wholly harnessed to immediate social purposes - particularly in the case of the humanities, which both attract and puzzle many people and are therefore the most difficult subjects to justify.

At a time when the future of higher education lies in the balance, What Are Universities For? Offers all of us a better, deeper and more enlightened understanding of why universities matter, to everyone.

Which statement best summarises the book's message?

A We do not necessarily need universities nowadays

B Universities should be harnessed for social purposes

C Universities must justify the money they are given

D We need to change our understanding of the role of universities

 第24题

Read the following passage about cognitive behavioural therapy. Choose the best headings for paragraphs A, B and C from this list:

1 A slow process

2 A new type of therapeutic approach

3 The benefits and drawbacks of CBT

4 A goal-oriented therapeutic approach

5 CBT therapists are always honest with their clients

6 The range of CBT interventions

A Cognitive behavioural therapy (CBT) is a psychotherapeutic approach:a talking therapy. CBT aims to solve problems concerning dysfunctional emotions, behaviours and cognitions through a goal-oriented, systematic procedure in the present.

B The particular therapeutic techniques vary, but commonly may include keeping a diary of significant events and associated feelings, thoughts and behaviours; questioning and testing cognitions, assumptions, evaluations and beliefs that might be unhelpful and unrealistic; gradually facing activities which may have been avoided; and trying out new ways of behaving and reacting. Relaxation, mindfulness and distraction techniques are also commonly included.

C Going through cognitive behavioural therapy is not an overnight process for clients; a typical course consists of 12-16 hour-long sessions. Even after clients have learned to recognise when and where their mental processes go awry, it can in some cases take considerable time or effort to replace a dysfunctional process or habit with a more reasonable and adaptive one. CBT is problem-focused and structured towards the client.

It requires honesty and openness between the client and therapist,as a therapist develops strategies for managing problems and guiding the client to a better life.

 第25题

The modern English alphabet is a Latin alphabet consisting of 26 letters, each having an upper- and lower-case form. It originated around the 7th century from the Latin script.

English is the only major modern European language that requires no diacritics for native words. Diacritic marks mainly appear in loanwords such as naïve and façade. Informal English writing tends to omit diacritics because of their absence from the keyboard, while professional copywriters and typesetters tend to include them.

As loanwords become naturalised in English, there is a tendency to drop the diacritics, as has happened with many older borrowings from French, such as hôtel. Words that are still perceived as foreign tend to retain them; for example, the only spelling of soupçon found in English dictionaries uses the diacritic. However, diacritics are likely to be retained even in naturalised words where they would otherwise be confused with a common native English word e.g. résumé rather than resume. Rarely, they may even be added to a loanword for this reason, as in maté, from the Spanish yerba mate but with the é to distinguish from the English word 'mate'.

Choose the best title from the list below.

A The English alphabet

B The use of diacritics in written English

C Disappearing diacritics in the English language

D How loanwords have entered the English language

 第26题

The setting is decidedly modest:a utility room in a red-brick house at the end of a cul-de-sac in Wales. But if the hype turns out to be right, this may be the starting point for an energy revolution in the UK. Householder Mark Kerr has become the first British owner of a Tesla Powerwall, a cutting-edge bit of kit that the makers say will provide a "missing link" in solar energy.

Like many owners of solar panels, Kerr and his family have a basic problem. They tend to be out at work and school when the sun is shining and the 16 solar panels on the roof of their home in Cardiff are producing power. The excess they miss out on is fed into the grid and they make a return on it but it does not seem right that they do not get to use the power from their panels. However, from now, energy produced but not used during the day will charge the Powerwall and can then be used to provide them with the energy they need when they're at home and their lights, music centres, computers, televisions and myriad other devices need feeding.

Choose title A, B, C or D. Can you explain why the others are wrong?

A The UK energy revolution.

B Wales at the forefront of technology.

C New device could herald energy revolution.

D The problem with solar panels.

 第27题

Finland's education system is considered one of the best in the world. In international ratings, it's always in the top ten. However, the authorities there aren't ready to rest on their laurels, and they've decided to carry through a real revolution in their school system. Finnish officials want to remove school subjects from the curriculum. There will no longer be any classes in physics, math, literature, history, or geography.

Instead of individual subjects, students will study events and phenomena in an interdisciplinary format. For example, the *Second World War* will be examined from the perspective of history, geography, and math. And by taking the course "Working in a Cafe", students will absorb a whole body of knowledge about the English language, economics, and communication skills.

The Finnish education system encourages collective work, which is why the changes will also affect teachers. The school reform will require a great deal of cooperation between teachers of different subjects. Around 70% of teachers in Helsinki have already undertaken preparatory work in line with the new system for presenting information, and, as a result, they'll get a pay increase. The changes are expected to be complete by 2020.

A The world's best education system.

B Finland plans to scrap school subjects.

C Teachers in Finland welcome education reform.

 第28题

A The hunt for intelligent species outside Earth may be a staple of literature and film - but it is happening in real life, too. NASA probes are on the lookout for planets outside our solar system, and astronomers are carefully listening for any messages being beamed through space. How awe-inspiring it would be to get confirmation that we are not alone in the universe, to finally speak to an alien race. Wouldn't it?

B Well no, according to the eminent physicist Stephen Hawking."If aliens visit us, the outcome would be much as when Columbus landed in America, which didn't turn out well for the Native Americans," Hawking has said in a forthcoming documentary made for the *Discovery Channel*. He argues that, instead of trying to find and communicate with life in the cosmos, humans would be better off doing everything they can to avoid contact.

C Hawking believes that, based on the sheer number of planets that scientists know must exist, we are not the only life-form in the universe. There are, after all, billions and billions of stars in our galaxy alone, with, it is reasonable to expect, an even greater number of planets orbiting them. And it is not unreasonable to expect some of that alien life to be intelligent, and capable of interstellar communication.

Match each paragraph with one of the headings below.

1 A pessimistic prediction.

2 The probability of life existing on other planets.

3 Astronomers send messages through space.

4 How to avoid contact with aliens.

5 The search for alien life-forms.

6 Life-forms exist on other planets.

（为什么霍金教授不希望人类尝试去寻找外星人？）

 第29题

A On February 10, 1996, Deep Blue became the first machine to win a chess game against a reigning world champion (Garry Kasparov) under regular time controls. However, Kasparov won three and drew two of the following five games, beating Deep Blue by a score of 4–2. Deep Blue was then heavily upgraded and played Kasparov again in May 1997, winning the six-game rematch 3½–2½. Deep Blue won the deciding game six, becoming the first computer system to defeat a reigning world champion in a match under standard chess tournament time controls.

B After the loss, Kasparov said that he sometimes saw deep intelligence and creativity in the machine's moves, suggesting that during the second game, human chess players had intervened on behalf of the machine, which would be a violation of the rules. IBM denied that it cheated, saying the only human intervention occurred between games. The rules provided for the developers to modify the program between games, an opportunity they said they used to shore up weaknesses in the computer's play that were revealed during the course of the match. This allowed the computer to avoid a trap in the final game that it had fallen for twice before. Kasparov demanded a rematch, but IBM refused and dismantled Deep Blue.

Choose the best heading for paragraph A and B from the list below.

1 The first chess-playing computer

2 Developers' intervention is questioned

3 Chess champion accepts defeat

4 Program developers caught cheating

5 A victory for artificial intelligence

（来听听卡斯帕罗夫自己是如何回忆当年的）

 第30题

Read the passage below and match each paragraph with one of the following headings:

1 Lobster habitats

2 Why lobsters must be measured when caught

3 Adult male lobsters are a prime catch

4 Lobster fishing methods

5 The world's heaviest lobster

6 Different types of American lobster

A The American lobster is a species of lobster found on the Atlantic coast of North America, chiefly from Labrador to New Jersey. It is also known as Atlantic lobster, Canadian lobster, true lobster, northern lobster, Canadian Reds, or Maine lobster. It can reach a body length of 64cm, and a mass of over 20 kilograms, making it not only the heaviest crustacean in the world, but also the heaviest of all living arthropod species.

B Most American lobsters come from the northeastern coast of North America, with the Atlantic Provinces of Canada and the U.S. state of Maine being the largest producers. They are caught primarily using lobster traps, although lobsters are also harvested as bycatch by bottom trawlers, fishermen using gillnets, and by scuba divers in some areas. Maine completely prohibits scuba divers from catching lobsters (violations could result in up to a $1,000 fine).

C In the United States, the lobster industry is regulated. Every lobster fisher is required to use a lobster gauge to measure the distance from the lobster's eye socket to the end of its carapace: if the lobster is less than 83mm long, it is too young to be sold and must be released back to the sea. There is also a legal maximum size of 130mm in Maine, meant to ensure the survival of a healthy breeding stock of adult males.

（一起感受一下抓大龙虾的乐趣）

 第31题

Read the following passage about migrating birds. Choose the best heading from the list below for each paragraph above.

   i Migration and food

   ii Survival of the fittest

   iii A record-setting bird

iv Other incredible animal migrations

v A new device for tracking bird migrations

vi How do migrating Arctic terns manage such a feat?

A A tiny bird from the Farne Islands off Northumberland, England has clocked up the longest migration ever recorded. The Arctic tern's meandering journey to Antarctica and back saw it clock up 59,650 miles, more than twice the circumference of the planet. The bird, which weighs just 100g, left its breeding grounds last July and flew down the west coast of Africa, rounded the Cape of Good Hope into the Indian Ocean and arrived in Antarctica in November. Its mammoth trek was recorded by a tiny device attached to its leg, weighing 0.7g - too light to affect its flight.

B "It's really quite humbling to see these tiny birds return when you consider the huge distances they've had to travel and how they've battled to survive," said Richard Bevan at Newcastle University and part of the tracking team. The birds survive the vast journey by dipping down to the sea surface to catch fish and other food as they travel. "They live in the fast lane all the time, constantly on the move," said Bevan. "They have to flap all the time. It is an incredibly energetic lifestyle."

C Like all migratory animals, the birds travel to take advantage of food that is available in particular seasons. Arctic terns perform the longest migrations but another bird, the bar-tailed godwit, completes its marathon from the Arctic to New Zealand in eight days straight, without stopping to feed. Whales undertake the longest mammal migrations and leatherback turtles and some dragonflies also travel over 9,321 miles. （资料来源于theguardian.com）

（科学家是如何跟踪北极燕鸥的呢？）

 第32题

Read the following passage and match each paragraph (A to E) with one of the headings from the list below.

i Think about what study tools you really need.

ii It's important to be in the right frame of mind.

iii Skim read to get an overview of relevant information.

iv Stick to a timetable.

v Where you study is key.

vi Develop your ability to concentrate for long periods.

vii Use notes to summarise and synthesise ideas.

Effective Study Habits

The key to effective studying isn't cramming or studying longer, but studying smarter. You can begin studying smarter with these proven and effective study habits.

A Too many people look at studying as a necessary task, not an enjoyment or opportunity to learn. That's fine, but researchers have found that how you approach something matters almost as much as what you do. Being in the right mindset is important in order to study smarter.

B A lot of people make the mistake of studying in a place that really isn't conducive to concentrating. A place with a lot of distractions makes for a poor study area. If you try and study in your dorm room, for instance, you may find the computer, TV, or a roommate more interesting than the reading material you're trying to digest.

C While it may seem ideal to type notes into a computer to refer back to later, computers are a powerful distraction for many people because they can do so many different things. Playing games, going online, and answering emails are all wonderful distractions that have nothing to do with studying. So ask yourself whether you really need a computer to take notes, or whether you can make do with the old-fashioned paper and pen or pencil.

D Most people find that keeping to a standard outline format helps them boil information down to its most basic components. People find that connecting similar concepts together makes it easier to remember when the exam comes around. The important thing to remember in writing outlines is that an outline only words as a learning tool when it is in your own words and structure.

E Too many people treat studying as the thing to do when you get around to it or have some spare time. But if you schedule study time just as your class time is scheduled, you'll find it becomes much less of a hassle in the long run.

 第33题

Adolescent Psychology

A Adolescent psychology is associated with notable changes in mood sometimes known as mood swings. Cognitive, emotional and attitudinal changes which are characteristic of adolescence, often take place during this period, and this can be a cause of conflict on one hand and positive personality development on the other. Because adolescents are experiencing various strong cognitive and physical changes, for the first time in their lives they may start to view their friends, their peer group, as more important and influential than their parents/guardians. Because of peer pressure, they may sometimes indulge in activities not deemed socially acceptable, although this may be more of a social phenomenon than a psychological one.

B The home is an important aspect of adolescent psychology. Home environment and family have a substantial impact on the developing minds of teenagers, and these developments may reach a climax during adolescence. Responsible parenting has a number of significant benefits for parents themselves, their communities, and most importantly, their children. For example, children who experience significant father involvement tend to exhibit higher scores on assessments of cognitive development, enhanced social skills and fewer behaviour problems.

C In the search for a unique social identity for themselves, adolescents are frequently confused about what is 'right' and what is 'wrong.' G.Stanley Hall denoted this period as one of "Storm and Stress" and, according to him, conflict at this developmental stage is normal and not unusual.

Margaret Mead, on the other hand, attributed the behaviour of adolescents to their culture and upbringing.

D Positive psychology is sometimes brought up when addressing adolescent psychology as well. This approach towards adolescents refers to providing them with motivation to become socially acceptable and notable individuals, since many adolescents find themselves bored, indecisive and/or unmotivated.

E Adolescents may be subject to peer pressure within their adolescent time span, consisting of the need to have relationships with the opposite sex, consume alcoholic beverages, use drugs, defy their parental figures, or commit any act which other people, particularly adults, may not deem appropriate. Peer pressure is a common experience between adolescents and may result briefly or on a larger scale.

It should also be noted that adolescence is the stage of a psychological breakthrough in a person's life when the cognitive development is rapid and the thoughts, ideas and concepts developed at this period of life greatly influence the individual's future life, playing a major role in character and personality formation.

Match the paragraphs below with one of the following headings

1 Parents' influence is a key factor

2 Encouragement to make their mark in society

3 The influence of friends

4 A difficult stage in life

5 Teenage culture

6 Trying to find out who they are

答案解析

填空题

第1题

词汇

filthy 污秽的   carcasses 动物尸体   microorganisms 微生物   antimicrobial 抗菌剂

pathogenic bacteria 致病细菌   compounds 化合物

○ 翻译&解析 ○

有一些昆虫甚至会利用一些肮脏的东西作为栖息地，比如粪便或尸体。这里会面临成千上万的微生物的挑战，而昆虫则拥有很多抗菌化合物来对付这些致病菌和真菌。人们可以利用这一特性找到新型抗生素的化合物。

1 They are also interested in compounds which insects use to protect themselves from pathogenic bacteria and fungi found in their ....

根据原文...**habitats**, ...where they are regularly challenged by thousands of microorganisms.

2 Piper hopes that these substances will be useful in the development of drugs such as ....

根据原文...suggesting that there is certainly potential to find many compounds that can serve as or inspire new **antibiotics**.

第2题

词汇

like-minded people 趣味相投的人   psychologically 心理学上的

○ 翻译&解析 ○

很多藏家是为了社交而收藏，他们参加藏家聚会并交换各种物品信息。这其实跟加入桥牌俱乐部或健身俱乐部的道理一样，都是让自己更多地和志同道合的人接触。

另一个收藏的动机是希望找到一些特别的东西，比如某一个特定歌手的早期录音。有些人一生都在找类似这样的东西。从心理学上来说，这会给人带来一个生活目标，让人生不至于漫无目的。

1 Collectors' clubs provide opportunities to share ....

根据原文...meetings of a group of collectors and exchanging **information** on items;

2 Collectors' clubs offer .... with people who have similar interests.

根据原文...and similarly brings them into **contact** with like-minded people.

3 Collecting sometimes involves a life-long .... for a special item.

根据原文...Some may spend their whole lives in a **hunt** for this.

4 Searching for something particular may prevent people from feeling their life is completely ....

根据原文...this can give a purpose to a life that otherwise feels **aimless**;

🔍 第3题

词汇

curriculum 课程　　liberal values 自由主义价值观　　modernity 现代性

predominantly 主要的

○ 翻译&解析 ○

宗教是早期欧洲大学的核心课程。不过在19世纪，它已经变得不再那么显著。到19世纪末，基于更自由的价值观的德国大学模式开始在世界各地流行起来。它拥有更多的科学科目，大众的接受度也越来越高。在英国，从工业革命到现代化的转变见证了以科学和工程为重点的城市大学的到来。

世界上不同国家的大学的赞助和组织结构差别非常大。在一些国家，大学主要由国家出资，而另一些国家，这笔经费来自校友捐赠或学费等。

1 The German university model, which became popular in the 19th century, promoted ....

根据原文...the German university model, based on **(more) liberal values**, had spread around the world.

2 Over the last 200 years, a university education has become .... the general public.

根据原文...Universities concentrated on science in the 19th and 20th centuries, and became **increasingly accessible** to the masses.

3 Depending on the country, universities may be funded by the state, by donors, or by fee-paying ....

根据原文...funding may come from donors or from fees which **students** attending the university must pay.

第4题

词 汇

provision 条件   verbal interactions 语言交流   self-regulation 自我管理

○ 翻译&解析 ○

当把孩子的智商与家庭教育条件进行比较时，我们发现了非常密切的正相关关系（费曼，2010）。高智商的孩子，特别是IQ分数超过130的孩子，拥有较好的教育条件。我们可以通过和他们父母的口头交流、孩子读过的书的数量和在家的活动了解到。

为了更有效的自我管理，帮助所有孩子找到自己的学习方式，我们可以使用反省认知这个方法，它是一个包括计划，监督，评估和选择合适内容来学习的一整套策略。情感意识也是反省认知的一部分，通过感受所在学习区域来增加自信心或好奇心。

1 One study found a strong connection between children's IQ and the availability of .... and .... at home.

根据原文...A very close positive relationship was found when children's IQ scores were compared with ...number of **books** and **activities** in their home etc.

2 Metacognition involves **children** understanding their own learning strategies, as well as developing ....

根据原文...can be helped to identify their own ways of learning...**Emotional awareness** is also part of metacognition.

 第5题

 词 汇

attributed to 归因于　　breakthrough 突破　　contaminated 被污染　　inhibited 抑制

substance 物质　　filtrate 过滤　　broth culture 培养物

○ **翻译&解析** ○

　　青霉素的发现要归功于苏格兰科学家亚历山大·弗莱明。佛莱明说，他是在1928年9月28日上午发现这个幸运的意外的：在伦敦圣玛丽医院的地下实验室里，弗莱明注意到一个装有葡萄球菌培养物的培养皿盖子没关。培养物已经被蓝绿色的霉菌污染了，霉菌周围有一圈光环。因此他得出结论，霉菌释放出一种抑制细菌生长的物质。他继续培养这种物质，发现它是一种青霉，也就是青霉菌。弗莱创造了"青霉素"这一词来指代青霉菌培养出的滤液。

1 Alexander Fleming discovered penicillin by .... on September 28,1928.

根据原文...The discovery of penicillin...Alexander Fleming...September 28, 1928. It was a lucky **accident**;

2 He found **that the growth of bacteria on a petri dish was** .... by a blue-green mould that had contaminated the culture.

根据原文...Fleming noticed...The culture had become contaminated by blue-green mould, and there was a halo of **inhibited** bacterial growth around the mould.

3 He realised that **the mould was** producing a substance that was responsible for .... bacterial growth.

根据原文...Fleming concluded that **the mould was** releasing **a substance that was repressing** the growth of the bacteria;

词 汇

literary families 文学世家　　launched 发起　　participants 参与者　　originality 独创性

novelty 新奇的　　plot development 情节发展　　sophistication 高水平　　inherited 遗传

heritability 遗传力

翻译&解析

人们发现文学世家中的写作能力是可以被"遗传"的。为了搞明白这个问题，美国耶鲁大学和俄罗斯莫斯科大学的研究者进行了一项研究，看看能否找到其中科学的原因，为什么著名作家会"繁衍"其他作家。

这项研究分析了511名8~17岁的儿童以及489名母亲和326名父亲的作品。所有参与者都进行了指定主题的写作。这些文章经原创性，新颖性，情节发展的质量，成熟度和创造性等几个维度考察后评分，研究人员还进行了详细的智力测试并分析了家庭的作用。

考虑到智力与家庭背景的关系，研究人员对创意写作的环境因素与遗传因素进行了计算，的确找到了所称的创意写作的遗传性因素。

1 Creative writing ability may be .... from parents, according to a new study.

根据原文...there may be an **inherited** element to writing good fiction;

2-3 Researchers compared .... written by children and their parents, looking at elements such as originality and use of ....

根据原文...The study ...All the participants wrote **stories** on particular themes. The stories were then scored and rated for originality and novelty,...and creative use of **prior knowledge**;

4-5 After conducting intelligence tests and allowing for ...., they concluded that there is a .... link between genetics and creative writing.

根据原文...Taking into account intelligence and **family background**, ...They found what they describe as a **modest** heritability element to creative writing.

词汇

nocturnality 夜行性　　adjective 形容词　　traits 特点　　predators 捕食者

illumination 光源　　compensate 补偿　　niche differentiation 生态位分化

partitioned 分割　　temporal division 时间分割　　meadow 牧场　　rodents 啮齿动物

翻译&解析

昼伏夜出是一种动物行为，说白话就是晚上出来找吃的，白天在家睡觉。常用的形容词是"nocturnal"，与之相反的是"diurnal"。

夜间活动的生物通常有高度发达的听觉和嗅觉，以及有适应力的视力。这些能力可以帮助动物，如飞蛾等避免捕食者。有些动物，比如猫和雪貂，它们的眼睛可以同时适应低光线的夜晚和白天的强光。而有些动物，如丛猴和蝙蝠，只能在夜间活动。有很多夜间动物，比如大部分猫头鹰都有一双大眼睛来聚光以适应夜间较低的光线。

夜间活动是生态分化的一种形式，一个物种的生态位不是按照自愿量划分的，而是按时间划分的。例如，鹰和猫头鹰可以在同一块草地上捕食同一种啮齿动物而不发生冲突，因为鹰在白天活动而猫头鹰在夜间活动。

1-2 Nocturnal animals sleep during the daytime, whereas .... animals are awake during the day and they .... at night.

根据原文... versus its opposite "**diurnal**"，这里第一个空应该填diurnal；而刚好与nocturnal相反，diurnal是**sleep** at night；注意，根据题干空格词性这里不可以填asleep这个形容词；

3-4 Animals that are active at night tend to have .... hearing and smell, and they may have .... eyesight.

根据原文...Nocturnal creatures generally have highly developed senses(**sensitive**) of hearing and smell, and specially(**exceptional**) adapted eyesight;

5 Nocturnality allows animals to hunt for prey without having to **5**................... with predators that are active during daylight hours.

根据原文...hunt the same field or meadow for the same rodents **without conflict** because hawks are diurnal and owls are nocturnal.

第8题

词 汇

thunderclouds 雷雨云   lightning strikes 雷击   revealing 揭露

○ 翻译&解析 ○

在20世纪60年代，研究人员试图向雷雨云发射带引线的火箭，试图让雷雨云中产生的巨大电荷找到放电路径。不过这种方法仅止步于实验研究，它并不能真正成为防雷电保护的措施。毕竟在人口稠密的地区发射火箭不是明智之举，火箭掉下来怎么办？

另一种方式是利用激光来安全释放雷雨云中的电量。这个想法大概始于20年前，当时发现高功率激光可以从原子钟提取电子并产生离子。如果激光能在空气中产生一条电离线直戳风暴云中心，那么这条导线就可以引导电子抵达地面，从而释放电量。而为了不被导回的电子击中，它不会直接对着云层。取而代之的是，激光会射向镜子并反射到云层。要实现这个想法，必须将激光发射器及其部件的价格降到足够便宜。

1 a laser is used to create a line of ionisation by removing electrons from ....

根据原文...when high-powered lasers were revealing their ability to extract electrons out of **atoms(B)** and create ions；

2 This laser is then directed at .... in order to control electrical charges

根据原文...If a laser could generate a line of ionisation in the air all the way up to a **storm cloud(C)**, this conducting path could be used to guide lightning to Earth.

3 a method which is less dangerous than using **3**..................

根据原文...who would want to fire streams of **rockets(G)**...Another project is trying to use lasers to discharge lightning safely，这道题无法用关键词定位得出，必须读懂原文第一段；

4 As a protection for the lasers, the beams are aimed firstly at ....

根据原文...To stop the laser itself being struck,... Instead it would be directed at a **mirror(D)**, and from there into the sky;

 第9题

词 汇

accompanied 伴随着　pedestrianised zone 步行街　interconnected 相互联系的

vehicular traffic 车流　infancy 婴儿期　cobblestones 鹅卵石　pavement bricks 路面砖

◦ 翻译&解析 ◦

　　自20世纪60年代初以来，很多欧洲的城镇将市中心规划成了步行街。一般在步行街的尽头都会有停车场和公交站。哥本哈根市中心就是一个最大且最古老的例子之一：以Strget为中心串联整片步行街道，形成了一个庞大的步行区。虽然也有车辆在街道间穿行，但大部分区域只允许送货卡车在清晨为企业服务，街道的清洁车辆也通常在大多数商店晚上关门后进行作业。

　　在北美，人们通常把这种区域叫做步行商业街，不过它还处于发展阶段。有步行街区的城市还很少，更多的只有一条步行街。一些步行街铺有鹅卵石或石砖，这会导致轮椅等非机动车无法通行且它们并不完全禁止机动车。

1 In some cases, people are encouraged to park .... of the town or city centre.

根据原文...car parks **on the edge** of the pedestrianised zone；

2 The only vehicles permitted in most pedestrian zones are those used for .... or

.... -cleaning.

根据原文...Most of these zones allow **delivery** trucks to service the businesses located there during the early morning, and **street**-cleaning ....

3 Certain types of road surface can be used to .... traffic.

根据原文...Many pedestrian streets are surfaced with cobblestones, or pavement bricks, which **discourage (any)** kind of **wheeled** traffic...

词 汇

jeopardising 危害　　presence 存在　　emerge 出现　　disturbance 干扰

destructive 破坏性的　　nocturnal 夜行的

○ 翻译&解析 ○

　　研究人员最新发现，人类活动正在导致鹿、老虎和熊等原本在日间活动的哺乳动物不得不昼伏夜出。人类活动会导致动物强烈的恐惧感，而人类活动覆盖了地球75%的面积，使得这种现象难以避免。由于白天无法活动，它们被迫夜间觅食。

　　加州大学伯克利分校Kaitlyn Gaynor教授领导的研究小组分析了来自六大洲近80个研究项目后得出这一结论。这项研究利用GPS跟踪器和运动相机监测各种哺乳动物的活动。科学家利用这些数据来评估不同人类干扰程度对动物的行为习惯的影响。

　　这些人类的干扰包括无害的徒步旅行和有害的狩猎活动等。同时更大规模的农业种植和道路建设也是干扰之一。总的来说，研究人员得出结论：无论是海狮还是狮子，只要动物的夜间行为增加，附近必然有人类活动。

1 A recent study has shown that many mammals are being forced to become .... due to the presence of humans.

根据原文...the researchers concluded that from beavers to lions, there was an increase in **nocturnal** behaviour when humans were in the vicinity;这道题的答案出现在文末最后一句;

2 Scientists reached these findings **by** ....

根据原文...arrived at this conclusion after...**monitored** ... **trackers** and motion-activated cameras；这里有两个动词可以填，但根据原文前的by，后面只能跟-ing形式，所以应该填 **tracking**；

3 and analysing the movements of mammals in areas with different levels of ....

...to assess the night time antics of the animals during periods of low and high **human disturbance**.

4 They showed that human activities, ranging from hiking to .... to road building

根据原文...harmless activities like hiking to overtly destructive ones like hunting,...farming and road construction；这里可以填写hunting或farming，但根据可选词，填**agriculture**(farming同义词)更合适；

5 made it more likely that mammals would **5**................... at night.

根据原文...mammals are forced to **emerge** during the night；

这道题的题干顺序并不与句子顺序一致，由于篇幅较短，更适合在读懂文章之后来做题；另外一个难点在于选词，要根据词性和匹配度进行一定的筛选；

第11题

词汇

aviation 航空　　pioneers 先驱　　fundamental breakthrough 根本性突破　　enabled 使能够
equilibrium 平衡　　aeronautical 航空的　　pilot control 飞行器控制　　emphasis 重视
wind tunnel 风道　　propellers 螺旋桨　　rival models 竞品　　essential 必要的
printing presses d印刷机

翻译&解析

莱特兄弟奥维尔和威尔是美国发明家和航空先驱，他们于1903年12月17日发明并成功制造了世界上第一架飞机。这是一架可控制，有动力切可持续的载人飞行器，两年后，他们又研发出第一架实用的固定翼飞机。

兄弟俩的创造性突破是对三轴控制的发明，它能够使飞行员有效操纵飞机并保持平衡。这个方法在当时已成所有固定翼飞机的标准配置。从开始研究飞机起，他们就致力于开发一种可靠的飞行员控制方法来解决最关键的"飞行控制问题"。这个方法和当时其他着力开发更大马力引擎完全不同。莱特兄弟利用一个小型的自制风洞，收集到比以往任何人都更准确的数据，这使得他们能够设计和制造比竞争对手更高效的机翼和螺旋桨。

他们经营自己的商店多年，熟练使用印刷机、自行车、马达和其他机械设备，以此获得了必要的机械技能。特别是对自行车的研究，让他们意识到不稳定的飞行器也可以通过练习来控制平衡。

1 In 1903, the Wright brothers completed development of the first airplane that was capable of sustaining controlled ⋯⋯⋯⋯⋯⋯ .

根据原文...building the world's first successful airplane and making the first controlled, powered and sustained heavier-than-air **human flight**

2 The key to their success was a system that gave the pilot the means to control and ⋯⋯⋯⋯⋯⋯ the airplane.

根据原文..The brothers' fundamental breakthrough was their invention of three-axis control, which enabled the pilot to **steer** the aircraft effectively...

3 This set them apart from other inventors who had focused on building ⋯⋯⋯⋯⋯⋯

根据原文...This approach differed significantly from other experimenters of the time who put more emphasis on developing **powerful engines**.

4 The brothers had previous experience with a wide variety of ⋯⋯⋯⋯⋯⋯

根据原文...They gained the mechanical skills essential for their success by working for years in their shop with printing presses, bicycles, motors, and other **machinery**.（请注意，这里不可以填写mechanical skills，因为题目已经说了experience with...）

5 but it was their work with ⋯⋯⋯⋯⋯⋯ that had the greatest influence on their ideas.

根据原文...Their work with **bicycles** in particular influenced their belief that...;

🔍 第12题

词汇

folklore 传说　hideout 藏身所　mythical 神话的　estimated 大约　canopy 树冠
public poll 公众投票　oddly 古怪的　fused 结合　sapling 幼苗　pruning 修剪
trunk 树干　massive 巨大的　limb 主枝　partial 部分的　elaborate 复杂的
illegally 违法的　acorns 橡子

"大橡树"是英国诺丁汉郡舍伍德林森里的一颗大型橡树。根据当地民间传说，罗宾汉和他的伙伴们把大橡树作为藏身之所。这棵树的大小和它的神话地位使它成为一个受欢迎的旅游景点。

"大橡树"重约23吨，周长10米，树冠高28米，树龄为800~1000年。在2002年的一项调查中，它被评为"英国最受欢迎的树"。2014年，在Woodland信托基金的评选中，它被评为"英国年度之树"。

关于"大橡树"为什么长得这么大且形状怪异的原因，有几种说法。一种说法是它其实是由几颗幼苗拼接而成，而另一种说法认为它之前被修剪过。修剪树木可以使树干和树枝长得又大又粗。由于树干的过大过重，它需要一个复杂的脚手架来进行支撑。早在维多利亚时代就已经建立起这个支撑系统了。

有意思的是，2002年，有人试图在网上非法拍卖大橡树的橡子。

1 Legend has it that the Major Oak was Robin Hood's ....

根据原文...According to local folklore, Robin Hood and his Merry Men used the Major Oak as their hideout(**den**).

2 The .... of the tree's trunk is 10 metres.

根据原文...The Major Oak weighs an estimated 23 tons, has a girth(**circumference**) of 10 metres

3 The tree may actually be more than one tree that .... together.

根据原文...the Major Oak may be several trees that fused(**joined**) together as saplings.

4 Some of the tree's .... have to be held up by props.

根据原文...the tree's massive limbs(**branch**) require the partial support of an elaborate system of scaffolding；

5 Acorns from the oak were once .... for auction on the Internet.

根据原文...someone attempted to illegally sell acorns from the Major Oak on an internet-based auction website；这里要填sell的同义词**put on**（挂出来），而不能填put in（提出）；

 第13题

 词 汇

spectacles 景象　nonstop 不间断的　pathways 路径　hatched 孵化　laboratory 实验室
cardinal direction 大方向　suspected 怀疑　genetic inheritance 基因遗传　hunches 预感
existence 存在　social interaction 社交

◯ **翻译&解析** ◯

动物迁徙是自然界最壮观的景象之一。每年角马和斑马都会在马拉河生态系统中随着雨水迁徙，而帝王蝶会沿着一条小径从墨西哥飞到加拿大，鸟类也会长途迁徙好几天。科学家现在已经弄清它们是如何知道去哪里，什么时候该出发。

科学家发现，有一些动物的迁徙路径是被写入基因里的。一只在实验室里孵化出来的鸟，虽然对自然界一无所知，但它仍然试图在一年中的正确时间段朝着正确方向开始迁徙。

但对于大角羊和驼鹿这样大型哺乳动物来说就是另一回事了。长期以来，野生动物学家长期怀疑它们的迁徙建立在经验之上，每年的迁徙活动其实是相互学习的结果而不是遗传。本周四在《科学》杂志上的一项新研究表明，这些判断是正确的——一些动物必须学会如何迁徙（而不是依靠基因遗传）。

研究人员解释说，集体信息和知识可以从年长的动物传递给年轻的动物，它其实是一种"文化"形式，当动物学通过社交与信息传递来学习时，这就是一种文化交流而不是基因遗传。

1 Scientists believe that .... are responsible for some animal migrations.

原文说到...Some of these animals, they've found, have their migration pathways written into their **genes**；

2 Songbirds, for example, do not need to learn when and in which .... to migrate.

原文说到...still attempts to begin migration at the right time of year and in the right cardinal direction；

3 bighorn sheep appear to **3**.................. migration habits from the herd.

原文说到...some animals must **learn** how to migrate；

4-5 They, and other mammals, seem to have a .... that is passed from one generation to the next through interaction and exchange of ....

原文说到...that can be passed from older animals to younger ones, is a form of "**culture**",...a result of social interaction and the transfer of this **information**；

第14题

词 汇

Cathedral 教堂　　dome 穹顶　　octagonal 八角形　　buttresses 支墩　　formula 配方
scaffolding 脚手架　　impractical 不实际的　　attributed 把...归因于

○ 翻译&解析 ○

　　到15世纪初，经过100年的建造，佛罗伦萨教堂仍然没有盖好圆顶。这个建筑需要一个八角形的穹顶，而且比任何一座建筑的穹顶都要高都要宽，并且没有任何外部墙壁来防止它由于自身重量的作用坠落。

　　这种砖石穹顶的建造有很多技术难题。现在被称为世界第一位建筑工程师和建筑界翘楚的菲利波，当时向罗马万神殿的大穹顶提出了解决方案。万神殿是一个混凝土外壳，而材料配方早已消失不见。它是由混合银币的泥土制成，但由于佛罗伦萨教堂的尺寸太大而导致过重，混凝土并不是好的解决方案。另一种解决方案是使用脚手架，但整个托斯卡纳地区缺乏足够的木材，所以这个方案也无法实施。

　　布鲁内莱斯基则采用砖来制造穹顶，因为它比石头轻，而且很容易成型，而且制造的时候下方不需要支撑。他最终的成功在很大程度上归功于他的数学和技术天赋，这个使用了400多万块砖建造的教堂仍是当今世界上最大的砖石穹顶。

1-2 Due to the .... and .... of the required structure, the construction of a dome for the cathedral in Florence **had challenged architects for many years.**

根据原文...The building required an octagonal dome **which would be higher(height) and wider (width) than any that had ever been built...；**

3 A method employed by the Romans, using .... to support a dome while it was being built, was not suitable....

根据原文....**Soil(earth) filled with silver coins** had held the Pantheon dome aloft while its concrete set. This could not be the solution **in the case....；** 请注意，这里填concrete就错了；

4 an insufficient supply of **4**................... meant that scaffolding could not be used either.

根据原文...the use of scaffolding, was also impractical **because there was** not enough timber(**wood**)....

5-6 The architect Brunelleschi finally .... in building **the largest** .... **dome in the world.**

根据原文...His eventual **success(succeeded)** can be attributed......**the largest** masonry(**brick**) **dome in the world.**

选择题

词 汇

confusion 困惑　　curious 好奇心　　distortions 歪曲　　perception 看法

○ 翻译&解析 ○

造成这种困惑的第三个原因是媒体的态度。人们对于坏消息的好奇心远大于好消息。报纸与广播只提供读者想要的内容。然而这会导致读者认知的严重扭曲。

1 媒体是打算：

A 教育读者；在原文中没有找到educate的同义词，媒体并不存在educate readers这个行为；

B 满足读者的期望；根据原文...to provide what the public wants, 刚好对应题干meet their readers' expectations；

C 鼓励读者反馈；根据原文newspapers and broadcasters并没有打算获得readers的feedback；

D 误导读者；这是一个迷惑项，很多同学会根据最后一句...can lead to significant distortions of perception是mislead的同义词而选D，但别忘了题干中有一个词：intended to（打算；意在），mislead readers可能是一个结果，但不是媒体并没有刻意去误导读者；

第2题

词 汇

stubborn 棘手的　　accomplish 完成　　rigging 绳索

○ 翻译&解析 ○

有一个棘手的问题考古学家尚未给出任何答案：拉皮塔人是如何多次完成难度堪比登月

的？没有人发现过能够揭露他们航行的独木舟或索具等证据。即使后来的波利尼西亚人的口述历史和传统中也没有提供任何见解，拉皮塔人早已成了神话。

1 为什么很难解释拉皮塔人的航行？

A 被发现的独木舟揭示了相关的线索；这个事实与原文相反，原文说：No-one has found one of their canoes or any rigging；

B 考古学家对于该领域的兴趣有限；这个判断在原文没有体现，原文只是说：There is one stubborn question for which archaeology has yet to provide any answers，至于考古学家到底感不感兴趣就无从得知了；

C 与这一时期有关的资料很少，因此无法推测出确切过程；这里的little information relating to this period对应原文的turn into myth；

D 技术的进步改变了人们看待这些成就的方式；原文中完全没有这个信息；

🔍 第3题

词 汇

placebo 安慰剂　medical intervention 治疗手段　general practitioner 全科医生
prescribed 给...开药　antibiotics 抗生素　viral infection 病毒感染　fatigue 疲劳

○ 翻译&解析 ○

安慰剂其实是一种假装的治疗手段。不过有时候接受安慰剂治疗的患者会感觉到有实际状况的改善，这种现象也被称为安慰剂效应。

一项针对丹麦全科医生的调查发现，48%的医生在过去一年中至少开过10次安慰剂。最常用的安慰剂是治疗病毒感染的抗生素治疗和缓解疲劳的维生素。医院医生和专家的使用率则要低得多。

1 安慰剂效应是指：

A 一种假装的医疗手段；这里其实是一个陷阱，因为题目问的不是placebo，而是The placebo effect；

B 通过假装的医疗手段来提升病人的健康；根据原文...have a perceived or actual improvement in a medical condition；

C 一种常见的医疗现象；placebo effect是一种现象，但并不是医疗现象；

2 根据研究，丹麦的安慰剂用来：

A 主要是医院的医生在使用；选项跟原文有对应的同义词，但完全与原文的意思相反，原文说：Specialists and hospital- based physicians reported much lower rates of placebo use，即医院所开的安慰剂比例很小；

B 代替抗生素；原文说了是antibiotics for viral infections，仅针对感染（轻症）的抗生素，而不是antibiotics；

C 治疗受病毒困扰的患者；与原文的vitamins for fatigue同义；

背景知识补充：General Practitioners，又称GP，全科医生。在国外，病人通常先找GP问诊，相当于疾病初筛，然后GP会根据病情介绍到不同的专科医生处就诊。这有点像国内的社区门诊，先帮你看病，然后根据病情将患者转到相应的三甲医院就诊。

第4题

○ **翻译&解析** ○

Pierre de Coubertin 顾拜旦，现代奥林匹克运动之父；

mens sana in corpore sano 拉丁文诗歌选句，高尚的灵魂寓于强健的体魄。

英国公立学校的贵族风气对顾拜旦产生了极大影响。学校信奉体育是教育的重要组成部分，用一句话来概括就是"mens sana in corpore sano"，即高尚的灵魂寓于强健的体魄。在这种风气中，绅士其实是一个多面手，而并不仅是在某一个方面做得突出的人。同时，公平是一个非常流行的概念，认为练习或训练无异于作弊。

1 顾拜旦认为

A 体育是绅士的运动；原文中提到了gentlemen和sport，但没有谈到二者是否为对应关系；

B 学校应当推动身心健康教育；原文中的a sound mind in a sound body对应选项中的both physical and mental health；

C 体育是儿童教育的重要环节；原文提到了…an important part of，但并没有说the most important part of，遇到most这种绝对的字眼要特别小心；

2 顾拜旦认为：

A 各项运动全面发展比只从事一项运动要简单；原文说...who became an all-rounder, not the best at one specific thing，但并没有说全面发展或单项突破哪个更简单；

B 如果要成为一个多面手就需要训练；原文提到了all-rounder，也提到了training，但是否 necessary并没有说；

C 训练使运动员拥有不公平的优势；原文的practising or training was considered tantamount to cheating对应题干中的training gives the athlete an unfair advantage；

第5题

词 汇

corpus 语料库   representative 代表

○ 翻译&解析 ○

在语言学中，语料库（复数语料库）是一个庞大且结构化的文本集合（现今以电子方式存储）。语料库可以用来帮助语言学家分析语言，也可以用来编写词典或进行语言教学。英国国家语料库（BNC）是一个拥有一亿字文本的语料库，来源于各种风格的书面语和口语。该语料库涵盖了二十世纪末英语的各种体裁，是当时英语口语和书面语的代表性样本。

1 什么是语料库？

A 一部大字典；原文中提及它是for the purpose of dictionary writing，而不是字典本身；

B A single written text. 一个单一文本；原文中说它是a large and structured set of texts，而不是single text，与原文相反；

C 一个语言分析工具；原文中说它是used to help linguists to analyse a language；

2 BNC是做什么的？

A 是为了语言教学的；原文中说的是：a corpus used to help language teaching而不是BNC；

B 记录某一特定时期的英语书面语与口语；这与原文中的：a representative sample of spoken and written British English of that time相同；

C 记录英语语言的历史；BNC并不是一个历史资料；

第6题

词汇

tragically 悲惨的　　threatened 威胁　　a formidable challenge 一个巨大的挑战

○ 翻译&解析 ○

　　艾格尔山是瑞士伯尔尼地区阿尔卑斯山脉的一座山峰。自1935年以来，至少有64名登山者在攀登山峰北麓时丧生，因此赢得了一个德语绰号Mordwand，意为"谋杀墙"，也是Nordwand（North Wall）的一语双关。在1938年被成功攀爬之前，大部分的攀登者的下场都很悲惨，伯尔尼当局甚至禁止攀登并威胁将对试图攀爬的人处以罚款。不过自从它被成功登顶以来，北麓已被攀登过多次，即便如此，它仍被认为是一个巨大的挑战。

　　1 根据原文，以下哪两个选项是正确的？

　　A 艾格尔山是阿尔卑斯山脉最危险的山；又是一个很绝对的词the most，原文并没有表明；

　　B 山的北麓有一段可怕的历史；原文中说：most of the attempts on the face ended tragically，对应选项中的infamous history；

　　C Nordwand终于在1938年被征服；这里的conquered对应原文中的the first successful attempt；

　　D 伯尔尼当局对试图攀爬北麓的登山者给予了处罚；原文说：...threatened to fine any party that should attempt it，所以当局只是威胁会处罚，我们并不知道是否真的有处罚过；

　　E 伯尔尼当局对试图攀爬北麓的登山者给予了处罚；原文说：...threatened to fine any party that should attempt it，所以当局只是威胁会处罚，我们并不知道是否真的有处罚过；

第7题

词汇

psychologist 心理学家　　intelligence tests 智力测验　　phenomenon 现象　　constant 持续

○ 翻译&解析 ○

　　"IQ"这个词来自德语"Intelligenz-Quotient",由德国心理学家William Stern于1912年发

明，它是一种儿童智力测验的方法。自从二十世纪以来，世界上大部分地区的IQ得分都在增加。这种现象意味着如果按照不变的评分标准来评分，IQ测试的分数将以每十年上升三点的平均速度持续增长。这个现象被弗林在书中称为钟形曲线，弗林的这一发现引起了心理学家的注意。

1 "IQ" refers to IQ是指

A 一种儿童智力测验；

B 智力测验评分方式；

很多同学会错误地选择A，A和B确实很接近但并不完全相同；IQ指的是a method of scoring children's intelligence tests，所以它说到底是一种method，也就是means的同义词，是一种算分方法，即constant standard scoring rule，而不是智力测验本身；

C 心理学的一个领域；原文只是说...bring this phenomenon to the attention of psychologists，并没有说这是心理学的一个领域；

2 弗林注意到

A IQ得分在世界范围恒定不变；这个结论显然是错的，因为原文说：IQ test scores have been rising at an average rate of around three IQ points per decade；

B IQ是一种全球现象；原文中提到的this phenomenon，指的并不是IQ本身，而是IQ分数逐年增长；

C 在过去十几年智力测试的分数在不断上升；这句话对应原文中的：IQ test scores have been rising at an average rate of around three IQ points per decade；

 第8题

词汇

fragile 脆弱的   pristine 处于原始状态的   undisturbed 未被打搅的

ecological conservation 生态保护   political empowerment 政治权利   foster 促进

occasionally 有时候   modest 不太大的   necessitates 使...成为必要

infrastructure 基础设施   water treatment plants 污水处理厂

sanitation facilities 卫生设施   utilisation 利用

生态旅游是一种旅行方式，游客在这里感受脆弱，原始和相对未受干扰的自然风景。它的目的可以是教育游客，为生态保护提供资金，直接有利于当地社会的经济发展和政治权利，抑或是促进对不同文化和人权的尊重。

然而，生态旅游有时并不能实现保护环境的目的。即使是人口的适度增长也会给当地环境带来额外的压力，因为需要建设更多的基础设施。污水处理厂，卫生设施和酒店的兴建将伴随着对不可再生资源的开发和对当地有限资源的利用。由于当地社区无法满足这些基础设施的需求，环境可能会受到破坏。

1 生态旅游的目的之一是：

A 让人们去到那些从未涉足的地区；生态旅游通常确实都发生在...relatively undisturbed natural areas，但这不是它的目的，原文说Its purpose may be to...所以这句话后面的才是ecotourism的目的；

B 对生态脆弱地区的社区提供教育服务；原文中提到...to educate the traveller，所以并不是对local communities的教育；

C 为保护区筹集环境保护资金；题干中的raise money for和environmental projects in natural areas是原文provide funds和ecological conservation的同义词组；

2 然而，生态旅游可能会导致一些问题：

A 当地人并不欢迎游客；虽然我们能从第二段感觉出来当地人不欢迎游客，但并没有直接信息提到了当地人不欢迎游客；

B 人口的增长导致需要兴建很多设施；

C 当地人没有资金来改善设施；根据原文...local communities are unable to meet these infrastructure demands，但并没有缺乏资金；

 第9题

词 汇

ethnography 人种志　　ethnos 民族　　systematic 系统的　　cultural phenomena 文化现象

ethnographic 人种学　　personal bias 个人偏见　　participant 参与者

人种志，来自希腊民族（包含民间，人民和民族）是对人种和文化的系统研究。它的目的是让研究者从不同角度观察社会，探索文化现象和文化氛围。

根据著名社会学家约翰布鲁尔所称，人种学数据收集方法旨在捕捉人们在"自然发生环境"中的"社会意义和日常活动"，他们通常被称为"告密者"。其目的是收集数据的方式使研究者施加最小的个人偏见。数据收集的方法可以包括参与者观察，实地记录，访谈和调查。

1 根据原文，以下哪两个判断是正确的？

A 人种学起源于希腊；原文说：Ethnography, from the Greek ethnos (folk, people, nation) and grapho，但并没有说它起源于希腊；

B 人种论研究是与古代文化与社会相关的；本文从头到尾都没有提到古代字眼；

C 人种学的研究对象被称为"告密者"；

D 人种论学者试图使他们的研究尽量客观；原文的a minimal amount of personal bias和题干中的as objective as possible是同义词；

E 观察是最有效的数据收集方式；原文说：Methods of data collection can include participant observation, field notes, interviews, and surveys. 但这个the most effective并没有体现；

🔍 第10题

词 汇

resides 坐落于　　atlases 地图册　　magnificent 壮丽的　　elaborate 精心制作的

cartography 制图　　fragile 易碎的　　magnifying glasses 放大镜　　prodigious 巨大的

instantly 立刻

○ **翻译&解析** ○

世界上最大的地图收藏坐落于华盛顿特区的国会图书馆，这里由460万张地图和6.3万个地图集组成，其中有宏伟的国界图和精美的地图，比如黄金时代的荷兰制图。在阅览室的学者们戴着轻薄的棉手套保护着这些碎片，用放大镜来研究这些古代地图。在隔壁房间，人们坐在电脑屏幕前研究着最新的地图。凭借着巨大的存储能力，电脑能够存储有关人、地点和环境的所有数据，地图上的所有信息，并且几乎可以立即在屏幕上显示所需的地理环境信息，而且只需要点一下就可以打印出来。

1 在国会图书馆你能够

A 借阅荷兰地图；在原文中的确提到了：the pride of the golden age of Dutch cartography，但并没有说明它是否提供借阅；

B 学习如何保存古代易碎地图；原文中提到了：scholars, wearing thin cotton gloves to protect the fragile sheets，但并没有说有机会可以学习；

C 享受阅览室的氛围；这个原文中完全没有提及；

D 购买计算机订制地图；原文中说：...people sit at their computer screens...and at the click of a button, a print-out of the map appears；

🔍 第11题

词 汇

etymology 词源学　　etymologists 词源学家　　comparative linguistics 比较语言学

inferences 推断

◦ 翻译&解析 ◦

词源学是研究词汇的历史、起源以及它们的形式和意义是如何随着时间的推移而变化的。对于那些有着悠久文字历史的语言，词源学家利用这些语言中的文本，收集有关单词在历史早期如何使用以及何时进入相关的语言体系的。

词源学家还会运用比较语言学的方法来重建那些古老而无法获得任何直接信息的语言。通过使用一种被称为比较法的技术来分析相关的语言，语言学家可以推断出他们共同的母语及其词汇。通过这种方式可以追溯到词根词缀的发源地是印欧语系。

Etymology一词源于希腊单词etymologia，意思是"真正的意义"，它的后缀-logia，是"研究"的意思。

1 以下哪两个选项是正确的？

A 词源学涉及对历史文本的研究；

B 有一些语言过于古老以至于词源学家无法理解；这个判断与原文相反：

C 古希腊人是首先研究单词起源的人；原文只提到了：The word etymology is derived from the Greek word etymologia，无从得知是否希腊人是最先研究单词词源的；

D 大多数单词都起源于印欧语系；原文中只是说道：word roots have been found that...the Indo-European language family；题干说的是words而原文说的是word roots，不是一回事；

E etymology这个单词的意思是"真正的意义"；

 第12题

词 汇

identifiable 可识别的　stimuli 反馈　individualised 个性化　enormous 极大的

proponents 支持者　efficacy 效用　extensively 广泛的　criticised 批评

hypothesis 假设　appropriate 恰当的　invalid 无效的

○ 翻译&解析 ○

"学习风格"指的是各种各样的学习方式。"学习风格"理论是基于以下这样一种观察：大多数人更喜欢和信息进行互动、接受和处理可识别的方法。个性化的"学习风格"这一理念起源于20世纪70年代，并获得广泛的推广。支持者说，教师应该评估学生的学习风格，调整课堂教学方法，以最适合每个学生的偏好。

这些提议的依据和有效性受到了广泛的批评。尽管儿童和成人都表达了个性偏好，但没有证据表明辨别出学习风格能提升产出效果。同时有证据表明，这种假设（以适合其学习风格的方式进行教学，学生的成绩会更好）可能是无效的。

1 人们应该根据各自的学习风格学习的观点

A 已经影响了所有的教师；这个选项里有一个很绝对的词：all 所有的，原文只提到了...acquired enormous popularity；

B 已经风行了40年；

C 从未有过争议；很显然与原文不符；

2 没有证据表明：

A 人们有各自的学习风格；

B 假设可能是错的；

C 判断出学生的学习风格会有帮助；

这道题的问法不多见，我们可以把"没有证据表明"理解为"以下哪个选项是错的"；

第13题

词汇

mass media 大众媒体 keep the money rolling in 维持运转 overstate 夸大
overwhelmingly 压倒性的 selfless folk 无私的人 nevertheless 尽管如此
lobby groups 游说团体 scepticism 怀疑态度 self-interested 自私的 altruistic 无私的

○ 翻译&解析 ○

其次，环保团体需要被大众媒体所关注。它们还需要足够的资金维持运转。所以，有时候，它们会言过其实。比如在1997年的时候，世界自然基金会在媒体上发布说"三分之二的森林将永久消失"，但实际上只有20%消失了。

虽说环保团体大部分都是由志愿者管理的，（这种无私性会扩大它的话语权）但它们的地位其实和其他团队是相同的。不过如果在涉及环保的议题上，人们对其他组织的怀疑程度要远大于环保组织。比如，对于加强污染管理来说，所谓公正的常理事实上可能弊大于利，但如果一个贸易组织提倡要放松管制，那它就会被视为自私自利，而一个主张加强污染控制的绿色组织就会被视为是无私利他的。

1 作者举世界自然基金会的例子想说明：

A 它可以影响到大众媒体；原文说：environmental groups need to be noticed by the mass media，所以它不仅不能影响到大众媒体反而不被重视；

B 它是一个有效率的环保组织；原文从始至终没有提到环保组织是否effective；

C 大众媒体可以帮助绿色组织筹集资金；原文并没有提到媒体会帮助绿色组织筹款；

D 环保组织会夸大他们的主张；题干中的exaggerate their claims是overstates their arguments 的同义词组；

2 作者关于其他游说组织的主要观点是？

A 它们更加主动；第二段中没有任何信息提到active；

B 它们组织得更好；没有任何信息提到organised；

C 它们受到了更多的怀疑；有些同学会排除这个选项，因为看到原文说...applied the same

degree of scepticism to...就得出environmental groups和lobby groups得到的criticism是一样的，但这其实是没有认真阅读原文；原文中说到A trade organisation...seen as self-interested, a green organisation...seen as altruistic，显然前者受到的批评更多；

D 它们支持更重要的议题；选择这个选项的同学一定是因为看到了...That would matter less if...，但根据原文，我们无法得出lobby groups support more important issues...这个判断；

🔍 第14题

词汇

life expectancy 寿命　　generosity 慷慨　　materialize 发生　　intimately 紧密的
incubate 孕育　　illustrate 表明　　remarkably 出乎意料的　　accounted for 导致

○ 翻译&解析 ○

年度《世界幸福报告》的研究人员发现，大约四分之三的人类幸福感来自以下六个因素：强劲的经济增长，健康的预期寿命，优质的社会关系，慷慨，信任和过上适合自己的生活的自由。这些因素不是自然产生的，它和一个国家的政府及其文化价值密切相关。换言之，最幸福的地方孕育着最幸福的人民。

为了说明地方的重要作用，该报告的编辑之一约翰赫利维尔分析了50万份问卷，这些问卷都是由移民完成的，他们在过去的40年中从100多个国家移居加拿大，其中很多被认为是不太幸福的国家。值得注意的是，赫利维尔和他的同事们发现，在抵达后的几年内，来自不幸福地区的移民的幸福水平比援助家庭更高了。似乎这种幸福感的增加只来自于环境因素。

1 根据原文以下哪两个判断是正确的？
A 个人自主权利是幸福感的来源之一；题干里的personal autonomy是原文freedom to...that`s right for you的同义词；
B 没有发现幸福与文化之间的关系；这与原文是完全相反的，intimately是紧密的意思；
C 加拿大是世界上最幸福的国家；这个题干中有一个很绝对的词：**happiest**；根据原文：Seemingly their environment alone accounted for their increased happiness；根据这个信息无法得出题干的结论；
D 搬到另一个国家会让一些人感觉更幸福；这个题干同时也是第二段的中心表达：环境让人更幸福；

E 与其他本地居民相比，移民的幸福感更少一些；这个题干是与原文完全相反的；

 第15题

词 汇

beneath 在...下面　　underneath 在...底部　　navigable river 适航河流　　triumph 巨大成就

exceeding 超过...的限制　　initial 最初的　　estimates 估价　　pedestrian 行人

scepticism 怀疑态度　　recognition 承认

翻译&解析

　　泰晤士河隧道始建于1825年至1843年间，位于伦敦泰晤士河下，全场396米，埋深23米，是已知的第一条通航河流下的隧道。

　　尽管泰晤士河隧道是土木工程的一个胜利，但它在财务上并没有取得成功，它的建造成本远超设计之初。原本扩建后可容纳车辆的提议失败了，只能供行人通行。不过，这条隧道最终变成了一个主要的旅游打卡地，每年吸引大约200万人，每个人都需缴纳1分钱门票。

　　尽管此前很多工程师对此持怀疑态度，但泰晤士河隧道的建造证明这是有可能的。在1995年3月24日，由于它的历史重要性被列为英国国家二级保护建筑。

1 下面哪三个判断是正确的?

　　A 泰晤士隧道是世界上第一条隧道；原文说...It was the first tunnel known to have been constructed successfully underneath a navigable river，但并没有说它是世界上第一条隧道；

　　B 建造隧道的成本比预测的贵；题干中的construction，more expensive，predicted分别对应原文中的building，exceeding和estimates；

　　C 原本有计划让汽车通过隧道；题干中的there were plans to对应原文的proposals；

　　D 游客让隧道变的有利可图；原文提到...each of whom paid a penny to pass under the river，但无法根据这个得出隧道是profitable的结论；

　　E 很多工程师曾尝试修建水下隧道；原文提及...despite the previous scepticism of many engineers，之前的工程师并不是tried而是scepticism，与原文相反；

　　F 泰晤士隧道现在是一个著名的建筑；题干的significant work对应原文的historic important；

词 汇

creative talents 创意人才　enraptured 兴高采烈的　prestigious 有威望的

programmer 程序员　sophisticated 复杂精妙的　computer code 代码

翻译&解析

"傻瓜都能画"这个程序是日益增长的电脑软件之一，他们的制作者声称，这些程序拥有创造性的才能。一个人工智能谱曲程序制作的古典音乐让观众欣喜若狂，甚至让大家差点相信人类谱曲已经过时了。由机器人绘制的艺术品已经可以卖到几千美元，并挂在著名的画廊里展出。甚至一些软件能够创造出连程序员都无法想象的艺术作品。

人类是能有规律的进行复杂创造行为的物种。如果我们能够把艺术创造这个过程分解成代码，那人类的创造性还有何用？"这是人类最核心的问题，"伦敦大学金史密斯学院运算创新研究员Geraint Wiggins说到，"这个问题吓坏了很多人，人们担心这会从人类意义上剥夺一些特别的东西。"

1 文章第一段，作者关于电脑制作的艺术品的看法是：

A 人们对它的接受程度各不相同；人们的反应是enraptured，说明接受程度是很高的；

B 在该领域已经取得了非常多的成就；

C 在特定的一些艺术体裁上，机器人比人还厉害；原文说的是even tricked them into believing，这个tricked就说明机器人作曲实际上还没有超过人类；

D 它们的先进程度并没有公众们期望的那么高；通读第一段，作者关于程序谱曲的解释都是比较积极的，并没有太多看空的成分；

2 根据Geraint Wiggins，为什么很多人会担心计算机艺术？

A 它会干扰人类的审美；全文并没有提到关于aesthetically inferior的问题；

B 它最终会取代人类艺术；原文说道：it is taking something special away from what it means to be human，但绝对不是完全取代；

C 它会逐渐削弱人类的基础品质；题干中的undermines对应原文中的where does that leave；

D 它最终会摧毁人类的能力；D选项说的比C选项还要严重，不过原文并没有提到；

翻译&解析

　　古英语，又称盎格鲁撒克逊语，是现代英语最早的历史形式，中世纪早期在英格兰、苏格兰南部和东部使用。它是由大约在公元5世纪中期由盎格鲁撒克逊殖民者带到英国的，而第一部古老的英国文学作品可以追溯到7世纪中期。

　　1066年英国被诺曼人征服后，古英语消失了。在那个时期，社会上层的流行语言是盎格鲁-诺曼语，这被认为标志着古英语时代的结束。因为在这一时期，英语收到盎格鲁-诺曼人的严重影响，逐步发展到现在被称为中古英语的阶段。

　　和其他古日耳曼语一样，古英语和现代英语有很大的不同，不经过学习是很难理解的。古英语语法和现代德语语法非常类似：名词、形容词、代词和动词有很多结尾和形式，词序更灵活。

　　1 7世纪发生了什么？
　　A 英语首先产生于英国；它并不是只诞生于Britain；
　　B 第一个由英语讲述的故事；原文并没有找到oral stories的信息；
　　C 最早由古英语创作的作品产生于那个时代；题干中的creating writing与原文的literary works是同义词组；

　　2 古英语：
　　A 与法语相关；原文说到的是Anglo-Norman, a relative of French，并不是Old English；
　　B 相较于英国人来说，德国人更好理解；原文提道：Old English grammar is quite similar to that of modern German...，古英语的语法与现代德语类似，但德国人能否理解，根据原文我们并不清楚；
　　C 对于现在的英语使用者来说已难以听懂；

词 汇

curriculum 课程　pedagogue 教师　parallels 相似的　foster 培养　dialects 方言

proficient 精通　prodigies 神童

○ 翻译&解析 ○

　　铃木方法是一种国际知名的音乐课程和教学理念，它可以追溯到20世纪中期，由日本小提琴家和教育家铃木信一（1898-1998）创立。这种方法旨在创造一种与母语学习类似的音乐学习环境。铃木相信这种环境也会有助于培养良好的道德品质。

　　作为一个熟练的小提琴手和一个挣扎在德语学习中的人，铃木发现，孩子们很快就能够学会母语，甚至五六岁的孩子就能够把成人认为是很"难学"的方言说出来。他据此推测，如果孩子有能力掌握语言的能力，他们也有精通乐器的必备能力。

　　铃木相信，如果教育得当，每个孩子都有能力取得高水平的音乐成就。他还明确表示，这种音乐教育的目标是培养一代又一代具有"高尚心灵"的孩子，而不是创造出所谓的音乐神童。

1 以下哪三点的正确的？

A 铃木发现了语言学习与音乐学习的共同点；题干里的similarities与原文的parallels是同义词组；

B 他使用自己的方法学习德语；原文只提到了...a beginner at the German language，并没有说他是使用何种方法学习德语的；

C 他觉得德语学起来很简单；这个选项与原文是完全相反的；

D 他认为每个孩子都有音乐潜质；选项中的musical potential和原文的capable of musical achievement是同义词组；

E 他的目标超越了简单的音乐教学；

F 他希望下一代都成为著名的音乐家；这个选项和原文是完全相反的；

词 汇

long-term effects 长期效应　proposition 提议　social reality 社会现实

align with 与...一致　portrayed 描绘　exposure 面临　subtly 微妙的

originators 首次提出者　assert 断定　socialisation 社会化　enculturation 文化适应

initial 最初的　establishes 建立　unprecedented 前所未有的　centrality 中心地位

diverse communities 多元化社区　bound together 密不可分

○ 翻译&解析 ○

　　培养理论关注电视的长期影响。它的主要观点是人们在电视世界中"生活"的时间越久，他们就越可能相信现实社会和电视上描绘的现实是一致的。

　　培养理论认为，随着时间的推移，接触电视会潜移默化地"培养"观众对现实世界的感知。研究员乔治·格布纳和拉里·格罗斯是这一看法的发起人。他们断言"电视是一种媒介，将大多数人社会化为标准的角色和行为。"一言以蔽之：文化浸润。

　　对这一理论的初步研究表明，人们对电视影响的关注源于电视在美国文化中前所未有的中心地位。格布纳认为，作为大众传播媒介的电视已经形成了一个共同的象征环境，将不同的社区联系在一起，使人们成为标准化的角色和行为。因此，他将电视和宗教的力量进行对比，指出电视对现代社会的作用就如同早期的宗教一样。

　　1 以下哪三个关于培养理论的判断是正确的?

　　A 它着眼于看太多电视对身体的影响；原文的确提到了the more time people spend 'living' in the television world，但具体有什么physical impact的影响，原文并没有提及；

　　B 它提出电视影响我们看待世界的方式；

　　C 它认为电视对人们的影响是逐渐产生的；题干中的occur gradually和原文的over time, subtly是同义词组；

　　D 这是一个被研究者广泛接受的既定理论；全文三段话都只是在解释这个理论，但是否是被学界广泛接受的公论，原文并未提及；

　　E 它指的是一种独特的美国现象；原文确实提到了...television in American culture，但这是不是只有美国有呢? 并没有提及；

F 它强调电视在社会中的作用；

 第20题

词汇

continuum 看似相邻却截然不同的　　implicit 含蓄的　　doggedness 坚持不懈的

incremental 递增的　　discerned 识别

○ 翻译&解析 ○

卡罗尔·德维克认为，可以根据个人关于自身能力来源看法的不同将他们分为两类。有些人认为自己的成功来自天生，他们的智力是固定的，即固定思维模型。而另一些人认为成功基于相反的思维模式，包括努力工作和学习，训练与坚持，这种人的智力是后天累加的，即成长思维模型。

个体可能对自己的思维模型并没有意识，但还是可以根据他们的行为辨别出来。特别是在看待失败这件事上。固定思维模式的人害怕失败，他们认为这是对自己能力的否定；而成长思维模式的人不介意或不害怕失败，因为他们认为自己的表现可以提高，失败让自己学到了很多东西。这两种思维模型在一个人的生活的方方面面中都扮演这重要的角色。德维克认为，拥有成长思维模式的人压力会更小，生活得更成功。

1 以下哪两个观点是正确的？

A 德维克相信成功基于人的天生；原文的确提道：Some believe their success is based on innate ability，但这并不是德维克的观点；

B 德维克根据人们关于能力与成功的看法将他们分类；

C 人们并不常意识到自己是哪一种思维模型；原文提到了：Individuals may not necessarily be aware of their own mindset；

D 固定思维模式的人比成长思维模式的人失败的更多一些；原文的确说到了：growth mindset...more successful life，成长思维模式的人会拥有一个更成功的人生，但原文并没有说固定思维模式的人失败会更频繁；

词汇

established 设立   industrialist 实业家   armaments manufacturer 武器制造商
fraternity 友好   abolition 废止   standing armies 常备军队   peace activist 反战人士
recipient 接受   profoundly 极大的   compensate 补偿   destructive force 破坏力

翻译&解析

诺贝尔和平奖是由瑞典实业家、发明家和武器制造商阿尔弗雷德·诺贝尔的遗嘱设立的五个诺贝尔奖之一，此外还有化学、物理、生理学、医学和文学奖。自1903年以来，它每年（除例外）会颁发给那些"为了国与国之间的友好发展、为废除或裁减常备军队以及为促进和平做出最大贡献或付出最多努力的人"。

诺贝尔于1896年去世，他并没有对和平奖做出具体的获奖解释。由于他是一名职业化学家，所以评定化学奖和物流学奖的标准非常清晰，但和平奖的评奖标准就很模糊了。根据挪威诺贝尔奖委员会称，他与和反战人士、后来获得诺贝尔奖和平奖的伯莎·冯·萨特纳私交很深，这深刻影响了他设立和平奖的决定。一些研究诺贝尔的学者认为，这是他对于不断发展的破坏力工具的一种补偿。诺贝尔的发明就包括无烟火药和甘油炸药，他亲历了这些发明的破坏性。

1 以下哪两个判断是正确的？

A 诺奖的创建者是一名武器制造商；题干的producer of weapons与原文的armaments manufacturer是同义词组；

B 诺奖是一个有争议的奖项；原文只是说The reasoning behind the peace prize is less clear，不清晰的是设立这个奖项的理由，而不是评奖的标准；

C 诺贝尔是一个反战人士；反战的是他朋友*Bertha von Suttner*不是诺贝尔本人；

D 和平奖是在诺贝尔朋友的建议下设立的；原文说：his friendship with…influenced his decision to include peace as a category，他确实受到朋友的影响，但是否是朋友直接建议的，根据原文未可知；

E 诺贝尔见到了自己发明的破坏性；原文的destructive application of与题干的used violently是同义词组；

词汇

life-supporting 维持生命的　　catchy name 好记的名字　　orbits 轨道

habitable 适宜居住的　Goldilocks 金发姑娘　sustain 维持　porridge 粥

constellation 星座

○ 翻译&解析 ○

　　一个新的"超级地球"被发现了，它可能有适合生命生存的气候和水。这颗星球被命名为HD40307D，它是在一个距离太阳42光年的太阳系中被发现的。它与恒星的距离刚好可以容纳液态的地表水。它的轨道在恒星的"宜居带"或称"金发姑娘带"，这个区域的温度既不冷也不热，适合生命生存。

　　来自赫特福德大学的Hugh Jones教授说："新行星的轨道越长意味着它的气候和大气刚好能够支持生命。就像童话里的金发姑娘喝的粥一样，既不太冷也不太热刚刚好。这颗行星的卫星轨道也与地球相似，这也增加了它的宜居可能性。""超级星球"是围绕着位于皮克托星座矮恒星HD40307的六颗行星之一的星球。其他的星球都位于宜居带之外，离母恒星太近，无法形成液态水。

　　1 为什么这是一颗宜居星球？

　　A 它有液态水；原文中说的是could have，所以是否真正液态水我们并不知道；

　　B 它离太阳有42光年；原文的确说到...42 light years from the Sun，但真正适合居住的原因是and后面的...lies at exactly the right distance from its star；

　　C 它以完美的距离环绕恒星运行；

　　D 它有几个卫星；原文提到了...this planet or indeed any moons that is has lie in an orbit comparable to Earth，但它宜居的根本原因还是因为它距离恒星的距离；

　　2 哪个对于"金发姑娘带"的描述是正确的？

　　A 有宜居气候的星球的区域；

　　B 距离母恒星较近的区域；"金发姑娘带"是不能离母行星太近的；

　　C 拥有数个卫星和长轨道的星球；它是一个zone，而不是一个planet；

　　D 它是一个与地球轨道类似的区域；

词 汇

groundbreaking discoveries 突破性的发现　　sizing up 打量　　freshman 大一新生

distilled into 形成　　grasp 理解　　reimagine 再定义　　quantum mechanics 量子力学

翻译&解析

物理学家理查德·费曼一次又一次地提出了突破性的想法。他的方法被加州理工学院的同事大卫·古德斯坦记录在《费曼遗失的物理讲座》（费曼1960年代的讲座）：

曾经又一次我对他说："迪克，给我解释一下，这样我就能理解了，为什么自旋半粒子要服从费米狄拉克统计？"费曼打量了一下听众，然后说："我会针对它准备一个新生讲座。"但几天后他说："我不能这么做，这不是新生的能力水平接受得了的，他们并不能够真正理解。"

费曼这么说并不意味着所有人类知识都必须提炼到大学入门课程中去。不过他认为如果要掌握一门科学技术就必须从理论开始学习，同时还要了解它的知识结构。在学生时代他就很有名了，他自己重做了很多物理学早期实验，以建立对该领域的基本理解。通过掌握这些第一性原理，费曼经常在量子力学，计算机学和核物理学中发现其他人看不到的东西，他在1965年获得了诺贝尔奖。

1 当被问到难以解释的概念时，费曼会：

A 迅速回复说他不懂；选择这个选项的同学是因为看到原文有...That means we don't really understand it，但这里的we指的是同学们，不是费曼自己；

B 已经为这个知识做过讲座了；根据原文，他最后其实没有做；

C 回复说他也不理解这个概念；这个错误原因同A；

D 承诺会做一个基础性课程；题干中的：freshman lecture和原文的an introductory lesson是同义词组；

2 费曼认为：

A 科学家应该掌握基础理论知识；题干中的...master basic scientific principles和原文中的build our grasp of science and technology from the ground up是同义词组；

B 早期物理实验需要重做；原文中说...redoing many of physics' early experiments himself,

但并不是说所有人都应当这么做；

C 很多科学专业的学生并没有一个好的物理学基础；原文中并没有提到这件事；

D 他凭借第一性原理知识赢得诺贝尔奖；原文中说...Feynman often saw things that others did not in...earning him the Nobel Prize in 1965，他是因为发现了其他人看不到的东西而获奖，并不是第一性原理；

 第24题

词汇

deforestation 砍伐森林　fertilisers 肥料　pesticides 杀虫剂　contaminate 污染

intensive farming 集约化农业　abandonment 放弃　fallow periods 休耕期

exacerbate 恶化　monoculture 单种栽培　highyielding varieties of crops 高产作物

topsoil 表土层　diminish 减少　subsequently 随后　meadow 草地　vanishing 消失

dramatic 突然的　scrapped 废弃的　conducted 执行　commodity 商品

diversify 多样化　compounded 恶化　subsidies 补贴　immense 巨大的

readily 便利的　enlightened 开明的　eliminate 消除　incentive 激励

crop residues 秸秆　competitive 竞争的

翻译&解析

以下这些活动都可能会环境造成破坏性影响。比如，毁林开荒是植被减少的主要原因；化肥和杀虫剂的使用会污染水源；集约化耕种与缩减休耕期会加剧土壤侵蚀；推广种植单一高产品种会导致一些传统粮食作物的消失，而它们本能为病虫害防治提供天然屏障。土壤侵蚀威胁着所有国家的土地产出。1982年，经过精确测算，美国有五分之一的农田的表层土正在流失，土壤肥力下降。随后美国实施了一项计划，将该国11%的耕地改为草地或林地。印度和中国的土壤流失速度比美国还要快。

1 1982年的研究表明美国土壤侵蚀：

A 减少粮食产量20%；错误选项，有20%的农田遭到破坏而导致粮食产量下降，而不是粮食产量下降20%；

B 跟印度和中国的情况一样严峻；错误选项，印度和中国的情况比美国情况更严重；

C 对20%的农田造成严重损失；正确选项，有五分之一的农田遭遇减产；

D 将农田转为林地或草地会降低侵蚀；错误选项，原文只提到了...convert 11 per cent of its cropped land to meadow or forest，但是否能够reduced原文并没有说；

政府的政策也在加剧农业发展可能造成的破坏。在发达国家，对粮食作物的补贴和对农产品价格的补贴推高了土地价格。这些补贴的数额巨大，约为2'500亿美元，超过了1980年代世界银行的所有贷款。为了增加每亩作物产量，农民最简单最便利的选择就是使用化肥和杀虫剂。1960到1985年间，丹麦化肥的施用量翻了一番，荷兰增加了150%。杀虫剂的施用量也增加了，丹麦1975-1984年间的施用量增加了69%，从1981年起的三年施用频率增加了115%。

2 自80年代中期以来，丹麦农民：
A 比荷兰农民少用50%的肥料；错误选项；原文提到的是增长比例，并不是绝对值；
B 比60年代多用两倍的肥料；正确选项；题干的twice和原文的doubled是同义词；
C 比60年代化肥使用更加频繁；
D 在过去3年中杀虫剂施用量增加了2倍；
这两个都是错误选项；根据原文，1984年比1981年确实是更频繁了，但是否比60年代更频繁原文并没有提及，同时也没有提及施用量；

80年代末到90年代初，各国为减少农业补贴做出了一些努力。最引人注目的例子是新西兰，它在1984年取消了大部分的农业补贴。1993年进行的一项环境评价发现，化肥补贴结束之后，施用量下降（由于大宗商品价格下跌致使农业收入减少，使这一下降更为严重）。取消补贴之后，土地过度囤积和清理的行为也随之停止，而这是之前造成水土流失的主因。农场开始变得多样化。之前对环境有害的补贴变为了对土地侵蚀的补偿。

3 下面哪一项是新西兰在1984年之后有增长的？
A 农民收入；错误选项，这个信息原文中完全没有提到；
B 化肥施用量；错误选项；原文明确说到施用量是下降的；
C 土地囤积量；错误选项；原文明确说到土地囤积在1984年之后停止了；
D 农田多样化；

还有一些不太开明的国家，如欧盟，他们选择减少而不是取消补贴。同时他们建立新的补贴方式，鼓励农民以更环保的方式对待土地或休耕。虽然有点难以理解，但这种补贴额度要必须高于现有鼓励农民种植粮食作物的补贴。农民们利用这些补贴款投资秸秆乙醇汽油，作为化石燃料的替代品，或是使用秸秆焚烧发电。这种燃料（如乙醇汽油）所排放的二氧化碳要远少于煤或石油，且在（玉米）生长过程中吸收二氧化碳，所以并不会造成温室效应。不过清洁能源（如乙醇汽油）只能依靠价格补贴存活，否则就无法与化石燃料抗衡，而且种植它们（如玉米）对环境的危害也不比其他作物低。

判 断 题

第1题

词 汇

notable figure 名人　　autobiographical literature 自传体文学　　transcribed 记录

○ 翻译&解析 ○

很多著名人物的传记已经出版，这是自传体文学的重要组成部分。塞廖尔·佩皮斯（1633-1703）是当今最著名且最早的日记作者。他的日记现在保存在剑桥大学的玛格塔林学院，是1825年首次被转录并出版的。佩皮斯是第一个将记事簿从单纯的记账功能变为个人生活记录的人。

1 塞廖尔佩皮斯现在的名声比有生之年更大；

NG 根据原文，我们只知道他现在名气挺大的，但并不知道他在世时的名气，所以无法比较；

2 佩皮斯是纯粹出于商业原因写日记；

F 佩皮斯写日记是为了记录生活而不是商业；注意一下原文中的beyond这个词；

第2题

词 汇

randomly assigned 随机分配　　emotional trauma 情绪创伤　　participant 参与者

○ 翻译&解析 ○

1971年，津巴多接受了斯坦福大学心理学终身教授职位。在那里他进行了斯坦福监狱的研究。在这项研究中，21名师范大学学生被随机分配到位于斯坦福大学心理学大楼地下室中的模拟监狱中，担任"囚犯"和"看守"。该实验计划研究监狱生活对心理的影响，不过仅维持了两周就结束了，因为所有的参与者都遭受了情绪创伤。

1 研究的参与者全部都是心理学专业的学生；

NG 我们并不知道这21名师范大学学生具体是学习什么专业的；

2 他们可以选择扮演囚犯或看守的角色；

F 学生并不能够指定角色扮演而是随机分配；

3 实验中使用了一座真正的监狱；

F 监狱并不是真的，只是在地下室中的一个模拟监狱；

4 该研究旨在调查监狱生活对心理和行为的影响；

T 题干中的the mental and behavioural effects对应原文中的the psychological impact；investigate对应study into；life in prison对应prison life；

 第3题

 词　汇

geographical location 地理位置　　visitor satisfaction 游客满意度
marae 毛利人的集会的会堂

○ **翻译&解析** ○

　　在新西兰旅游网站上，游客不仅可以按地理位置信息去搜索附近的活动，还可以按活动的种类进行分类搜索。这是非常重要的，因为研究表明，活动对于游客满意度的贡献为74%，而住宿和交通占其余的26%。游客参加的活动越多，他们的满意度就越高。研究还发现，游客最喜欢的活动是文化活动，比如参观毛利会堂了解他们的生活。

　　1 大部分的游客在搜索活动时都是基于地理位置信息的；

　　NG 原文说到网站不仅可以提供基于地理位置信息的搜索方式，还可以按照活动类型进行搜索，但并没有说大部分游客首选何种搜索方式；

　　2 根据研究，有26%的游客满意度是和住宿有关的；

F 很显然这与原文不符，是住宿和交通占比26%，而不是只有住宿；

3 在新西兰的游客喜欢参与当地的文化活动；
T 题干中的like to become involved是原文中enjoy...most；

🔍 第4题

词汇

minority language 方言　　marginalised 边缘化　　uncultured（人）没有文化的

primitive 原始的　　separatism 分离主义　　indicative 表现　　non-integration 非一体化的

notion 观念　　exclusion 排斥

○ 翻译&解析 ○

　　方言在国内被逐渐边缘化的原因有很多。首先，说方言的人不多且不断减少，与通用语言相比，它们被认为是没有文化，原始的或简单的语言。此外，支持方言有时会被认为是民族主义。少数族裔的语言被看做是一种威胁，是一种不融入社区的表现。这些行为都会认为是排斥通用语言的做法。通常情况下，在国家系统中也无法给予方言支持（比如教育系统或司法系统）。

　　注：在教育领域，通用教材不大可能使用方言去教学，而司法条文或政策也太可能使用方言写著。

1 方言有时候会消失；
NG 原文提到了方言正在被边缘化，但并没有提到消失；

2 方言比通用语更容易学；
NG 原文提到了方言更简单，但并没有直接说它是否容易学；

3 方言有时被看做是有害的；
T 题干中的considered to be harmful与原文的seen as a threat是同义词组；

词 汇

marshmallow 棉花糖　　deferred gratification 延迟满足

○ 翻译&解析 ○

　　斯坦福棉花糖实验是一个关于延迟满足的研究项目。这项实验是在1972年由斯坦福大学心理学家沃尔特谢米尔实施的。从那以后，这项实验又重复过很多次，但这次最初的研究仍被认为是人类行为学研究中最成功的实验之一。实验中，每个孩子都可以得到一个棉花糖。如果这个孩子能够忍住不吃棉花糖，他之后就可以得到两个。科学家们分析了每个孩子抵抗棉花糖诱惑的时间，以及这些决定是否会影响到他们未来的成功。该项实验研究结果为研究人员提供了关于自我控制心理的深刻见解。

1 当研究人员重复这个实验时，结果不太成功；

NG 原文中只说到了第一次的实验仍具有里程碑的意义，但并没有提及之后的几次的实验是否失败或是否成功；所以这道题也不可以选N；

2 孩子如果不吃第一个棉花糖，他之后可以得到两个；

T 题干中的were offered对应原文的was promised，managed not to eat the first one对应resist eating the marshmallow；

3 科学家们发现了抵制诱惑和未来成功之间的关联性；

NG 科学家只是分析关联性，原文并没有给出任何答案（比如是正向关联或是负向关联或是毫无关联）

 第6题

词 汇

identification 识别　　characteristics 特点　　traits 特征　　identifiers 标识　　versus 和

　　"生物特征识别"是指通过生物特征对人类进行识别。生物特征识别码通常分为生理特征和行为特征。生理特征与身体部位的形状有关。比如人们的指纹、人脸、DNA、掌纹、手部几何图形和虹膜识别。行为特征与人的行为有关，包括打字节奏、步态和声音。

　　传统的身份识别手段包括基于令牌的系统，如驾照或护照，以及基于内容的密码或身份证号码。生物特征识别码是每个人独有的，因此与传统的令牌和基于内容的密码相比，它在身份验证方面更可靠；然而，收集生物特征识别码引起了公众的隐私担忧和对最终用途的担心。

　　1 生物识别码主要有两种；

　　T 题干中的 types 与原文中的 categorised 是同义词组；两种 biometric identifier 分别是：physiological characteristics 和 behavioural characteristics；

　　2 指纹识别是最著名的生物识别系统；

　　NG 指纹只是生理特征之一，并没有最著名；这道题也不能选 N，因为根据原文也无法证明指纹不是最著名的生物识别系统；

　　（虽然根据人们的常识，指纹识别应该是应用最广泛且最著名的生物识别特征，但雅思阅读的判断题判断依据必须来自原文内容而不是读者常识）

　　3 密码的使用是生物识别的另一个例子；

　　F 根据原文，密码是基于内容的传统身份识别手段，在第一段所列的所有关于生物识别的例子中都不包含密码；

　　4 有些人会担心生物识别码被滥用；

　　T 题干中的 worry about 对应原文的 raises privacy concerns about，how biometric data is used 对应原文中的 the ultimate use of this information；

 第7题

词 汇

amusement 娱乐活动　　underestimated 被低估　　amorphous 无形的　　estimate 预测

旅游业包括：酒店、汽车旅馆和其他类型的住宿；餐馆和其他餐饮服务；运输服务和设施；娱乐、景区和其他休闲设施；礼品店和其他企业。由于这些企业也为当地的居民提供服务，游客消费的影响很容易被忽视或被低估。此外，Meis指出，旅游业所涉及的概念对于分析师和政策制定者来说是无形的。这个问题导致所有国家在做旅游业的信息统计时，难以测算旅游业对当地、国家和全球经济的贡献。

1 游客消费始终大于景区当地居民的消费；

NG 根据原文，游客消费的影响被低估了，所以我们并不知道游客消费是否一直大于居民消费；这道题也不能选F，因为原文说的是影响(the impact)而不是题干说的具体数字；

（不得不说这道题是有点烧脑的，至少比下面这道题要难很多）

2 从统计上很容易说明旅游业如何影响各个经济体；

F 题干里的It is easy to show statistically...与原文中的...has made it difficult for...是反义词组，题干表达的意思与原文完全相反；

第8题

词 汇

patent 专利　　intended 为...设计　　functional and practical 兼具功能性与实用性
reminiscent 使回忆起（人或事）

○ 翻译&解析 ○

据早期的办公室博物馆称，1867年，费伊在美国获得了历史上第一个弯曲金属回形针专利。这个夹子的最初目的是用来把票据贴在织物上，专利里也提到，它还可以用来夹纸。这种设计兼具功能性与实用性，但费伊的设计以及1899年之前所有获得专利的其他50种设计都不被认为是现代回形针的鼻祖。

据美国技术创新专家亨利彼得罗斯基教授介绍，目前仍在使用的最常见的金属回形针-宝石回形针从未获得过专利，比较可信的说法是在19世纪70年代初由"宝石制造公司"在英国生产出来的。

1 费伊的回形针只获得了一个特殊用途专利；

F 根据原文，这个回形针除了夹织物还可以夹纸，所以它不是只有一个用途；

2 费伊的回形针没有我们今天使用的回形针那么实用；

NG 根据原文，费伊的回形针是兼具实用性与功能性的，但和今天的相比较哪中更实用，这个原文并没有给出；这道题不能选F，因为我们在原文中并不能够找到否定题干或和题干完全相反的信息，比如原文确实提到了现在的回形针比当年的实用；

（根据读者的常识，现今的回形针肯定会比当时的更实用，这毋庸置疑。但这不是原文给我们的信息，我们不能用常识去做题，雅思考试考的是对原文的阅读理解并不是常识考试）

3 现如今大部分人使用的回形针是没有专利的；

T 题干中的most people use today对应原文中的the most common type of;nobody has a patent对应原文中的never patented;

第9题

词 汇

minimal 极小的　　state 声明　longitudinal study 长期研究　　moderate 适量的

midlife 中年的

翻译&解析

喝咖啡已经被证实对癌症病情的影响非常小，无论是积极的还是消极的。不过，参与哈佛大学公共卫生院一项持续22年的研究人员表示，"总体上来说，喝咖啡是利大于弊的。"

其他研究表明，喝咖啡可有效降低患阿尔茨海默病、帕金森病、心脏病、2型糖尿病、肝硬化和痛风的风险。2009年的一项长期研究表明，与那些很少喝咖啡或完全不喝咖啡的人相比，喝适量的咖啡或茶（每天3~5杯）的中年人在晚年患老年痴呆症的可能性更小。

1 科学家们将喝咖啡与癌症的加速发展联系起来了；

F 题干的信息与原文完全相反；

2 一些科学家认为喝咖啡的好处大于坏处；

T 题干中的the benefits of...outweigh the drawbacks对应原文中的on the side of benefits；

3 最近的科学研究将喝咖啡与降低某些疾病的风险联系起来了；

T 题干中的coffee consumption对应原文中的...consumed a moderate amount of coffee；题干中的a reduced risk of some illnesses对应原文中的less likely to develop dementia and Alzheimer's disease；

 第10题

词 汇

groundwork 基础工作　　the most influential people 最有影响力的人

the greatest genius who ever lived 有史以来最伟大的天才　　famously 著名的

○ 翻译&解析 ○

牛顿是英国著名物理学家、数学家、天文学家、自然哲学家、炼金术师和神学家。他的哲学著作《自然数学原理》（拉丁文，意为"自然哲学的数学原理"，简称《原理》）出版于1687年，是有史以来最重要的科学著作之一。它为大多数经典力学奠定了基础。

牛顿被许多学者和公众认为是人类历史上最有影响力的人物之一。法国数学家约瑟夫认为牛顿是有史以来最伟大的天才。而牛顿本人对自己的成就相当谦虚，1676年2月，他在给罗伯特胡克的一封信中写出了那句著名的话："如果我看得更远，那是因为站在了巨人的肩膀上。"

1 牛顿的《原理》一书使其所在领域的奠基之作；

T 题干与原文意思完全一致；题干中的groundbreaking与原文中的It lays the groundwork for...表达的意思一致；

（有的同学会查字典，发现groundbreaking的意思是"创新性"，认为与groundwork不符，这样的理解过于片面。如果你通读上下文，你会发现题干所说的意思与原文是一致的。）

2 很多专家都认为牛顿是世界上最伟大的天才；

NG 题干最大的问题就出在很多，根据原文，我们只知道只有一位专家是这么认为的；我们并不知道其他专家是怎么认为的；有些同学会根据常识而选择T，但雅思考试并不是对常识的测试而是基于对阅读原文的考察；

3 牛顿自己认为他的成就不来自任何人的帮助；

F 牛顿这句著名的话，用的是具象的拟人写法，题干中的he had achieved everything对应原文中的I have seen further，而without the help of others与原文中的it is by standing on the shoulders完全相反；

 第11题

词 汇

common wisdom 普遍观念　instinct-driven 天性使然　　migration pattern 洄游路线
powerful problem-solving skills 强大的解决问题的能力　curiosity 好奇心　anecdotal 传闻

○ 翻译&解析 ○

与鲨鱼只是简单的"猎杀机器"的大众观念不同，最近的研究表明，很多动物具有强大的解决问题的能力以及社交能力和好奇心。鲨鱼的脑体比跟哺乳动物和鸟类相似，但鲨鱼的迁徙路径可能比鸟类还要复杂，很多鲨鱼的洄游路线会覆盖整个海洋。不过，对鲨鱼的行为研究才刚刚开始，所以我们还有很多东西有待了解。

一个流传甚广的神话是说鲨鱼对疾病和癌症免疫；当然，这还有待证明。那些所谓鲨鱼能够抵抗癌症和疾病的消息大多都只是传闻，因为果真如此的话，学界或统计研究早该有相应的研究结果了。

1 研究表明鲨鱼比大多数人认为的要更聪明；

T 题干中的most people think就是原文中的the common wisdom；题干中的more intelligent和原文中的powerful problem-solving skills, social skills and curiosity是同义词组；大部分人都认为鲨鱼只是没有什么智商的捕猎机器，但实际上它们有很强大的脑力（好奇心，社交，解决问题）；这道题是不能选择**NG**的，因为原文提到的many species自然是包含shakes的，而intelligent其实就是泛指problem-solving skills, social skill；

2 参考体型来说，鲨鱼的脑袋比鸟类要大；

F 请注意题干中有参考体型这几个字，也就是原文中所提到的"the brain-to body-mass

ratios"，即脑体比（脑袋大小和身体的比值）；原文中提到了它们是一样的；有的同学会选择**NG**，因为TA认为原文是mass，而题干中是size，这个就有点抠字眼了，毕竟咱们雅思阅读不是科学教材；

3 没有真正的证据表明鲨鱼对疾病有抵抗力；

T 题干中的there is no real evidence proving that与原文中的this remains to be proven是同义词组；

 第12题

词 汇

well-considered decision making 深思熟虑后的决定　　work routines 日常工作

have enormous impacts on 对……有巨大影响　　productivity 生产力

financial security 财务安全

○ 翻译&解析 ○

　　威廉·詹姆斯在1892年写道："我们所有的生活，只要有明确的形式，其实是一堆习惯，"我们每天做出的大多数选择可能感觉像是经过深思熟虑的决策产物，但其实不是。它们是一种习惯。虽然每一个习惯本身的意义非常小，但随着时间的推移，我们如何点菜，每晚对孩子说什么话，我们喜欢存钱还是花钱，我们是否经常锻炼以及我们组织思想和每天工作的方式都会对自身的健康、生产力、财务安全和幸福产生巨大影响。杜克大学的一位研究人员在2006年发表的一篇论文中说，人们每天所做的行为中有40%并不是根据实际情况决定，而是习惯所决定。

　　1 我们每天做出的大多数选择都是有意识的决定；

　　F

　　2 存钱是财务安全的关键；

　　NG 原文中的确提到了我们的习惯会影响到自身的财务安全，但并没有提及是否需要存钱；这道题有些同学会选择T，其实是把自己的常识带入了解题，因为大部分都有这个常识：要财务安全就得存钱，月月光是不会财务安全的。不过雅思阅读并不是对我们常识的考察，它只对文章原文考察。

3 习惯至少决定我们每天所做事情的40%；

T 这并不是一个难题，但很多同学会卡在一个词上面：account for，觉得似乎跟decision没有关系；account for即"对……负责"/"导致……"，其实就是决定；

第13题

翻译&解析

美国宇航局发布了一些令人惊叹的照片，比如火星上的"尼亚加拉大瀑布"比地球上的那个更令人惊艳。这些熔岩流是由曾经在这颗红色星球表面流动的熔岩构成的，并在令人惊叹的全新3D图像中被描述出来。这些照片是由火星轨道侦察器（简称MRO）拍摄发回的。MRO于2005年发射，此后不久就一直在回传火星表面的图像。

美国宇航局注意到，人们花了很多时间去寻找火星上液态水的证据，这是生命存在的迹象。但新的照片显示，这颗行星可能曾经更有生命力，它表面遍布流动的熔岩。

1 火星上的熔岩流比地球上最著名的瀑布之一还要美丽；

T 题干中的one of Earth's most famous waterfalls对应原文中的Niagara falls，题干中的more beautiful than对应原文中的more stunning than；

2 美国宇航局刚刚发布了有史以来第一张火星的3D图像；

NG 原文中提到的是新的3D图片，但并没有说它是否是第一张火星的3D图像；这道题不能选**F**，因为根据原文我们也不能排除它是第一张火星3D图像的可能；

3 新照片证明火星可能存在液态水；

NG 根据原文，新照片只能证明火星表面有熔岩流，并不能证明其存在液态水；

（有的同学可能会较真说熔岩流中难道不含有水吗？对，熔岩流虽然是"流"但其中并没有水）

4 照片显示现在的火星表面比以往任何时刻都更加活跃；

N 题干信息很明显是与原文相反的，它是once (in the past) far more active，而不是more active than ever；

词 汇

（请注意，twins是指孪生兄弟中的之一，不是一对）

翻译&解析

在最近发表在《科学运动》杂志上的一项研究中，研究人员观察了10对30岁的男性同卵双胞胎。他们在很多方面都和自己的兄弟非常像，甚至包括饮食习惯，除了其中一个在成年后就停止了定期锻炼以外。

虽然不怎么运动的那个人和他的兄弟有着相同的DNA，但停止锻炼三年之后，就产生了胰岛素抵抗（糖尿病先兆），身体脂肪增多，耐力下降。同时最显著的是，大脑中负责运动控制和协调的区域灰质较少。虽然这项研究的规模不大，但有证据表明，锻炼对人的健康的影响和基因一样大。

1 研究中的双胞胎非常相似，但他们的饮食不同；

F 题干与原文内容完全相反；

2 体格较好的那个比他兄弟体脂少；

T 原文中说到不爱运动的那个身体脂肪增多，那也就意味着爱运动（体格好）的那位体脂率自然较低；有些同学会选择NG，理由是原文中并没有写明体格好的兄弟比对方体脂少，这样的理解有些"认死理"了；

3 不爱运动的那个人在协调测试中表现不佳；

NG 原文中并没有提到协调测试这个内容，只是说不爱运动的那个人协调能力较差；

4 研究的规模意味着无法得出结论；

F 显然这与原文完全相反，原文已经得出了明确的结论；

词 汇

the evidence is crystal clear... 证据清晰表明　　school performance 成绩

○ 翻译&解析 ○

证据清晰表明：体育活动对孩子们很有好处。世界各地的学者都认为，爱锻炼的小孩拥有更好的脑机能、更有尊严、更有活力以及更好的学习成绩。

在学校期间，孩子们不需要长时间的锻炼。2011年发表的一项研究回顾表明，短时间的体育活动，比如10分钟或者更少，会增加学生在课堂上的注意力。那些因为体育活动而得到短暂休息的孩子在学校的成绩表现也会更好，他们表现出更抗压和更稳定的情绪。

把体育活动与教学联系起来怎么样？2015年发表的一篇文章指出：当儿童一边运动一边学习时，他们在标准化考试中的表现明显更好。有很多种方式都可以做到这一点，比如一边跳高一边拼写单词。

1 体育锻炼可以让孩子自我感觉更好；

T 题干中的Physical exercise对应原文中的young people who are active；feel better about themselves对应原文中的higher self-esteem；这道题有些同学会选**NG**，理由是feel better about themselves和higher self-esteem不是一个意思；这里的feel better其实指代的就是原文的这句话...better brain function, higher self-esteem, more motivation and better school performance，是一个比较宽泛的意思；

2 儿童的最佳运动量是10分钟；

NG 原文提到了运动10分钟会提高孩子在课堂的注意力，但并没有信息给出说明10分钟是儿童的最佳运动时间，所以这道题不能选**T**；

3 脑力劳动与体力劳动结合的任务会让孩子收益；

T 题干中的tasks provide both mental and physical stimulation与原文中的when children learn while moving their bodies是同义词组；题干中的children can benefit与原文中的they perform significantly better是同义词组；

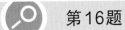

词汇

frigid 寒冷的   natural predators 天敌   sophisticated 复杂精妙的   manifestations 表示

○ 翻译&解析 ○

　　虎鲸，通常又称为逆戟鲸，或又被称为黑鱼，是一种海豚系的齿鲸。从寒冷的北极到南极再到热带海洋，虎鲸几乎遍布所有海洋。作为一个物种，虽然虎鲸通常会专门捕食特定类型的猎物，但他们的饮食结构也可以多样化。有些虎鲸只捕食鱼类，而另一些则以海狮、海豹、海象甚至是大型鲸鱼等海洋哺乳动物为食。虎鲸是公认的顶级猎手，几乎没有天敌，它们有时甚至会捕食大鲨鱼。

　　虎鲸是高度群居动物；有一些族群是家族，这也是动物种群中最稳定的。他们拥有复杂的捕猎技能和发声技巧，并在特定的族群中世代相传，这是一种文化的表现。

　　1 虎鲸主要分布于寒带海洋中；

　　NG 这道题有些同学会选择F，但题干的信息并没有与原文相反；如果这个题干表达的是"虎鲸只分布于寒/热带海洋"我们才能选择F；

　　2 一些虎鲸族群只吃鱼；

　　T 题干中的only eat fish与原文中的feed exclusively on fish是同义词组；

　　3 他们甚至会捕食大鲨鱼；

　　T 题干中的may even eat large sharks对应原文中的preying on even large sharks；

　　4 虎鲸可以将自己的技能传授给幼鲸；

　　T 题干中的pass on skills to their young对应原文中的techniques and vocal behaviors...passed across generations；

词 汇

further afield 在远方　synonymous 等同于……的　enterprise 事业　Renaissance 文艺复兴
permanently 永久的　unrestricted 没有限制　circulation 传递　transcended 超越
monopoly 垄断　bolstered 改善

翻译&解析

印刷业发源于德国小镇美因茨，在十几年间传遍了十几个欧洲国家的200多个城市。到1500年，西欧各地的印刷机已经印刷了2 000多万册书。16世纪，随着印刷机向更远的地方传播，它们的印刷量增加了十倍，约有1.5亿册到2亿册。图书印刷业务几乎等同于印刷业务了，甚至这个名词代表了媒体的一个分支：报刊业。

在文艺复兴时期的欧洲，活字印刷术的到来让社会进入了大众传播的时代，它永久地改变了社会结构。相对不受限制的信息和思想的传播跨越国界，威胁到了政治和宗教当局的权利。识字率快速升高打破了精英阶层对教育和学习的垄断，并提振了新兴的中产阶级。

1 在16世纪之初，印刷机在多个国家被使用；

T 其实在15世纪时，印刷机就已传到多个国家，16世纪则传播到了更远的地方；

2 印刷机之所以流行是因为它操作便利；

NG 原文没有提到关于印刷机的操作，所以我们也不知道到底是难还是便利；

3 活字印刷术和当时人们的识字率提升有很大关系；

T 活字印刷术促进了大众信息传播，从而提升了人们的识字率；

4 印刷对中产阶级有消极影响；

F 这很显然是与原文完全相反的；题干中的negative effect与原文中的bolstered是反义词组；

第18题

词汇

explosion 爆发　digital communication 数字媒体　controversial 有争议的
...gave rise to the question 引发了一个问题　mass medium 大众媒介　distinct 独特的
in the sense that 从某种意义上来说　ideologies 意识形态　subdivided 分为

翻译&解析

在20世纪末，大众传媒可以分为八个途径：图书、互联网、杂志、电影、报纸、广播、录音和电视。20世纪末和21世纪初数字通信技术的爆发引出了一个问题：到底什么形式的媒体应该被归为"大众媒体"？手机和视频游戏是否算作大众媒体也一直颇有争议。

每一种大众媒介都有自己的内容类型、作者、技术和商业模式。举例来说，互联网包括博客、播客、网页和基于分发网络技术之上的其他平台。互联网和手机通常被称为数字媒体，广播和电视通常被称为传统媒体。一些人认为，视频游戏已经发展称为独特的大众媒体形式，因为他们为全球数百万人提供了相同的体验，并向所有用户传达了相同的信息和意识形态。

1 在21世纪，人们普遍认为至少有8种以上的传播媒介；

NG 首先原文中的确说到了8种传播方式，问题就是手机和视频游戏是否应该算作大众媒体仍有争论，题干中的it is widely accepted that和原文的it is controversial whether是反义词组；这道题不能选择T或F，因为原文并没有否定也没有肯定；

2 数字媒体可细分为各种内容类型；

T 互联网就是数字媒体，而数字媒体是大众媒体的一部分；

3 视频游戏是最新的大众媒体平台；

NG 根据原文，视频游戏是否为大众媒体平台仍存争议，文末也只是描述了一些人的看法，并不代表作者观点；这道题不能选T，因为根据原文尚不能得出结论（虽然根据我们的常识视频游戏肯定已经属于大众媒体平台的一部分，但根据原文得不出这个结论）；当然也不能选F，因为从始至终作者都没有否定；

词汇

empirical 经验主义的　　devised 发明　　standard scale 衡量标准　　subjective 主观的

qualitative 定量的　　frigate 护卫舰

○ 翻译&解析 ○

蒲福风级表是一种经验测量法，它将风速与海上或陆地的观测结合起来。它的全称是蒲福风力等级表，尽管它只是风速的一种度量方式而不是科学意义上的风力。

这种测量方式是由爱尔兰皇家海军军官佛朗西斯博·福特于1805年创造。在19世纪早期，海军军官会定期对天气进行观测，但并没有一个标准的尺度，导致他们（的风力评定）都非常主观。最初定的十三级风力（0到12级）并没有参考风速数字而是根据风对护卫舰（当时皇家海军主力舰）的帆的影响来评定的。

1916年，为了适应蒸汽动力的发展，人们将风力等级描述从帆船改为海洋。1946年，蒲福风级扩大了，从13级增加到了17级。现今，飓风风力有时位于蒲福风级的12级到16级。

1 蒲福风级是风力的科学测量等级；

F 这很显然是与原文信息相反的，它只是一种风速测量而不是科学的风力测量；

2 在19世纪早期，海军军官需要一种更精准的方法来测量天气状况；

NG 这道题很多同学会选T，理由是这种观测方式过于主观，所以肯定需要升级；但原文并没有信息给出已有军官提出需求；

3 原始的测量方法是看风对船帆的影响；

T 题干中的the original对应原文的the initial，题干中的ship's sails对应原文中的sails of a frigate；

4 现如今，蒲福风级仍然是描述风力等级的主流指标；

NG 根据原文并不能得出蒲福风级是否还是主流的风力测量指标；

词汇

erupted 喷发　combination 混合体　hotspot 热点地区　astride 在……之上
boundary 边界　submerged 淹没在水下的　submarine 水下的；海底的

○ 翻译&解析 ○

由于独特的地质条件，冰岛的活火山高度集中。该岛约有130座活火山，自公元900年冰岛人定居以来已有18座火山喷发。在过去500年中，冰岛火山喷发总量占全球熔岩总产量的三分之一。

地质学家解释说，火山活动的高度集中是因为该岛位于大西洋中脊和岛下的火山热点结合在一起。该岛横跨欧亚板块和北美板块之间的边界，大部分火山活动集中在板块边界沿线，从岛的西南到东北贯穿该岛。一些火山活动发生在近海，特别是南部海岸。这包括完全淹没的海底火山，甚至包括一些新形成的火山岛，比如苏尔特西火山和乔尼尔火山。

冰岛最近的一次火山喷发是2010年4月14日的Eyjafjallajokull火山喷发，上次喷发是3月20日。

1 大约在10世纪初，人们首次在冰岛定居；
T 这里困扰大家的，应该是公元900年即10世纪初；

2 该岛位于两个地球板块的交汇点；
T 题干中的situated at the point...对应原文中的sits astride...；

3 冰岛附近的海洋也有火山活动；
T 题干中的takes place和in the ocean near Iceland与原文中的occurs和offshore是同义词组；

第21题

词汇

tackle climate change 解决气候变化问题　think-tank 智库　pollsters 民意调查员
clean energy 清洁能源　carbon emissions 碳排放

○ 翻译&解析 ○

美国一位全球变暖政策的主要倡导者昨日表示，深水地平线漏油事件正在促使美国人更多地思考清洁能源的未来 - 但还不至于为气候变化买单的地步。

美国最重要的气候智囊团，总部设在华盛顿的皮尤全球气候变化中心主席艾琳克劳森表示，美国公民对墨西哥湾的污染感到"震惊"，并开始更多地考虑风能和波浪能等清洁能源。

但她也表示，当民意调查问消费者是否愿意为这样的未来支付更多费用时，得到的答案都是不，并认为政府应该为此买单。此外，克劳森女士表示，海湾灾难给了美国能源政策在清洁能源方向上"一个巨大推动，而不是根本转变"，至少就目前而言，还不足以推动立法来遏制碳排放。

1 墨西哥湾的石油泄漏是人为造成的；

NG 题干里的The oil spill in the Gulf of Mexico就是原文的The Deepwater Horizon oil spill，但根据原文，并没有给出造成这个事件的原因；

（虽然根据常识，我们大概率都可以判断出这一定是由于人为失误造成的，但雅思考试只考察我们对原文的掌握）

2 美国公民愿意为清洁能源的未来买单；

F 题干中的US Citizens就是原文中的consumers，原文中明确写明老百姓不愿意为此买单，认为这是政府的事；

3 尽管发生了灾难，政府也不太可能出台减少碳排放的法律；

T 题干中的unlikely to, introduce laws和reduce分别对应原文中的 it would probably not be enough to, bring forward legislation to和reduce；

 第22题

词汇

toddlers 学步的儿童   fatter 肥胖的   stupider 糊涂的   pre-school children 学龄前儿童
bullied 恐吓   cognitive development 认知发展   paediatricians 儿科专家
critical time 关键时期   incremental 递增的

一项最新研究表明，看电视会让初学走路的儿童在小学变得更胖、更傻。跟踪学龄前儿童学习进展的科学家发现，他们看得电视越多，就会导致数学成绩越差，垃圾食品吃得更多，受其他学生欺负的次数也越多。

这一发现支持了早期的证据，表明电视不利于儿童的认知发展，这促使人们呼吁政府应该限制儿童收看电视。美国儿科医生建议两岁以下儿童不要看电视，年龄较大的儿童每天最多看一到两个小时的电视。法国已禁止针对三岁以下儿童的电视节目，澳大利亚建议三到五岁的儿童每天观看节目不超过一小时。而英国没有官方建议。

研究人员说，学龄前是儿童大脑发育的关键期，看电视取代了那些花在"丰富任务拓展"上的时间。蒙特利尔大学琳达帕加尼博士说，即使是逐渐接触电视也会延缓发育。

1 科学家们认为，孩子看电视的次数与他们的智力之间存在关系；

T 题干中的mental ability就是原文中的mathematics和cognitive development；这道题有些同学会选NG，理由是mental ability并不完全等同于mathematics，这有些抠字眼，其实它们是一个意思；

2 在美国，禁止针对两岁以下孩子的节目播放；

NG 原文说儿科医生建议对两岁以下孩子不要看电视，但并没有禁止；

3 法国对儿童节目的控制比英国更加严格；

T 根据原文，英国对儿童节目没有任何管控；

第23题

词 汇

subtle 不明显的　　illuminated 发光的　　immediately 立即

○ 翻译&解析 ○

为了研究饥饿与口渴是如何影响动物的偏好决策，人们做了很多实验研究。研究结果是一致的：动物对食品或水的细微差异有高度的敏感性。

让我们来看一个饥饿鸽子的实验。鸽子被训练啄食笼壁上的发光按钮，实验人员会在它啄食按钮后喂食少量的谷物。鸽子很快学会了啄食按钮。接着实验人员在墙上并排放上两个发光按钮，一个红色一个绿色。如果鸽子啄食了一下红色按钮，它会得到2盎司食物；如果它啄食绿色按钮，它会得到1盎司食物。几乎所有的鸽子都会很快学会啄食红色按钮而忽略绿色按钮。

然而，当红色按钮被啄食后延迟掉落时，结果就完全不同了。几乎所有的鸽子都强烈选择立即送到的1盎司食物而不是延迟四秒的2盎司食物。

1 针对动物饥饿与口渴的实验得到的结果是不一致的；

F 题干中的inconsistent与原文中的universal是一对反义词；

2 鸽子可以被训练做一些简单的动作来赢得奖励；

T 题干中的taught与原文中的trained是同义词；

3 鸽子会选择更大的奖励，无论是否需要等待；

F 这个题干很显然是与原文事实不相符的；鸽子们不想等待；

🔍 第24题

词 汇

ceased 停止　　deviate 违背

◎ 翻译&解析 ◎

27年来，哲学家亚瑟·叔本华遵循着相同的作息。他每天早上7点起床后洗澡，不吃早餐；接着他会喝一杯浓咖啡，然后坐在办公桌前一直工作到中午。中午时他已结束一天的工作，会花上半小时练习长笛，这使他成了一个相当熟练的演奏者。接着他会去他最喜欢的餐馆吃午饭。饭后他会回家读书，一直读到四点，然后每天出去散步；不管天气如何，他都会走了两个小时。六点钟，他会去图书馆的阅览室阅读《泰晤士报》。晚上他会去看戏或听音乐会，然后在酒店或餐馆吃饭。晚上九点到十点之间回家，很早就上床睡觉。只有有访客来访时他才会改变日程。

1 叔本华每天都同一时间起床； **T**

2 他把一整天的时间都花在工作上；
F 根据原文，他中午便会结束一天的工作；

3 他每天晚上都吃同一个套餐；
NG 原文只说到他会去酒店或餐馆用餐，但是否每天都吃同一个菜（或套菜），我们并不清楚；

4 叔本华不允许任何事情打断他的日常生活；
F 很显然根据原文，receive visitors是可以改变他的作息的；

第25题

词 汇

equation 方程式　　hypothesised 猜测　　substance 物质　　partially accurate 部分正确

○翻译&解析○

尽管光合作用的一些步骤还没有完全被人理解，但从19世纪开始，人们就知道了整个光合作用的过程。

赫尔蒙特在17世纪中期开始了这一过程的研究，当时他仔细测量了植物使用的土壤质量和植物生长的质量。在发现土壤质量变化很小之后，他猜测生长中的植物的质量一定来自水，因为这是他唯一加入盆栽中的物质。他的猜想在一定程度上是正确的，大部分植物增长的质量都来自二氧化碳和水。

1796年，瑞士牧师、植物学家和博物学家吉恩证明了绿色植物在光的影响下消耗二氧化碳并释放氧气。不久之后，德·索绪尔证明，随着植物的生长，其质量的增加不仅仅因为吸收了二氧化碳，还有水。

1 我们现在完全了解光合作用的过程；
F 题干中的fully understand与原文中的still not completely understood是反义词组；

2 赫尔蒙特的假设没有考虑到植物消耗的二氧化碳；

T 原文指出二氧化碳和水是植物质量的来源；

3 德·索绪尔证明，二氧化碳和水都有助于植物生长时质量的增加；

T 题干中的both...and...contribute to对应原文中的could not be due only to...but also...；

第26题

词汇

conceived 构想　　executed 实施　　the essential components 最核心的部分

dialects 方言　　proficient 精通的　　scaled down 按比例缩小

翻译&解析

　　铃木教学法是日本小提琴家铃木信一（生于1898年，卒于1998年）从20世纪中期构思并演奏的一种音乐教学方法。铃木教学法的核心理念是所有的人都能从所在环境中习得。这个方法最核心的部分是源于创造学习音乐的良好环境的出发点。他还相信，这种积极的学习环境也有助于培养学生的性格。

　　作为一个熟练的小提琴手和努力的德语初学者，铃木注意到，孩子们会很快学会自己的母语，甚至那些被成年人认为是非常难学的方言都很容易被一个五岁的孩子习得。他认为，如果孩子们有掌握母语的技能，那么他们肯定也有精通乐器的必要能力。他开创了这样一种学习方法，把每一个学习步骤分解到足够小，并把小提琴缩小以适合孩子的身体，让学龄前儿童就开始学习小提琴。

1 铃木相信环境对任何学习乐器的人来说都是至关重要的；

T 题干与原文表达的意思是一致的；

2 他用这种方法去学习德语；

NG 原文只是提到了他在学习德语，但并没有说他使用了铃木教学法；

3 铃木将语言学习与乐器学习进行比较；

T 题干信息与原文相符；

4 他发明了一个新的音乐教学方法；

T 这道题困扰同学们的其实是一个单词infant，它到底是不是pre-school age children，因为在绝大部分同学会认为infant就是婴儿，但实际也可以指a person who is not of full age；

第27题

词 汇

constitutes 构成　merely 仅仅　financial system crashed 金融危机　tackles 解决
head-on 迎面的　envisioned 展望　strayed from 偏离　wide of the mark 大错特错

○ 翻译&解析 ○

什么构成了美好的生活？金钱的真正价值是什么？为什么我们工作这么长时间只是为了获得更多的财富？这是2008年金融危机发生后许多人问自己的一些问题。这本书正面讨论了这些问题。作者从伟大的经济学家凯恩斯开始说起。1930年，凯恩斯预言在一个世纪内，人们的基础需求将得到满足，没有人每周工作超过15小时。

很显然，他预测错了：虽然人们的收入如他所设想的增加了，但人们的需求似乎没有得到满足，人们还是继续工作很长时间。作者解释了为什么凯恩斯是错的。然后，作者从经济学是一门道德科学的前提出发，追溯到亚里士多德提出的美好生活理念，并展示了过去半个世纪我们的生活是如何偏离这个理想的。最后，作者呼吁我们重新思考生活中真正重要的是什么，以及如何实现它。

1 在2008年之前，人们对经济不太关心；

NG 文中提到了2008年经济危机之后，人们开始关心经济的问题，如金钱的价值到底是什么，但并没有说2008年之前人们就不关心经济；

2 凯恩斯关于工作时间的预测太离谱了；

T 这道题有些同学可能会选F，理由是题干里的wide of the mark和原文的wrong表达意思有些许不同，但这其实过于钻牛角尖，它们的大意是一致的，都是表示错误的意思；

3 这本书让我们思考生命中什么是重要的；

T 题干中的asks us to consider和what is important in life与原文中的issue a call to think anew about和what is important in life是同义词组；

第28题

词汇

perceived 认为　invariably 一成不变　mental agility 心智敏锐度

minority languages 方言　enhanced 增强的　detrimental 有害的

○ 翻译&解析 ○

科学家认为，学校和大学应该积极鼓励方言的发展，他们认为，学习第二语言可以提高思维敏捷性，延缓大脑老化。研究发现，学习或说另一种语言的儿童和成人可以从处理两套词汇和语法规则所需的额外努力中获益。

爱丁堡大学的索拉切教授说："很少有家长是因为自己的孩子缺少可使用的语言而对他们说方言。很多人仍然认为让孩子讲方言会让他们感到困惑，使他们在学校被排挤。"这些想法其实与关于双语研究的结果相冲突。研究表明，当单语儿童与双语儿童之间存在差异时，对的往往都是双语儿童。

她跟华盛顿美国科学促进会说："双语儿童往往有更强的语言能力，更好地理解他人的观点，在处理复杂情况时有更大的灵活性。"

1 一些科学家认为应该促进方言教学；

T 题干中的promoted与原文中should be positively encouraged是同义词组；

2 双语研究支持学习两种语言对儿童有害的观点；

F 原文说到，家长们认为讲方言对孩子有害，但这与实际研究结果相左，原文用词是clash；

3 双语儿童往往在智力测验中获得高分；

NG 原文说到了，双语儿童在处理复杂问题时更加灵活，并没有提及他们参加智力测验会获得更高分数；

词 汇

co-occur 一起出现　　restriction 限制　　preposition 介词

○ 翻译&解析 ○

固定搭配指的是一系列的单词或术语，它们一起出现的频率比单独出现的频率要高。固定搭配对一起使用的单词是有限制的，例如哪些介词与特定动词一起使用，或哪些动词与名词一起使用。举一个例子（来自语言学家*Michael Halliday*）说明，strong tea这个搭配。虽然这词组的意思用powerful tea也能表达，但事实上，英国人更喜欢使用strong tea来形容浓茶而不是powerful tea。类似的固定表达也适用于powerful computer，人们不习惯使用strong computers。

如果你经常听到一个固定表达，这些词就会"粘"在你的脑海里"crystal clear"（像水晶般清澈），类似的固定搭配还有"middle management"（中层管理），"nuclear family"（小家庭），和"cosmetic surgery"（整形手术）等。有一些词经常一起出现以至于它们构成了一个新的复合词，如"text message"（短信）和"motor cyclist"（摩托车手）。

1 "powerful tea" 可以用，但并不常见；
T possible对应原文的roughly equivalent，but对应原文的the fact is that；

2 在英语中，"powerful computers" 和 "strong computers" 都是同样接受的；
F 题干与原文给出的信息不同，equally acceptable的意思是同样适用，与原文的preferred over...并不是同义词（当然，也不完全反义）；

3 我们的大脑对一些词组的印象比其他词组要深；
NG 原文并没有给出这个信息，只是说到我们的大脑对经常听到的单词会更加有印象；

第30题

词 汇

embrace 欣然接受　　prosperity 繁荣　　alternative 可供替代的　　standpoint 立场
disastrous 极糟糕的　　city dwellers 城市居民　　sewers 下水道

其实很容易理解为什么经济学家会将城市和它的缺点，以及它的所有东西视为繁荣的引擎。但环保主义者要理解这一点可能需要多花一点时间。城市居民的收入增加伴随着消费和污染的增加。如果你最看重的是自然，那么城市看起来就像破坏的集中体；但考虑到另一种方案，则是破坏的蔓延。《全球概览》杂志创办人斯图尔特布兰德说，从生态学的角度来说，回到农村的开放居住的理论是毁灭性的。城市容纳了一半的人类居民但只占用了4%的耕地，留下了更多的开阔的土地资源。

正如大卫·欧文在《绿色城市》中所解释的那样，城市居民的人均能耗更低。他们所需的道路、下水道和电线都比较短，因此使用的资源也较少。公寓用来加热、制冷和照明的能源使用比别墅要少。更重要的是，密集型城市人们的通勤较少。他们的目的地足够近，可以步行前往，而且有足够多的人前往相同的地方，使公共交通变得实用。在纽约这样的城市，人均能源使用量和碳排量远低于全国平均水平。

1 经济学家和环保主义者现在都能看到城市的好处；

T 这道题困扰同学们的应该是It has taken a bit longer for...，意思是环保主义者最终也接受了城市是对环境有好处的；这道题不能选F，原文中没有说到环保主义者反对城市；

2 从生态角度来说，回到农村是个坏主意；

T 原文中的from an ecological standpoint, a back-to-the-land ethic, disastrous是题干中ecologically speaking, a return to rural living, a bad idea的同义词组；

3 城市居民比普通人更注重环境保护；

NG 原文只是说到，城市居民的人居消耗比普通人少，但并没有说这是因为它们注重环保带来的，所以也不能选择T；

第31题

词 汇

predominantly 主要的   academic term in English 英语学术词汇   competence 胜任
conscious 有意识的   innate 天生的   underlying 底层的   parentage 出身
ethnic origin 族裔

○ 翻译&解析 ○

在20世纪之前，"philology"一词通常被用来指代语言科学，当时语言学主要以语言历史研究为主。然而，这一点重点已经转移，"philology"这个词现在普遍用于"研究语言的语法、历史和文学"，尤以美国学界为主。"语言学"这个词现在指在英语中对语言进行科学研究的常用学术术语。

语言学是关于描述和解释人类语言的本质，以及与此相关的问题，比如什么是语言的普遍性，语言如何变化，以及人类如何认识语言。人类在成长过程中能够掌握周围人所说的任何语言，显然他们不需要明确的有意识的指导。

语言学家认为，获得和使用语言的能力是人类天生的，基于生物的潜能，类似于行走的能力。人们普遍认为，语言学习之间并不存在明显的遗传差异：一个人将获得他/她在童年时接触到的任何语言，而不管其父母或种族出身。

1 直到20世纪，语言学通常被称为"philology"；

T 题干中的up until the 1900s与原文中的before the twentieth century的同义词组；

2 为了学习一门语言，孩子们需要大量的指导；

F 题干中的in order to learn a language与原文中的acquire whatever language是同义词组，而a significant amount of instruction与原文中的explicit conscious instruction也是同义词组，而原文中有**little need for**，也就是说孩子们是不需要大量指导的，题干信息与原文信息完全相反；

3 研究表明，人类具有天生的语言学习能力；

NG 这道题很多同学都会选择T，因为题干中的an inbuilt capacity for和原文中的innate是同义词；但这道题实际的陷阱是原文说的是assume that，即认为，假设，侧重于主观；而题干中说的是research has shown that，侧重于客观；所以这道题我们只能选择NG；

（虽然根据常识，这个题干肯定是对的，但我们在做阅读题时只能严格根据原文所提供的信息进行判断，而不能添加自己的背景知识；）

词 汇

formal education 正规教育　　experimentalist 实验家　　apprentice 学徒

bookbinder 装订工人　　bookseller 书商　　apprenticeship 学徒制

enthusiastically 热情的　　therein 在其中　　eminent 著名的

subsequently 随后　　favourable 有助于的　　sacked 炒鱿鱼

○ 翻译&解析 ○

迈克尔·法拉第（1791-1867）是一位对电磁学和电化学领域做出突出贡献的英国科学家。尽管法拉第没有接受过正规教育，但他仍是历史上最有影响力的科学家之一，科学史学家称他为科学史上最好的实验家。

小时候的法拉第在家中四个孩子里排老三，只接受过最基本的学校教育，大部分时间他只能自学。14岁时，他成为当地图书装订与销售商乔治的学徒。在他七年的学徒生涯中，他读了很多书，包括瓦茨的《心灵的改善》，他对其中的原则和建议深信不疑。

1812年，法拉第20岁，学徒期结束，他参加了著名英国化学家戴维的讲座。法拉第随后根据他在课堂上所做的笔记，寄给戴维一本300页的书。戴维立即给他回信，语言亲切且对其有帮助。随后当皇家研究所的一名助手被解雇后，戴维要寻找替代者，他就雇用了法拉第作为皇家研究所的化学助理。

1 许多专家认为法拉第是有史以来最重要的实验家；

T 题干中的foremost和of all time对应原文中的best和of all time；而experts即指代原文中的historians of science；

2 法拉第通过阅读乔治推荐给他的书来自学；

NG 原文只是说到了法拉第给乔治当学徒，也在这期间读了很多书，但并没有信息表明这些书是乔治推荐的；

3 法拉第根据一位化学家的课程写了一本书之后，成功引起了他的注意；

T 题干中的famous与原文的eminent是同义词，而came to the attention即对应原文的

Davy's reply was immediate, kind, and favourable；这道题有些同学会选择NG，理由是rely was immediate, kind and favourable并不能代表came to attention，这样的理解有些过于狭隘；

第33题

词汇

ancestors 祖先　　clan 家族　　invading 入侵的　　In parallel 并行的　　plethora 过量的

Uni-tasking 单一任务　　Multi-tasking的反义词　　bombarded 提供过量信息

equivalent 等于　　tame 克服　　immerse 沉浸于

翻译&解析

人类的大脑进化是为了专注一次只做一件事情。这使得我们的祖先能够捕猎动物，创造工具，保护他们的部族免受捕食者或邻居的侵害。同时，自身的注意力过滤也在进化，它能够帮助我们完成手头的任务，只让那些重要到足以打乱我们思路的信息通过。

在迈向21世纪的道路上发生了一件有趣的事情：大量作用于我们大脑的信息和服务改变了我们用脑方式。人们被要求将注意力同时集中到几件事情上。想集中注意力太难了。信息时代让我们被来自四面八方的数据埋没。我们收到的信息比历史上任何时候都多——相当于每天175份报纸，这是30年前的5倍。

如果人们需要更高的生产力和更好的创造力，且拥有更多的精力，科学家建议我们应该克服多重任务，而让自己持续地沉浸于单一任务中，比如说持续工作30分钟至50分钟。

1 The human brain is set up to perform many tasks at once. ....

2 The information age is characterised by our exposure to an abundance of data. ....

3 Multi-tasking may reduce human performance. ....

1 人类的大脑被设置为可以一次完成多种任务；

F 题干中的set up to与原文的evolved to是同义词，但perform many tasks at once和focus on one thing at a time的意思是完全相反的；

2 信息时代的特点就是我们会接触大量的信息；

T 题干中的exposure to an abundance of data与原文中的buries us in data coming at us from every which way对应的；

3 多重任务会降低人们的表现；

T 题干中的human performance对应原文中的more productive and creative，而原文说如果需要更好的表现则需要克服多重任务，所以多重任务会降低人们的表现；

🔍 第34题

词 汇

approximately 大约　　alternatively 或者

◦ **翻译&解析** ◦

"人才"一词来自拉丁语"talentum"，它意思是一笔钱，而这个词又来自于希腊语"talanton"，它的意思是一种钱或重量单位。在古希腊，一个talent指的是26公斤，差不多是装满一个双耳瓶（古代的一种水罐）所需水的重量。

当被用作金钱的度量单位时，"talent"一词通常指的是黄金或白银的重量。在罗马，一个talent约为33公斤黄金；在埃及，一个talent约为27公斤黄金；在巴比伦，一个talent约为30.3公斤。按照目前每克黄金38美元价格计算，一个talent的价值大约为125万美元。

另一种计算talent的方法是用它来估算军饷。在古希腊罗伯奔尼撒战争期间，talent是支付trrireme（一种需要170名桨手的战舰）所有船员一个月所需的银币。或者说，一个talent相当于一个技术工人9年的价值。

1 对于古希腊人来说，talent指的是特定容器中水的重量；

T 题干中的particular container指的就是原文中的amphora - an ancient jar or jug；

2 从现代意义上来说，罗马的talent相当于一大笔钱；

T 原文中说到在罗马，1个talent等于33公斤黄金，一克黄金是38美元，这是相当大的一笔钱；

3 Trireme是一群古希腊战士的名字；

F 原文中括号已经解释了，Trireme指的是一种战舰；

4 希腊人最早使用现代意义上的"人才"一词；

NG 整篇文章都在讲"talent"这个词古代的用法和含义，没有提到现代意义上的talent；

第35题

词 汇

paleontologists 古生物学家　　refuge 收容所　　stumbled 被...绊倒　　remain 遗骸

intact 完整的　　backbone 脊梁骨　　rarity 罕见的　　juvenile 青少年

翻译&解析

地狱溪是古生物学家的天堂。蒙大拿野生动物保护区到处都是泥土和石头，这些泥土和石头为我们提供了很多史前线索。就是在这里，堪萨斯大学的研究人员最近偶然发现了一条年轻霸王龙雷克斯的遗骸。

在那里发现了不同时期的化石，这不是第一个发现霸王龙化石的地方，但堪萨斯大学科学家认为它可能是最完整的化石之一。这条恐龙的上颚，连同它所有的牙齿，都保存完好。古生物学家还挖出了它的部分头骨、脚、臀部和脊柱。如果这些遗骸确实属于霸王龙的，那它们的年龄就有6'600万岁左右。更为罕见的是，这些化石可能还属于青少年。

科学家还将做进一步的研究来确定它们其中是否真的有一只霸王龙，或是矮暴龙（一种暴龙的分支），这一点科学界还存在争议。许多古生物学家认为，所谓的矮暴龙化石其实就是年幼的霸王龙的化石。

1 研究人员在蒙大拿州的地狱溪发现了一块新化石；

T 题干里的Researchers指代的就是原文的researchers from the University of Kansas；

2 据称出土的骨骼属于一只成熟的霸王龙；

F 题干中的the unearthed bones对应原文的fossils，而mature与原文的juvenile是一对反义词；

3 一些古生物学家怀疑矮暴龙是否真的存在；

T 根据原文，确实有一些科学家认为矮暴龙实际就是年幼的霸王龙，即它们并不存在；

🔍 第36题

词 汇

Britons 英国人   agenda 议程   hijacked 操纵   ploy 花招   committed 承诺

green policies 绿色政策，环保政策   publicly fund 公共基金

renewable resources 可再生资源   firms 公司   urge 敦促

take the essential action 采取必要措施

○ 翻译&解析 ○

根据一项调查，大多数英国人认为对4X4吉普车、塑料袋和其他消费品征收"绿色"税是为了募资而非改变人们的行为，且三分之二的英国人认为整个绿色协定都被操纵了，完全是为了征税。

英国政府承诺到2050年将碳排放量减少60%，大多数专家都认为这一目标恐难以实现。领先的民调公司Opinium的问卷调查结果表明，保持公众对绿色政策的支持可能是一项难以实现的行动，未来限制燃油车的使用和将公共资金投入到可再生能源的尝试将被证明是不受公众欢迎的。

威尔士亲王昨日呼吁英国商界领袖要采取"必要行动"，使他们的企业更具可持续性。查尔斯王子在伦敦市中心对该国一些大企业家发表讲话时说："我现在急切地敦促在座各位，我们国家的商业领袖们，现在就要采取必要的行动，使得你们的企业更具可持续性。反复强调已使我疲惫不堪，我们真的没有时间可以浪费了。"

1 大多数英国人认为政府是想改变人们的行为的；

F 原文说得很清楚，大部分英国人认为政府的这些行为...raise cash rather than change our behaviour；

2 到2050年，政府将征收更高的环保税；

NG 原文只提到了到2050年英国要减碳60%，但并没有提及征收更多环保税；（虽然根据常识判断，英国政府肯定会上调碳税，但原文中并没有提及）

3 调查预测，人们对燃油车的依赖将很难改变；

T 题干中people's dependence on cars指的就是原文中的car use；而it will be difficult to change即等同于原文中的prove deeply unpopular；

4 威尔士亲王认为大多数企业是不可持续的；

NG 根据原文，他说的是...make your businesses more sustainable，而并没有说businesses are not sustainable；这道题也不能选择F，因为原文也没有说到这些企业less（more的反义词）sustainable，只有当我们发现题干与原文信息相反时才能选F；

 第37题

词 汇

contemporary 当代的　　ethologists 动物行为学家　　neurons 神经元

connectivity 连通性　　manifest 表现　　grief 悲伤　　mimicry 悲伤　　altruism 利他主义

compassion 怜悯　　self-awareness 自我意识　　nonverbally 用非语言的方式交流

in distress 处于危难之中　　hold-up 延误

翻译&解析

很多当代动物行为学家都认为大象是世界上最聪明的动物之一。大象的大脑重量超过了5公斤，比任何陆地上的动物的大脑都要重。尽管最大的鲸鱼的体重是普通大象的20倍，但鲸鱼的脑质量却只有大象的两倍。此外，大象总共有3 000亿个神经元。大象大脑的连通性与功能分区与人类和许多其他哺乳动物类似。

大象可以表现出各种不同的行为，包括悲伤、学习、模仿、玩耍、帮助、使用工具、同情、合作、自我意识、记忆和交流相关的行为。此外，有证据表明，大象还能理解手势指点，即通过伸手指或其他等效物以非语言方式与物体交流的能力。

大象被认为是高度利他主义的动物，它们甚至会帮助包括人类在内的其他动物。在印度，有一头大象跟随一辆卡车，按照驯象师的指示，将原木放到预先挖好的洞里。但有一个洞，大象没有把原木放进去。驯象人发现其实是因为洞里面有一只正在睡觉的狗。等狗走后，大象就把原木放进洞了。

1 大象的大脑比鲸鱼的还大；

F 原文中明确说到，鲸鱼的脑质量是大象的两倍，题干信息与原文不相符；

2 在某些方面，大象的大脑与人类相似；

T 题干中的resembles与原文中的similar to是同义词；

3 大象可以模仿人类的行为；

NG 原文只提到了大象会表现出各种不同的行为，但并没有说大象会模仿人类；

4 大象可以理解某种类型的肢体语言；

T 题干中所说的a certain type of body language即指的原文中的pointing；

5 作者为了说明大象的利他主义，说了一个印度大象的故事；

T 整个第三段，都是在举例说明大象是有利他主义的表现的；

第38题

词 汇

metropolitan area 都市区　　conurbation 集合城市　　metropolis 首府

metroplex 大都会区　　inhabitant 居民　respectively 分别的　　comprehensive 综合的

○ 翻译&解析 ○

"megacity"通常被定义为总人口超过1 000万的大都市。一个特大城市可以是一个单一的大都市区，也可以是两个或多个会聚在一起的大都市区。城市化、大都市和大都会也适用于后者。截至2017年，全球现有37个特大城市。其中最大的是东京和上海这两个大都市，每一个都超过3 000万居民，分别为3 880万和3 550万。东京是世界上最大的都市区，而上海拥有世界上最大的城市人口。联合国预测到2030年全球将有41个特大城市。

相比之下，"global city"，也称为"世界城市"，有时也称为"阿尔法城市"或"世界中心"，是一个通常被认为全球经济体系中重要节点的城市。东京莫里纪念基金会城市战略研究所于2016年发布了全球城市综合研究报告。该排名基于六大类：经济、研发、文化互动、宜居性、环境和便利性。根据这一特定的排名体系，目前排名前三位的"global city"是伦敦、纽约和东京。

1 "megacity"指的是人口规模，而"global city"主要用于表示经济的重要性；

T 这道题没有什么悬念；聪明的同学也能看出来，这个题干其实是对全文的总结；

2 目前全球有37个城市，人口超过1 000万；

T 这道题很多同学会选NG，因为会认为题干指的是"目前"，而原文中是2017年；

3 伦敦被称为特大城市和全球城市；

NG 这道题很多同学会选择F，其实是一个逻辑错误；即原文是否有与题干完全相反的信息给出；具体的说，是否有提到London是megacity，如果没有的话，我们只能选NG；

 第39题

词 汇

blind tests 盲测　　acoustic 声学的　　comparable 类似的

○ 翻译&解析 ○

　　斯特拉迪瓦里小提琴是17世纪和18世纪由斯特拉迪瓦家族制造的乐器，特别是安东尼奥斯特拉迪瓦里制作的小提琴，大提琴和其他管弦乐器。盛名之下，它们的音质其实很难评定或名不如实，当然这个看法也存在争议。"Stradivarius"这个名字已经成为一个高级的词，通常与卓越联系在一起，而斯特拉迪瓦里乐器的名气也非常大，出现在很多小说作品当中。

　　根据情况，在1700年到1725年斯特拉迪瓦里的"黄金时期"，他们所制造的乐器价值数百万美元。2011年，他在1721年制作的"布朗特夫人"小提琴在塔里西奥拍卖会上以980万英镑的价格售出，该小提琴保持完好无损的状态。

　　这些乐器以其音质好而闻名。然而，从1817年至今的许多盲测从未发现斯特拉迪瓦里小提琴与同时期其他高质量制造商的小提琴在音质上有何差异，声学分析也没有区别。1977年，在英国广播公司的一个广播节目中，小提琴手艾萨克斯特恩和平查斯祖克曼以及小提琴家专家兼经销商查尔斯贝尔在一次特别著名的测试中，试图区分Chaconne，Stradivarius和其他三把小提琴。它们其中有一把是1976年制造的，由专业独奏家在屏幕后演奏。在这四个乐器中，没有一个专家能够正确识别两种以上的乐器，其中有两个专家把20世纪的小提琴听成了斯特拉迪瓦里乌斯。

1 斯特拉迪瓦里乌斯乐器的卓越声誉从未受到质疑；

F 这很显然是和原文相反的；原文说到the quality of their sound has defied attempts to explain or equal it；

2 "布朗特夫人"是斯特拉迪瓦里乌斯琴里最贵的一把；

NG 原文只是提到了这把琴的拍卖历史，但是并没有说这是最贵的一次拍卖；

3 盲测表明，专家们能够辨别出著名的斯特拉迪瓦里乌斯的音质；

F 根据原文，专家们并不能够分别出它们之间音质的区别；

🔍 第40题

词汇

inactive 不活跃的　　premature death 过早死亡　　prolonged sitting 长期久坐
shortening 缩短　　lifespan 寿命　　sedentary 久坐不动　　vigorous 激烈的
longevity 寿命　　untimely 过早的　　pursuits 消遣

◦ 翻译&解析 ◦

工作日的轻松可能是以我们的寿命为代价的。《美国预防医学杂志》对老年妇女的一项新研究发现，长时间坐着会增加过早死亡的概率。在研究中，工作，开车，躺在沙发上看电视或从事其他休闲活动的时间越多，她们因各种原因（包括心脏病和癌症）过早死亡的概率就越大。

即使是经常锻炼的女性，如果他们每天大部分时间都是久坐的话，也有短寿的风险。该研究的作者之一，曼森博士说"即使你做了中等强度的剧烈运动，如果你坐的时间太长了，你仍然有较高的死亡风险。"

那么一天坐多久是合适的呢？在这项研究当中，每天静坐11小时或以上的女性表现最差，面临12%的早死风险，但即使不活动的时间少也会引发问题。曼森博士说"一旦你一天坐6-8小时以上，这肯定会对身体产生不良影响。你要避免久坐，并增加每天的运动量。"

1 这项研究只研究了坐姿对老年女性的影响；

T 题干中的looked at the effects of elderly women对应原文中的a new study of older women...finds that；（通常当阅读判断的题干中包含only这样比较绝对的字眼时，大概率是出题人的陷阱，不过本题是例外）

2 在久坐的时间和严重的健康问题之间发现了联系；

T 题干中的A link体现在原文的the more...the more...；而serious health problems则对应着dying early from all causes, including heart disease and cancer；

3 关于久坐的警告不适用于经常锻炼的人；

F 这很显然是和原文信息相反的；

4 每天久坐的时间不宜超过6小时；

NG 原文虽然提到了6~8小时以上久坐是危害健康的，但并没有说a safe amount of sitting是多长时间；

第41题

词汇

breaking down 分解　　pervasive 普遍的　　harbour 包含　　toxic substances 有害物质
ingesting 摄入　　alarming quantities 惊人的数量　　potential 潜在的　　disposable 一次性的
in the firing line 禁止的目标（打算抛弃……）　　magnitude 重要性

◦ 翻译&解析 ◦

微型塑料是尺寸小于五毫米的小块塑料。有一些微型塑料是特别制造的，例如添加到健康和美容产品中的微珠，而另一些则是由较大的塑料逐渐分解而成的。这些微型塑料广泛存在于海洋环境中，它们含有重金属和邻苯二甲酸等有害物质。

由于很多动物都吃了微塑料，科学家们担心其含有的有毒物质，以及毒素在动物体内积累并阻碍它们正常吸收影响的能力。

即使是最大的海洋生物也受到散布在世界各地海洋中塑料碎片的影响。一项新的研究发现，鲸鱼和鲸鲨-这两种世界上最大的鱼类-正在摄入数量惊人的微塑料。这些动物都是滤食者，这意味着它们是通过过滤海水来捕食大量的小猎物。在这个过程中，它们每天吞下数百到数千立方米的海水，它们有可能已经吸收了大量漂浮在水中的微塑料。

近年来，塑料污染因其对海洋动物的影响而备受关注。在英国，微珠已经被禁止使用，其他塑料制品，如水瓶和一次性咖啡杯也逐渐被淘汰。不过，虽然科学家们都认同塑料污染对海洋生物来说是一个大问题，但他们仍然不知道这种污染的影响到底有多大。

1 有害微塑料在各地海洋中广泛存在；

T 题干中的widespread和world's oceans and seas与原文的pervasive和marine environments是同义词组；

2 较大的鱼类最有可能受到这些有毒塑料的伤害；

NG 原文谈到了微塑料的对鱼类的危害是无论大小的，所以不存在体积较大的鱼更有可能收到这些危害；

3 唯一能吞食微塑料的鱼类是那些能吞水滤食的鱼；

NG 根据原文，我们并不能确定是否滤食者是唯一的受塑料危害的鱼类；

（虽然根据常识，我们可以非常确定，一定是所有鱼类都收到了微塑料的危害，但原文并没有提到这一点，所以我们只能选择NG而不是F；此外，在题干中碰到The only类似非常绝对的字眼要非常注意，可能是出题陷阱）

4 水瓶和一次性纸杯在英国被禁止使用；

F 先通过water bottles and disposable cups定位原文信息点，题干中说的是have been banned，而原文中说的是have also been in the firing line，其实就在考 in the firing line这个词，它的意思是target for banning，即打算淘汰，但不是真正已经被禁止或淘汰；

5 科学家还没有发现微塑料问题到底有多严重；

T 题干中的yet to discover和how serious the ...problem is对应原文的there is still a lot they do not know about 和 the magnitude of its impact；

 第42题

exaggerated 夸张　　drawn-out 冗长　　apparently 明显的　　phonetic 音标

tutorial 辅导　　exceptionally 破例　　infant 婴儿　　over-articulation 刻意强调发音

stretch out 延展　　unconsciously 无意识的

翻译&解析

"父母语"是父母用来与自己的婴儿交流的一种夸张、拖拉的语言形式，它是一种通用语言，在帮助婴儿分析和吸收父母对话中的语音要素方面起着至关重要的作用。一项国际研究表明，婴儿非常善于分析这种语言，到他们20周大的时候，会发出所有人类语言共有的三个元音"ee"、"ah"、"uu"。

华盛顿大学的神经科学家Kuhl解释说"父母语是有旋律的。这个旋律中包含了一种婴儿的教程，是一个非常好的语言构建模块。"

这项新的研究调查了美国、俄罗斯和瑞典的母亲对婴儿和其他成年人说话方式的差异。研究表明，"父母语"的特点是发音过度，夸大了单词中的发音。事实上，参与研究的母亲们发出"超级元音"来帮助婴儿学习语言的语音部分。

"在正常情况下，成年人的日常语言是以非常快的速度进行的，但如果他的发音刻意延长一些的时候，我们会更容易听懂。比如我们在课堂上或跟陌生人交谈时，往往会说得更慢，更仔细，以助于对方的理解。我们也会在婴儿身上下意识的这样做，通过放慢语速和过度发音，给他们一个更好的语言信号。"

1 "父母语"并非所有文化都通用；

F 题干中的not common to all与原文中的apparently is universal是反义词；

2 父母在对婴儿说话时，往往会延长或过度强调某些声音；

T 题干中的tend to和lengthen and over-emphasise certain sounds对应原文中的characterised by和over-articulation that exaggerates the sounds contained in words；

3 成年人在与婴儿说话时有目的使用"父母语"；

F 题干中的aware that与原文中的do this unconsciously是反义词组；

 第43题

词汇

Sustainable 可持续的　accommodate 为……提供空间　apocalyptic warnings 天启警告
water scarcity 水资源匮乏　stampede 促使……行事　do its bit 做点什么
charlatans 江湖骗子　peddling 兜售　bewildering 令人糊涂的　frustrating 令人懊恼的
greenwash 绿色外衣（特指公司为树立支持环保的形象而做的有关捐赠或公关的活动）
minimising or negating the damage 将危害降至最低

◦ 翻译&解析 ◦

请问你有兴趣让自己的假期变得更环保、更可持续，确保当地居民从你付的钱中获得公平的回报，同时你的旅行不会导致河流干涸或森林被砍伐吗？如果答案是肯定的，祝贺你，正在成为一个善意的少数派。

英国旅行度假协会最近的一项调查发现，仅有20%的旅行社曾被游客问及关于度假的可持续性问题，虽然他们确实报告了一些苗头，即游客对可持续性旅行的兴趣正在增长。尽管有关气候变化、水资源短缺、污染和石油峰值等问题甚嚣尘上，但社会似乎并没有要求旅游业发挥什么应尽的义务。

旅游业基金会首席执行官Sue说："行业都觉得客户对可持续旅旅行的需求不大，他们并不会敲门告诉我们需要一个更环保的假期。"

其他人则说的更具体，如独立学术研究中心-国际旅游责任中心的哈罗德教授说"价值观和方法发生了重大转变——这不仅仅是旅游，而是一种普遍的消费趋势。如果你担心家里的猪肉是否是环保猪肉，为什么不担心自己的度假是否环保呢？"

对我们这些感到困扰的游客来说，知道旅游业有哪些应尽的环保义务，什么时候没有尽到责任，同时把优秀的经营者和那些打着绿色环保幌子的骗子区分开来的确是一件令人困惑和沮丧的经历。仅在英格兰地区就有大约20个行业认证或标识可供使用，它们一般分为两类：奖项、酒店和运营方自己的等级；以及认证，通常需要付费才可以获得认证。这些都有利于了解该行业的发展方向。不过行业讨论的还不是纯粹的生态旅游，它其实是一个非常小众的细分市场，业界更喜欢称之为"可持续发展"或"负责任的"旅游业。

"很多人错误地认为，当任何人将一项业务或活动描述为绿色时，他们就认为它们是环保的。"Visit England的经理杰森说到。"绿色，可持续或负责任是指确保经济可行性，社会包容性和对自然环境的贡献。"一个可持续发展的企业将尽最大的努力提高财务收入，同时为当地的经济做出贡献，并尽量减少或消除对环境或社区造成的损害。

1 旅行社发现很少有人对可持续发展的旅行感兴趣；

T 通过sustainability这个词可以定位到原文第二段开头，20 percent of travel agents have ever been asked for……对应题干的 few people express an interest……；

2 在英国，认证计划使得消费者很轻松地就能判断酒店和经营者是否绿色；

F 我们可以用题干中的certification schemes定位到原文的信息点，make it easy for consumers to judge与原文中的a bewildering and frustrating experience是反义词；

3 可持续发展的企业在财务上比不环保的企业更成功；

NG 原文中并没有将环保与不环保企业的财务收入进行比较；虽然通过常识判断，可持续发展的企业在长期财务回报会高于不环保的企业，但这并不体现在本文中；

标题配对题

第1题

词汇

villagers 村民   rural inhabitants 农民   district authorities 地区当局

翻译&解析

MIRTP项目初期采用了"上级命令下级"的执行办法，这种办法没有采纳基层的意见，而是由上头的专家和政府官员拍板决定。这样的做法招致了很多非议，但从政府高层指导实施又非常有必要，因为没有当局的支持和理解，就无法满足村民的需求。

虽然这种做法收到了很多批评，但从政府层面开始贯彻实施又非常有必要。

A 政府的合作；这显然和本文不符，政府并没有选择采纳基层的意见；

B 政府的理解与支持；题干中的co-operation对应原文中的support and understanding；本段内容主要就是在解释MIRTP项目的执行办法的合理性；

第2题

词汇

estuary 河口   the most heavily populated areas 人口最稠密的地区   degradation 恶化
overgrazing 过度放牧   overfishing 过度捕捞   drainage 排放   flood control 防洪
water diversion 引水（灌溉）

翻译&解析

所谓河口是指一个部分封闭的海岸水体，有一条或多条河流或溪流注入，并与公海连接。河口是世界上人口分布最稠密的地区之一，大约60%的世界人口居住在河口和海岸线。这直接导致河口地区环境因为以下多种因素而不断退化，包括过度放牧，过度耕种，过度捕捞等；湿地污染排放；污染物与污水的流入；还有为了防洪或饮水而筑起的堤坝。

A 河口对环境的影响；这里注意一下the environmental impact of estuaries是指河口对环境的影响，而不是环境对河口的影响；本文很明显讲的是人类活动对河口的影响；

B 人类活动对特定海岸的影响；本段中As a result之后的内容其实就是说哪些因素导致了河口的退化，而所有这些因素都属于人类活动；

C 为什么河口消失了；的确在退化但还不至于消失；

 第3题

词 汇

underwent 经历　intensively 集中的　extensively 广泛的　occasionally 偶尔的
patron 老主顾

○ 翻译&解析 ○

　　阅读这件事在18世纪经历了很大的变化。直到1750年，阅读一直是"集中"进行的：人们只有少量书籍可供阅读，且习惯反复阅读，通常也是一小撮人一起读。直到1750年之后，人们开始"广泛"阅读，可供阅读的书越来越多，且更多倾向于独自阅读。以低价出借图书的图书馆开始出现，书店也会向顾客提供借阅服务。咖啡馆也会向顾客提供书籍、杂志甚至是流行小说来阅读。

A 第一个公共图书馆的出现；原文没有说到这是first public libraries且这也不是本段大意；

B 集中与广泛的阅读习惯；原文这部分确实是在讲intensively reading和extensively reading，但这不是全段大意；

C 阅读革命；整段话其实就在围绕第一句话展开，题干的revolution与原文的underwent serious changes是同义词组；

 第4题

词 汇

incorporating 使并入　lexicographers 词典编纂者　vibrant 充满生机的
vernacular 方言　discreetly 谨慎的　transcribed 抄录　computerised 数据化的

词典出版者有史以来第一次将真实的口语词汇收录到他们的数据中。这项计划可以让词典编纂者能够接触到一种更具活力的、最新的、以前从未研究过的白话文。在一个研究项目中，150名志愿者将录音机别在腰上，记录他们两周内的所有谈话。 当所有数据被回收时，录音带的长度是大西洋是深度的35倍，打字员将录音整理了成了1 000万字的数据。

A 一种新的研究方法；

B 第一次对口语的研究；

这两个答案看似很接近。但是，整段话其实并不是对于口语的研究，而是第一次将英语口语作为编著字典的数据来源。换句话说，这是语言学家使用一种新的方法来编著字典，而不是对口语的研究。

🔍 **第5题**

词 汇

blend 混合　　approximate 近似　　decode 理解

"语音"指的是教讲英语的如何说该语言的方法。年轻的学习者被教导将口语的发音与字母或字母组合联系到一起。比如，他们可能被教导说/k/可以用拼写c, k, ck, ch或q来表示。通过使用语音，老师向学习者展示如何将字母的发音混合在一起，这样即使是不认识的单词也能够读出来。它是一种广泛使用的教授儿童说文解字的方法。儿童通常在5岁或6岁开始学习使用语音进行朗读。

A 一种语言学习的新方法；原文中提到它已经方法使用了，所以绝对不是一种新的方法；

B 发音如何帮助英国儿童；本段中完全没有指定特定国家的儿童，发音并不仅仅帮助英国儿童（虽然人们潜意识认为英语就是英国）；

C 儿童将发音与拼写联系起来；本段中主要在解释这种方法；

D 儿童学习拼写的规则（rule）；全文中反复提到的都是method，而不是rule；

第6题

词汇

mock-up 实体模型　　devise 发明　　gauge 测量　　painstaking work 艰苦的工作
hands-on experience 第一手的经验

○ 翻译&解析 ○

　　MIT的John领导的一个小组利用3D激光打印技术将法国的布尔日大教堂进行了精确的1:50复制。研究人员希望通过这个模型设计出一种方法来检测砖石古建筑的稳定性，从而检测其安全性。

　　制作复制品是一项艰苦的工作，但John认为，这个过程本身就非常有价值。因为对于建筑学和结构工程学专业的学生来说，实际操作经验在很大程度上已经没有计算机建模重要了。3D打印技术可能是将科学与工艺结合起来的一种新方式。

　　A 3D打印一座古建筑；本文第一句话就统领了全文，这正是本文标题；

　　B 3D打印的好处；原文中说到了学生通过这个过程能学到很多知识，很有价值，但它并不能代表3D打印的好处，全文也没有提到3D打印的好处（虽然我们通过文字能感觉出来）；

　　C 计算机建模还是实际操作经验；原文的确给出了这个问题的答案，但这并不是全文的主体内容；

　　D 危房教堂的重建；原文只是说到用3D打印的方法检测教堂的安全性，但并没有说教堂已经是危房，并且这也不是本文的主题；

 第7题

○ 翻译&解析 ○

　　托马斯·爱迪生是一位美国发明家和商人。他开发了很多设备，对世界各地的生活产生了重大影响。他的发明包括留声机、摄影机和耐用的灯泡。爱迪生是最早将大规模生产和大规模团队合作的原则应用于发明过程的发明家之一。因此，他也被认为是第一个工业研究实验室的创立者。爱迪生是历史上排名第四的多产发明家，名下拥有1093项美国专利，以及英国，法国和德国的多项专利。他在电信领域也有很多发明，为大众传播作出极大贡献。

A 世界上第一个工业实验室的发明人；这句话在文中有所体现，但不能代表全文；

B 一个具有开拓性的多产发明家；整篇文章都在围绕他发明家的身份做介绍；

C 爱迪生对于大众媒体的贡献；这个内容只出现在本文最后一句；

 第8题

词汇

challenging children 调皮捣蛋的孩子　　consequence 后果　　expulsion 开除

suspension 停学　　corporal punishment 体罚　　contemporary psychological 当代心理学

children's behaviour problems 儿童行为不端问题　　disciplinary methods 惩戒措施

exacerbate 加剧　　sacrifice 牺牲　　definitively 最终的　　momentary 片刻的

○ 翻译&解析 ○

　　对付调皮捣蛋的学生的宗旨一直植根于20世纪中期斯金纳的哲学中，即人类的行为由后果决定，而不端的行为必须受到惩罚。2011到12学年，美国教育部做了一个统计，在4 900万中小学生中有13万人被开除学籍，约700万人被停学，也就是说，七个孩子里面就有一个被停学过。此外，据估计，美国校园内每年发生25万起体罚事件。

　　不过当代心理学研究表明，这些标准的惩罚方法非但不能解决儿童行为不端的问题，反而往往会加剧问题的恶化。这种做法其实是牺牲长期目标（学生行为的改善）来换取课堂上短暂的安宁。

　　A 美国学校的行为管理可能弊大于利；本文第一段描述了当下美国教育系统是如何规范学生行为的，第二段谈到了这种做法是弊大于利的；

　　B 如何更好规范学生的行为；原文已经说到目前的手段其实是加剧问题的恶化，所以并没有提到一个更好的解决办法（也许在接下来的几个自然段会给出）；

　　C 美国教育系统崩溃了；原文并没有这么悲观；

　　D 学校纪律规范的长期目标；本文只在第二段提到了学校纪律规范的长期目标是学生行为改善，但这并不是全文的主要内容；

词 汇

politician 从政者　　underperforming 表现不佳的　　pupil 学生　　tightly 牢固的

crunching 运算　　tweak 调整　　narrowly 狭隘的　　watchword 口号

technocrats 技术官僚

○ 翻译&解析 ○

"大数据"一词越来越多地被政客们使用。它指的是这样一种概念，即不管任何问题-从学习成绩不好的学生到管理不善的医院-都可以通过收集一些高度集中的数据并加以分析处理并做出调整（如给学生调班或给护士轮班等）来解决。这其实是一种狭隘的关注"什么在起作用"的解决表面问题的方法，而不是费心地问"为什么会起作用"的根本方法。它是一种"小聪明"，很容易取得效果，但并不正确。民众信任受过高等教育的技术官僚，自然对公开辩论不感兴趣。受过高等教育的技术官僚也没有兴趣向公众进行解释。

A 数据如何促进社会发展；整篇义章其实更多的是在批评政客使用大数据而不是数据促进社会发展；

B 大数据：一种适用于所有人的高明的政治手段；但很显然作者其实是持批评观点的；

C 对大数据持怀疑态度的观点；本文在这句话之前是在描述大数据的好处，然后作者给出了自己的观点，对大数据持怀疑态度；同时在后面做了进一步的解释；

D 为什么公众更信任技术官僚而不是政客；这并不是全文的中心思想；

词 汇

pressing 紧迫的　　sheer 单纯的　　prosperity 兴旺　　boosting 使增长　　whammy 厄运

○ 翻译&解析 ○

农业给环境带来的挑战是巨大的，当我们努力满足全世界日益增长的粮食需求时，我们的环境也在变得更加糟糕。到本世纪中叶 - 我们还需要养活额外的20亿人口 - 也就是总共超过90亿。单纯人口的增长还不是我们需要更多食物的唯一原因。世界经济快速发展，特别是印度和中国，这带动了人们对肉蛋和奶制品的需求，从而增加了更多玉米、大豆的种植来以喂养牛、猪和鸡。如果这个趋势继续下去，人口增长和饮食结构不断丰富将导致到2050年全球作物种植翻一番。

A 两个导致全球食物需求增长的关键因素；本文前两句话在讲人口增长对食物的需求，这是第一个原因；后两句话说到饮食结构的不断丰富也导致了食物需求的增长；

B 农业对于自然环境的影响；这句话出现本段开头，但整段话并不是围绕环境而是围绕食品需求增长的；（选这个选项的同学应该只读了段首句）

C 人口增长对于食物的需求；本文中特别说到人口增长并不是我们需要更多食物的唯一原因，接下来解释了第二个原因；

 第11题

词 汇

immutable 极限的　　theoretical 理论的　　verified 证实的

infant mortality 婴儿出生死亡率　　longevity 长寿　　salubrious 更有益于健康的

○ 翻译&解析 ○

A 人类衰老的一个根本问题就是：人和其他动物是否拥有一个极限寿命？一项理论研究表明，人类的终极寿命是125年。根据吉尼斯世界纪录的现代标准，按照出生日期和死亡日期计算，世界上最长寿的人是法国人珍妮·卡尔门特，她活到了122岁。

本段标题：**iv** Is there a maximum age for humans?

这句话其实就是A段的第一句话：A fundamental question in ageing research is whether humans and other species possess an immutable lifespan limit.

ii 人的寿命有一个极值；这个问题在A段被提出来，但原文并没有给出确定的答案；

B 婴儿死亡率降低是群体平均寿命延长的主要原因，但自1960年以来，80岁以上老年人的死亡率每年下降1.5%。在延长寿命和缓解衰老方面取得的进展完全归功于医疗和公共卫生的努力、生活水平的提高、更优质的教育、更健康的饮食和更好生活方式。

本段标题：**i** Why the elderly are living longer；

B段这句话those over 80 years ...lengthening lifespans and postponing senescence is entirely due to之后的内容其实就是对这个问题的解释；

iii 自1960年以来的医疗条件的改善；它只是寿命延长的原因之一而并不能代表全部；

 第12题

○ 翻译&解析 ○

A 根据弗吉尼亚州艾灵顿的员工援助专业人员协会的统计数据，员工提出的与工作压力相关的劳工索赔数量已经翻番。75%~90%的就诊都与压力有关。根据美国职业压力协会的数据，压力对于全行业带来的损失约超2 000亿~3 000亿美元。

本段标题：**2** 工作导致的压力在增长；这是A段的主要内容；increase in work-related stress 和stress related claims by employees has doubled是同义词组；

3 看病人数在增加；这不能作为A段的标题，因为原文只提到了stress-related disability claims，并没有说他们是否visits to physicians；

B 显然，由于工作压力引起的问题已经引起雇主与雇员的重视。压力会导致生理和心理问题。持续的压力会导致心血管疾病，免疫系统减弱和频繁的头疼、肌肉僵硬或背痛。同时，它还可能导致应对能力变差、易怒、神经质、不安全感、疲惫和难以集中注意力。压力还会导致暴饮暴食、吸烟和酗酒。

本段标题：**4** 压力对人身体和心理都有很多副作用；这是B段的标题，B段第2句话是生理问题，第3句话是心理问题；

1 导致雇员和雇主工作压力的原因；B段主要在说症状，并没有解释原因；

 第13题

词 汇

visionary 有眼见的　　enhanced 加强　　aggregation 聚合　　transformative 改革的
ripple 扩散的　　came to prominence 崭露头角　　precise 精确的　　pedagogy 教学法

○ 翻译&解析 ○

英国奥运会自行车教练戴夫·布雷斯福德有一个简单而又高效的训练方式。他相信通过分解和识别运动员表现的每个微小细节，然后提升这些小细节哪怕1%，就可以使得整体表现得到显著提高。他所带领的自行车队这几年开始崭露头角，他的"边际收益聚合"理念也在学术界逐渐风靡。

布雷斯福德的边际收益概念之所以如此出色是因为它非常灵活。它提供了一种通俗易懂、精确且有用的语言，能够以各种方式帮助到学校：从学生改进学习，到教师寻求提升教学方法，甚至是学校领导希望作出微小但非常显著的改进。

A 一个有洞见的自行车教练的故事；选这个标题的同学应该只读了第一句话，认为它能够统领全文，但从整体内容来看，更多的还是关于边际效益的理论与实践，而不是布雷斯福德本人；

B 自行车的"边际效益"理论在学校中的实践；本文分为两段，第一段解释了什么是"边际效益"理论，第二段解释了它是如何帮助学校改进各项工作的；

C 英国自行车在奥运会的成功背后的男人；这句话作为第一段的标题是合格的，但并没有概括第二段的内容；

D 自行车运动员是如何执行"边际效益"理论的；即使在本文第一段也没有提到运动员是具体如何执行边际效益的；

E 奥运会之后学校做了哪些改变；本文中提到了Olympic Games，也说到了Schools，但二者之间并不存在时间先后关系；

🔍 第14题

词 汇

dispute 争论　patented 获得专利权　coined 创造　conceptualise 概念化

○ 翻译&解析 ○

摄像机是一种移动图像摄影机，它还可以作为电影放映机或胶卷显影。它发明于19世纪90年代，关于发明者的身份有很多争议。

有人认为，这种装置是由法国发明家Léon Bouly于1982年2月12日首次发明并获得专利"Cinématographe Léon Bouly"。他还创造了"cinematograph"这个单词，用希腊语翻译就是"在运动中写作"。据说由于Bouly无法支付第二年的专利费，Auguste和Louis Lumiere兄弟购买了该专利。

而另一个更为流行的说法是Louis Lumière是第一个发明这个概念的人。随后他公开了这份专利，于1894年拍摄了他们的第一部电影"Sortie de l'usine Lumière de Lyon"。

A 摄影机是如何发明的；全文中并没有任何内容透露了摄影机的发明过程；

B 第一台电影放映机；原文只是在第一段提到了摄影机可以作为放映机，但这并不是全文内容；

C 谁发明了摄影机；本文三段话全部围绕这一话题，在第一段抛出疑问，二段和三段分别给出两个不同的解释；

D 摄影机是什么；全文只有第一句话解释了什么是摄影机，余下的内容并不围绕摄影机而是发明摄影机的人；这是很多同学会选错的选项，犯这个错误的同学会机械地认为每篇文章第一句话就是统领全文的，但这其实不尽然；

第15题

词 汇

perception 看法　undergoing 经历　enormous 巨大的　overwhelms 击垮

accelerated 加速　shattering 令人难过的　symptoms 症状　component 组成部分

翻译&解析

《未来冲击》是未来学家阿尔文·托夫勒在1970年写的一本书，托夫勒在书中把"未来冲击"定义为个人和整个社会的一种心理状态。简单地说，它是指"在极短时间内发生太多变化"的看法。这本书后来成了全球畅销书，销量超过600万册，并被翻译为多国语言出版。

托夫勒认为，我们的社会正在经历一场巨大的结构变革，一场从工业社会转变为"超级工业社会"的革命。他认为，这种巨大的变化击垮了人们，技术和社会的变革让人们失去往日的联系，遭受"粉碎性的压力并迷失方向"-和对未来的震惊。他说，大多数社会问题其实都是未来冲击的症状。在讨论此类冲击的是由什么造成时，他科普了一个名词"信息过载"。

A 令人震惊的对未来的想象；两段话都是关于人们对于未来的反应的，并不是关于对未来想象；

B 什么是"未来冲击"？；第一段话是对未来冲击的定义，第二段话介绍未来冲击会导致什么；

C 未来学家托夫勒的职业；原文中只提到了托夫勒是一个未来学家，但完全没有介绍他的工作内容和职业；

D 一个正在变革的社会；全文中只有这部分是涉及社会变革及其影响的，这个标题并不能代表全文；

 第16题

词 汇

unconscious mind 无意识　　dramatically 显著的

non-task oriented behaviour 非目标导向的行为　　essential component 主要成分

implicit memory 内隐记忆　　reveals 揭露　　phenomenon 现象　　involvement 参与

○ 翻译&解析 ○

近年来，科学界对无意识思维的看法发生了巨大的改变。它曾经被认为是一种惰性记忆和无意识导向，但现在却被视为决策过程中的一个积极且重要的组成部分。

从历史上看，无意识思维被认为是梦或是内隐记忆的来源（比如人在不需要思考的情况下就可以走路或骑着行车），以及对于过去记忆的存储。但最新的研究表明，无意识思维在大脑决策、解决问题、创造力和批判性思维方面都发挥着积极作用。无意识在解决问题中比较熟知的一个例子就是"尤里卡时刻"，即当一个问题出现时还没来得及动脑筋就已经有解决方案的情况。

A 科学家提出关于无意识的新发现；

B 我们对无意识的理解不断加深；

标题A和标题B有很多同学会混淆，因为两个标题都围绕着本段的主题：unconscious mind；但仔细一看就会发现，A标题更侧重于new findings，而B标题更侧重于growing understanding；根据原文，我们对unconscious mind的理解是发生了改变，是一个看法上的改变，并不是任何新的科学发现，所以不选A；

C 人类是如何解决问题的；本文的主要内容都是围绕无意识这种解决问题的方式，但它并不是人类解决问题的唯一方式；

D 什么是"尤里卡时刻"？选择这个选项的同学，应该是只读了最后一句话，本段中只是举了一个无意识的例子，叫"尤里卡时刻"，但不是整段内容；

第17题

词 汇

substantially 非常　　rehabilitation 康复　　prevention 预防　　beneficial 有益的

desirable 可取的　　strenuously 费力的

○ 翻译&解析 ○

根据一项有关于跑步与健康的最新研究，每周慢跑5~6英里可以大大改善一个人的健康状况。新奥尔良的Ochsner医疗中心心脏健康与预防医学主任Carl.J.Lavie博士说"跑步的最大好处似乎发生在低强度，"他说，"只要每周跑一到两次，或者每周跑三到六英里，每周少于一小时，这会非常有益健康"。

然而，如果你的主要目标是变得更加健康，那么跑步的里程数应该有一个上限。有证据表明，每天剧烈跑步超过一小时可能会略微增加一个人患心脏病的风险，以及与跑步有关的受伤和残疾的风险。

A 慢跑对健康有益；这个标题显然不能代表全文，因为在第二段明确提到了过度慢跑的危害；

B 跑多少是最好的；本文其实是由这句话承前启后的，它连接的两段话。本文在第一段讨论了低强度慢跑的优势，在第二段谈到了高强度慢跑的弊端；

C 关于跑步的惊人发现；这个标题只适合第一段，不适合统领全文；选这个选项的同学可能只读了第一段的第一句话；

D 常规慢跑的优缺点；本文讨论的是慢跑的程度，而不是慢跑本身的优缺点；

 第18题

词 汇

respectively 分别的　　infrastructure 基础设施

○ 翻译&解析 ○

据《经济学人》智库的一份最新报告显示，墨尔本已跻身成为世界最佳居住的城市榜首。在全球最宜居城市排名中，奥地利的维也纳和加拿大的温哥华分别位居第二和第三。生活在世界各地城市里的市民根据自己的生活情况打分。得分依据治安、医疗保健、文化、环境、教育与基础设施等方面。这是澳洲城市第三次登上榜首。很不幸的是，英国的城市排名非常不好，伦敦在140个城市中排名55，而曼城排名51。报告还显示，全世界的总体宜居水平下降0.6%。

A 全球宜居城市调查的结果令人惊讶；通读整段其实作者并没有表达出surprising的态度；

B 城市是如何排名的？本段中提到了排名的依据，但这不是全文的重点；

C 最新"全球最宜居城市排名"结果；本文就是对全球最宜居城市排名的介绍，提到了各个城市的排名；

D 墨尔本是全球最佳旅游城市；原文只提到了墨尔本是全球最宜居城市榜首，但并不代表它是最佳旅游城市（虽然这二者可能有一些联系，但不在本文讨论范围内）；

第19题

词汇

spreading further afield 广泛传播　synonymous 同义的　enterprise 企业经营

movable type printing 活字印刷　mass communication 大众传播　permanently 永久的

transcended 超出　political and religious authorities 政治与宗教当局　monopoly 垄断

literate elite 文化精英　bolstered 改善

○ 翻译&解析 ○

A 印刷业起源于德国美因茨地区，在几十年的时间内扩展到十几个欧洲国家的两百多个城市。到1500年，西欧各国的印刷厂已经印刷了2 000多万册读物。到了16世纪，随着印刷机向更远地区的传播，它们的产量增加了10倍，总印册大约达到了1.5亿到2亿册。以至于"Press"这个单词直接代表了它的媒体分支-新闻业。

（编者注：press这个单词可作印刷之意，也可指新闻业）

本段标题：4 印刷业大爆发；这个标题的重点是爆发，这正好对应A段的内容；

1 印刷业销售额的上升；很多同学会把这个选项作为第一段的标题，但大家需要仔细看，这里说的是sales，也就是销售额，但原文中只提到了印量（或产量），并不是销量（或销售额）；

B 在文艺复兴时期的欧洲，活字印刷术的到来也催生了大众传播时代，它从根本上改变了社会结构。相对不受限制的信息和思想的传播超越了国界，这威胁到了当时的政治和宗教当局的权力。识字率的急剧上升打破了精英对教育和学习的垄断，提振了新兴中产阶级。

本段标题：**2** 印刷业带来的革命性影响；很显然重点会落到革命性影响这几个字，这很显然对应着B段的内容；而 **3** 新信息与新想法；这个标题有点太笼统了，完全无法代表B段；

第20题

词汇

reveal 揭示　　ingredient 成分　　sibling 兄弟姐妹

翻译&解析

一项最新的调查显示，家人一起吃晚饭会降低青少年尝试或使用酒精、香烟和毒品的风险。这项研究调查了1 000多名青少年，发现那些每周与家人一起吃饭5-7次青少年比那些每周与家人吃饭不到3次的青少年在饮酒、吸烟或吸食大麻的可能性低4倍。

英国最新的一项调查还表明，和家人一起吃饭是确保孩子幸福的关键因素。在调查中孩子们表示，当他们每周与家人一起吃饭三次及以上时，他们的幸福感会更高。"与人们普遍认为孩子只想花时间打电子游戏或看电视相反，我们发现，当他们和父母或兄弟姐妹互动时，他们是最幸福的。"埃塞克斯大学的研究者Maris博士如是说。

A 儿童的幸福；关于儿童幸福这件事，在本文第二段有提到，但仅仅是提到；

B 为什么青少年会有饮酒、抽烟和毒品问题；本文第一段提到了青少年有饮酒，抽烟和毒品的问题，但并没有对其原因进行解释；

C 什么才孩子最想要的？这句话可以作为第二段后半部分的概括，但无法统领全文；

D 为什么要跟孩子一起吃饭？本文其实由两个调查结果组合而成，第一项（第一段）说明一起吃饭能有效降低青少年行为不端的概率，第二项（第二段）表明一起吃饭是确保孩子幸福的关键；

第21题

词 汇

potential 潜在的　　infection 感染　　wounds 伤口　　disarm 消除　　virulent 致病

antibiotics 抗生素　　resistance 抵抗　　tenacious 顽固的　　deploy 部署

unconventional 非常规的　　tactic 手段　　toxin 毒素

翻译&解析

巴西胡椒树是美国南部的一个外来品种，在对抗抗生素细菌感染方面显示出巨大的潜力。早在1684年，一组科学家就研究了它在南美古老医学中的应用历史。据说胡椒树的种子可以治疗伤口，科学家从中提取出一种能够消除致病性的葡萄球菌。

现代抗生素是用来杀死细菌的。但一些细菌细胞存活下来之后会把耐药性遗传给下一代，这使得医生越来越难以对抗威胁患者生命的细菌。巴西胡椒树的提取物是一种非传统的抗感染策略。它阻止了细菌细胞间的交流，从而阻止它们联合起来产生破坏阻止的毒素。这反过来又使得人体的免疫系统发生变化，增强了自身对细菌的防御功能。

A 一种能消灭细菌的植物；题干中的weed与invasive plant是同义词组，busts bacteria与fight against antibiotic-resistant bacterial infections是同义词组；本文从头到尾都在讲述一种对抗耐药性细菌的植物；

B 传统草药东山再起；第一段确实提到了从胡椒树中提取抗病毒药物的事情，但并不是全文的重点；

C 耐药性的问题；这个内容在第二段有提到，但不能代表全文；

D 基于新植物的药品正在研发当中；这只能作为第一段的标题；

第22题

词 汇

multimillionaire 千万富翁　　candidate 候选人　　primarily 主要的

inappropriate 不恰当的　　private citizens 个人公民

丹尼斯蒂托是一个美国工程师和千万富翁，他是第一个资助自己太空旅行的太空游客。2001年，他作为EP-1国际空间站的访问游客，与机组成员在太空轨道上呆了近8天。之后他还被俄罗斯联邦宇航局选定为商业航天飞行的候选人。发射前，时任美国宇航局局长丹尼尔·戈尔丁批评了蒂托的太空旅游计划，他认为游客不应该坐飞机进入太空。

自丹尼斯蒂托到达国际空间站的后10年，又有8个游客支付了2 000万美元太空旅行费用，而且这个数字很有可能到2020年增加15倍。一项网络调查表明，有70%以上的受访者对太空旅行感兴趣，88%的人想到太空行走，21%的人想住太空旅馆。

A 21世纪旅游业的巨大跨越；整篇文章其实都在围绕space travel这个关键词展开；

B 第一次太空旅行；这个标题特别适合第一段，但不能统领全文；

C 太空旅行的利弊；这肯定不能作为本文的标题，因为全文是没有提到任何有利面与不利面的；

第23题

词 汇

numerous 众多的　　unprecedented 前所未有的　　confusion 困惑　　scepticism 怀疑态度
spirited 坚定地　　compelling 令人信服的　　institution 机构　　distinctive 独特的
disciplined 遵守纪律　　intellectual 智力　　harnessed 利用（产生价值）
humanities 人文　　in the balance 悬而未决的　　enlightened 开明的

○ 翻译&解析 ○

纵观全球，大学的数量比以往任何时候都多。但与此同时，人们对大学的办学宗旨产生了前所未有的困惑，对大学存在的价值产生了怀疑。大学到底是做什么的？本书将彻底反思我们看待大学的方式并给出一个为什么我们需要大学的令人信服的理由。

在书中，斯特凡·科里尼对一种普遍的说法提出了质疑，即之所以要给大学投资是因为它们是能够赚钱的。相反他认为，我们必须反思不同类型的机构以及它们所扮演的独特角色。特别是，我们必须意识到，为了扩展人类的理解能力-大学是有纪律的智力研究中心-它并不能简单直接的服务于社会目的-特别是人文教育领域。它的价值很难被衡量，因此也是最难证明自己价值的学科。

在高等教育的未来不确定的当下，大学存在的意义到底是什么？让我们大家更好、更深入、更开明的理解大学对每个人的重要性。

A 我们现在不太需要大学了；原文中的确谈到了对于大学作用的怀疑，但这很显然是跟作者观点相左；

B 大学应该服务于社会目的；文中已经明确说明，大学并不完全服务于社会目的；

C 大学必须证明给它们钱是有回报的；这个意思在原文有所表达，但和作者观点相反，且无法统领全文；

D 我们必须改变对于大学作用的认知；本文最后一句话其实就是在对文章进行总结；

第24题

词 汇

psychotherapeutic 心理治疗学　therapeutic 治疗的　dysfunctional 机能失调
mindfulness 正念解压法　distraction 消遣　overnight process 一蹴而就的过程
adaptive 适应的

翻译&解析

本题比较适合用同义词替换的解法来做题，请注意观察对应颜色的字体。

A 认知行为疗法（简称CBT）是一种心理治疗法，也就是谈话治疗。目前，CBT旨在通过目标导向的系统程序来解决与功能失调的情绪、行为和认知有关的问题

本段标题：**4.**A goal-oriented therapeutic approach；根据原文...CBT aims to solve problems concerning dysfunctional emotions, behaviours and cognitions through a goal-oriented, systematic procedure in the present.

B CBT的具体疗法各不相同，但通常可能包括记录重大事件及其相关的感觉、想法和行为；质疑和测试可能没有帮助和不现实的认知、假设、评估和信念；逐渐面对可能被避免的活动；尝试新的行为和反应方式。放松、正念解压和分心术也通常包括在内。

本段标题：**6**.The range of CBT interventions；根据原文...The particular therapeutic techniques vary, but commonly may include...are also commonly included.

C 对于患者来说，接受CBT并不是一蹴而就的过程；一个治疗阶段通常需要经历12-16小时。即使在患者已经学会识别心理过程何时何地会出错之后，在一些情况下，用一个更合理、更适应的过程或习惯来取代一个功能失调的过程与习惯还是会耗费患者很长的时间和精力。CBT是一个以解决患者问题为中心，个性化定制治疗方案的过程。

本段标题：**1**.A slow process；根据原文...Going through cognitive behavioural therapy is not an overnight process for clients

第25题

词 汇

alphabet 字母表 diacritics 音调符号 loanwords 舶来词 omit 省略
absence 不存在 naturalised 归化 perceived 被认为

○ 翻译&解析 ○

现代英语字母表是由26个字母组成的拉丁字母表，每个字母都有大小写形式。它起源于大约公元7世纪的拉丁文字。

英语是现代欧洲唯一一个不需要变音符号的主要语言。变音符号主要出现于naïve和façade等外来词中。在非正式英语写作中声调符号通常被省略，因为键盘上没有。而如果是专业文案的打字员则会将符号添上。

随着外来词在英语中的归化，有一种倾向是减少变音符号，很多历史久远的法语借词如hôtel就已经取消了变音符号。而有一些仍被看做是外来词的则会保留，比如soupçon是唯一使用拼写符号的英文单词。同时，变音符号还是会长期保留下来，因为有些单词没有变音符号之后就会和原本的单词混淆，比如résumé和resume。甚至有一些外来词需要加音标来区别于英文单词，比如maté，指耶巴马黛茶，后面的é就是为了区分与英语的mate。

A 英语字母表；本文只是在第一段提到了字母表；虽然段首句有很大可能是统领全篇，但这个规律并不是放之四海而皆准的，还是要结合全文来看；

B 书写英文中的音调使用；整篇文章，特别是第二和第三段都在讲音调符号，音调符号的保留和取消；

C 英语中消失的音调；原文的确提到了取消音调符号，但并不是主要内容；

D 舶来词是如何进入英语的；原文提到了舶来词常出现音调符号，但并未有任何内容讲述关于舶来词是如何进入英语的；

 第26题

词 汇

decidedly 显然　　utility room 杂物室　　hype 促销广告　　grid 电网　　myriad 各式各样的

○ 翻译&解析 ○

这里的环境非常简朴：在威尔士的一条死胡同里的一个杂物间。但是如果风口被证明是正确的，那这间红砖房就是英国新能源革命的起点。房屋的主人叫马克·克尔，他成了特斯拉Powerwall的第一位英国所有者。特斯拉Powerwall是一款先进的太阳能设备，厂家声称它是太阳能利用中重要一环。

和其他太阳能电池板的用户一样，克尔和他的家人也有一个头疼的问题。当阳光明媚的时候，他家屋顶上的16块太阳能板正在发电，但他们往往在外上学或工作。他们白天多余的电力会被输送回电网，从而获得报酬。可是自家发电自家却用不上总觉得有点奇怪。现在好了，白天发的电可以给Powerwall充电，而当晚上Powerwall则可以给家庭供电，满足灯光、音响、电脑、电视和无数其他设备的用电。

A 英国的能源革命；原文只是说Powerwall可能成为英国能源革命的起点，但并没有说是全过程，本文也不是英国能源革命的介绍；

B 威尔士走在科技前沿；全文仅仅只是提到了威尔士，没有谈及威尔士的科技发展情况；

C 新设备预示着能源革命 New device could herald energy revolution；根据原文...this may be the starting point for an energy revolution in the UK. ... a cutting-edge bit of kit that the makers say will provide a "missing link" in solar energy；这句话能很好地统领全文；

D 太阳能面板的问题；原文的确提到了大家都面临的太阳能板的问题，这个标题作为第二段的大意是可以的，但它不能概括第一段话的大意；

词汇

laurel 荣誉　　curriculum 课程　　phenomena 现象　　interdisciplinary 跨学科的

perspective 态度　　collective work 集体合作　　preparatory work 筹备工作　　scrap 取消

○ 翻译&解析 ○

　　芬兰的教育体系被认为是世界上最好的教育体系之一，常年稳居排名前十。不过，芬兰教育局并没有安于现状，他们决定在学校系统中进行一场真正的革命。教育局的官员希望从学校的课表中删除学科类科目，比如物理、数学、文学、历史或地理课程。

　　学生将不再学习单一学科，而是以跨学科的形式研究各种现象和事件。比如从历史、地理和数学的角度分析"二战"。又比如通过在咖啡馆实习，学习到有关英语、经济和沟通技能的全部知识。

　　芬兰的教育制度鼓励团队合作，所以混合式教学的变革也会影响到老师。学校改革需要不同学科教师之间的大量合作。大约70%的赫尔辛基教师已经按照新的教学方式开始备课，与此同时，他们也将因此加薪。这些变化将在2020年完成。

　　A 世界上最好的教育系统；选这个标题的同学肯定只看到了第一段的第一句话，认为它就是中心句。但实际上整篇文章是围绕着一个教育改革来进行的；（并且原文只是说"one of the best"）

　　B 芬兰计划取消专业课；全文其实都在围绕取消专业课这件事情，第一段交代背景，第二段介绍形式，第三段谈到对教师的影响；

　　C 芬兰教师喜迎教改；原文的确提到了芬兰大部分教师开始筹备新的课程，但并没有说他们是否全都欢迎；

词汇

intelligent species　智慧生物　　beamed 发射（电波）　　awe-inspiring 令人惊惊叹的

eminent 著名的　　forthcoming 即将发生的　　documentary 纪录片　　cosmos 宇宙

the sheer number of 大量的　　life-form 生命形式　　billions and billions of 数以亿计的

an even greater number of 数量巨大的　　interstellar communication 星际通信

A 在外太空寻找智慧生物似乎是文学和电影的主要内容，但这也发生在现实生活中。美国宇航局的探测器正在寻找太阳系以外的行星，天文学家们正在仔细聆听通过太空传送的任何信息。如果我们在宇宙中其实并不孤单，能够与一个外星种族对话，那将是多么令人惊叹的事情，对吧？

本段标题：**5** 搜寻外星生命；（原文"The hunt for"对应题干"The search for"）；这里不能选择**3** 天文学家在太空中通信，因为它只代表了一部分A段的内容；

B 不过根据著名物理学家史蒂芬霍金的说法"如果外星人造访我们，结果会类似哥伦布登陆美洲一样，原住民会遭殃，"这段话是霍金在即将出版的探索频道纪录片中说的。他认为，与其试图寻找宇宙中的生命并与之交流，不如尽一切努力避免接触。

本段标题：**1** 悲观的预测；霍金对探寻外星人持悲观态度；本段其实并没有谈到**4** 如何避免与外星人沟通，人类不是不知道如何避免，而是不知道应不应该避免；

C 霍金相信，基于目前科学家所掌握的已存在的行星数量，我们应该不是宇宙中唯一的生命形式。毕竟我们所在的银河系就有十几亿颗恒星，（像地球一样）围绕它们的行星更是不计其数。此外，指望能和具有智慧的外星生命进行星际通信也有些不切实际。

本段标题：**2** 在其他行星存在生命的可能性；（原文"believes that"对应题干"probability"）；这也就意味着不能选择**6** 其他行星有外星人；

🔍 第29题

词 汇

reigning（冠军）现任　defeat 击败　tournament 锦标赛　intelligence 智慧

intervened 干预　violation 违反　intervention 干预　revealed 揭示　dismantled 解散

○ 翻译&解析 ○

A 1996年2月10日，"深蓝"成为第一台在常规时间内赢得国际象棋比赛的计算机，对手是世界卫冕冠军加里·卡斯帕罗夫。不过，卡斯帕罗夫在随后的五场比赛中赢了三场，平了两场，以4-2的总比分击败了深蓝。1997年5月，深蓝进行了大幅升级，再次与卡斯帕罗夫交锋，并成功拿下赛点。在决定性的第六局，深蓝终于赢了，成为第一个击败国际象棋卫冕冠军的计算机系统。

本段标题：**5.人工智能的胜利**；整段话其实都在讲深蓝取得了最后的胜利；这里不能选**1.第一个会下国际象棋的计算机**，因为A段并没有告诉我们，深蓝是否是第一个会下国际象棋的系统；

B 失利后的卡斯帕罗夫说，他从机器的落子中察觉到深度思考和创造力，在第二局的比赛时人类选手干预了机器的行为，这应该被算作犯规。IBM否认他们作弊，并称唯一的人为干预发生在中场休息时间，因为比赛规则规定计算机开发者可以在中场休息的时候修改程序。他们利用了这个机会，弥补了计算机在比赛过程中暴露出来的弱点。这使得深蓝在最后一局比赛中避免了曾两次掉入的一个"陷阱"中。卡斯帕罗夫要求重赛，但IBM拒绝了并随后解散了深蓝团队。

本段标题：**2.开发团队的人工干预受到质疑**；整段话其实都在说人工干预这件事；这里不能选**4.开发团队作弊被发现**，因为是否算作作弊还没有定论；也不能选**3.象棋冠军承认了失败**，因为他是否承认这个成绩从原文中也无法得到；

第30题

词汇

chiefly 主要的　crustacean 甲壳纲动物　arthropod 节肢动物　primarily 主要的

bycatch 副渔获（捕捞鱼时的意外收获）　bottom trawler 底拖网渔船

gillnets 刺网　violation 违章　gauge 测量仪　carapace 外壳

翻译&解析

A 美洲龙虾是在北美洲大西洋海岸发现的一种龙虾，主要分布于拉布拉多至新泽西海域。它也被称为大西洋龙虾、加拿大龙虾、北方龙虾、加拿大红龙虾或缅因州龙虾。它身长可达64厘米，体重超过20公斤，不仅是世界上最重的甲壳类动物，也是所有现存节肢动物重最重的。

本段标题：**5.世界上最重的龙虾**

B 大多数美国龙虾产自北美东北海岸，其中加拿大大西洋省份和美国缅因州是最大的龙虾产地。它们主要是通过捕虾器捕获。当然，在某些地区，用底拖网渔船、使用刺网的渔民和带水肺的潜水员也会捕获一些龙虾作为副渔获物。缅因州完全禁止水肺潜水员捕捉龙虾，违者依照规定将被处以高达1000美元罚款。

本段标题：**4.龙虾的捕捞方式**

C 在美国，龙虾业受到监管。每一个捕虾人都需要使用龙虾测量仪测量龙虾眼窝到外壳末端的距离。如果龙虾长度小于83毫米就必须放归大海。缅因州也有130毫米的法定最大尺寸，以确保成年龙虾健康繁殖。

本段标题：**2.**为什么抓龙虾的时候要测量；

 第31题

词 汇

clock up 达到　　meandering 蜿蜒而行　　circumference 圆周长　　mammoth 庞大的

humbling 令人震撼的（这里不作"羞辱"之意）　　dipping down 迅速潜入

constantly 不断的　　energetic 需要能量的　　migratory animals 迁徙动物

marathon 马拉松　　survival of the fittest 适者生存

○ 翻译&解析 ○

A 一只来自于英格兰诺森伯兰附近法恩群岛的小鸟完成了有记录以来的最长迁徙。这只北极燕鸥蜿蜒地往返于南极洲，行程长达59 650英里，是地球周长的两倍多。这只体重只有100克的鸟去年7月离开繁殖地，沿着非洲西海岸飞行，绕过好望角进入印度洋，11月抵达南极洲。它的这些长途飞行是由一个装在腿上的微型设备记录的，重量仅为0.7g——很轻，所以不会影响它的飞行。

这段的标题是：**iii** 一种打破纪录的鸟；本段的主要内容就是在讲述一只小鸟是如何打破迁徙记录同时科学家是如何记录这一过程的；题干中的record-setting与原文的clocked up... ever recorded是同义词词组；文中确实也提到了 **v** 一种跟踪鸟类迁徙的新设备，但并不是主要内容；

B 纽卡斯尔大学的 Richard Bevan 和他的追踪小组的一名成员说："看到这些小鸟穿越了这么长的距离以及看到它们是如何挣扎着生存时会令你感到震惊，"这些小鸟在漫长的旅途中幸存下来，在旅游中俯冲到海面捕捉鱼和其他生物来充饥。"它们一直在快车道行驶，不断移动，"Bevan 说，"它们必须时刻保持活力，这真是一种令人难以置信的充满活力的生活方式。"

这段的标题是：**vi** 北极燕鸥是如何完成长途迁徙的壮举？；本段主要来自Richard的描述，他详述了北极燕鸥的飞行过程；在本段中确实提到了 **ii** 适者生存 和 **i** 迁徙与食物，但都不是本段的主要内容；

C 和所有的迁徙动物一样，鸟类飞行是为了在特定季节觅食。北极燕鸥的迁徙时间最长，而另一种鸟——长尾燕鸥，则连续八天完成从北极到新西兰的"马拉松"，其间没有停下来觅食。鲸鱼是哺乳动物迁徙时间最长的物种，棱皮龟和一些蜻蜓的迁徙距离可达9 321英里。

这段的标题是：iv 其他令人惊叹的迁徙动物；在本段提到了各种不同动物的迁徙记录；

 第32题

词 汇

mindset 心态   conducive 有利于   distraction 分散注意力

basic component 基本组成部分   boil down to 将……归结为   hassle 麻烦

○ 翻译&解析 ○

A 太多的人把学习看作是一个逼不得已的任务，而并不享受其本身；这本身没什么问题，但研究人员发现，你如何看待一件事情和你选择做什么事情同等重要。也就是说，为了更好的学习，你需要保持一个积极的正确的心态。

本段标题：ii 学习者需要一个正确的心态 进行；题干中的in the right frame of mind与原文中的being in the right mindset是同义词组；

B 很多人犯了一个错误，他们会在一个不利于集中注意力的地方学习。一个有很多分散注意力的地方是一个糟糕的学习区。如果你尝试在寝室学习，你就会发现电脑、电视或室友会比你要读的材料更有意思。

本段标题：v 在哪学习挺重要的；本段的中心是围绕学习的地点；题干中的where you study对应原文中的studying in a place；本段虽然提到了专注力，但并不涉及 vi 训练自己长时间专注的能力；

C 用平板或电脑来记笔记似乎是更先进了，但实际上平板和电脑对很多人来说其实是一个更强大的分散注意力的工具，因为它们不是只用来学习的。打游戏，上网，聊天这些都是与学习无关的消遣。所以我们需要反问自己，是否真的需要一台平板或电脑来做笔记，用传统的纸笔不行吗？

本段标题：i 思考一下你到底需要什么样的学习工具；题干中的what study tools you really need其实就是指的原文中的the old-fashioned paper and pen or pencil；本段作者建议读者不要使用电子笔记工具而要用传统工具；本段的内容不涉及 vii 使用笔记去归纳和整理观点；

D 大多数人都认为，有一个给定的标准目录有助于自己将信息归结为最基本的部分。当考试来临时，将相似的概念联系在一起会更方便记忆。写提纲的时候一定要注意，只有用自己的语言总结出来的提纲才能帮助你更好的记忆。

本段标题：**vii** 使用笔记来总结和归纳观点；题干中的summarise and synthesise与原文中的outline, connecting similar concepts是同义词组；本段的

E 绝大部分人把学习看做是自己有闲时间才做的事情。不过如果你能像上课一样安排自己的学习时间，从长远来看，你会发现这会减少很多麻烦。

本段标题：**iv** 要有一个课程表；题干中的stick to a timetable对应原文中的schedule study time；本段的主要内容是围绕学习安排的；

🔍 第33题

词汇

notable 显著的	attitudinal 态度上的	mood swing 情绪波动	cognitive 认知
guardian 监护人	indulge 沉迷于	phenomenon 现象	aspect 方面
substantial 巨大的	involvement 参与	confused 混淆	upbringing 教养
brought up 提出	indecisive 无决断力的	unmotivated 动机不明的	time span 时期
alcoholic beverages 酒精饮料	defy 蔑视	deem 认为	briefly 短暂的

翻译&解析

青少年的心理活动与情绪的变化相关，通常被称作情绪波动。认知、情绪和态度变化经常发生在这一期特殊时期，这一方面可能会导致一些冲突，另一方面也会促成一些性格上积极发展。由于青少年正在经历各种强烈的认知和身体变化，他们可能在一生中第一次开始将朋友、同龄人视为比父母/监护人更重要、更具影响力的人。由于同伴压力，他们可能会沉溺于一些反社会的活动，虽然这是一种社会现象，但并不是心理原因。

家庭是青春期心理学的一个重要方面。家庭环境和家人对青少年的心智发展有重大影响，这些影响将在青春期达到最高潮。负责任的养育方式对父母和社区，当然最重要的，对孩子都有很多好处。比如一个拥有父亲的童年的孩子往往在认知发展，社交技能和规范行为方面都有较高的分数。

在寻找独特社会身份时，青少年经常混淆什么是"对"什么是"错"。斯坦利·霍尔将这一时期称为"风暴和压力"时期，他认为这一发展阶段的冲突是正常的，并不罕见。另一方面，玛格丽特·米德将青少年的行为归因于他们的文化和教养。

在处理青少年问题时积极心理学也提供了一些观点。他们人为要为青少年提供动机，鼓励他们成为被社会所接受的人，一个著名的人。因为有很多青少年发现自己很无聊，没有做事情的动力。

青少年可能在其青春期受到同龄人的压力，而导致与异性发生关系、饮酒、吸毒、蔑视父母或作出其他人，特别是成年人看来不适当的行为。同伴压力是青少年之间的一种常见经历，这会导致短暂或长期的压力。

我们还需要注意，青春期是一个人在心理上取得重大进展的阶段，此时的认知发展迅速，在这一阶段形成的思想、想法和概念对个人未来的生活影响巨大，在性格和人格形成中起着重要作用。

这道题比较适合用同义替换来解题：

A Adolescent psychology...and this can be a cause of conflict...

4 A difficult stage in life；

B ...Responsible parenting has a number of significant benefits for parents themselves...

1 Parents' influence is a key factor；

C In the search for a unique social identity for themselves...

6 Trying to find out who they are

D ...refers to providing them with motivation to become socially acceptable and notable individuals...

2 Encouragement to make their mark in society

E Adolescents may be subject to peer pressure within their adolescent time span...

3 The influence of friends

阅读官方算分/能力描述/建议

正确题数	对应分数	能力描述	提升建议
40	9	该分数段的考生通常能够轻松阅读各种内容复杂且信息量大的事实类和论述类文本。能就通用类、专业性的和技术性的广泛话题，自如地运用广博的词汇知识建构意义，其理解可从句子到通篇文章。能够非常顺畅地理解复杂的论证，区分主旨和支撑细节，理解态度、观点和隐含意义。能够熟练地选择和运用包括略读和浏览在内的策略，顺利理解各种文本。	无建议
38~39	8.5	该分数段的考生通常能够有效地阅读各种事实类和论述类文本，该类文本通常内容复杂且信息量大。能就通用类、专业性的和技术性的诸多话题，熟练地运用十分宽泛的词汇知识建构意义，其理解可从句子到通篇文章。能较好地理解复杂的论证，区分主旨和支撑细节，理解态度、观点和隐含意义；能较好地运用略读和浏览等恰当的阅读策略，并能较好地综合信息和进行推断。	你的阅读能力已经相当不错，但要继续提高根据不同文本类型选用不同阅读方式的意识。某种特定类型的文本通常具有何种特征？该类文本中的信息是如何构成并组织起来的？要学会运用这些知识，并以恰当的方式完成阅读任务。阅读文本时，可给自己限制一下时间。 作为练习，可找几篇关于同一话题的文本，找出各方的观点、看法、定义和把想法形成概念的异同。学者们经常对这些方面做出细微的区分，看看你能否做到。甚至可以试着用一句话来总结，看看能否抓住那些差异。
35~37	8		
33~34	7.5	该分数段的考生通常能够阅读各种事实类和论述类文本，该类文本可能内容复杂且信息量大。能就通用类和专业性的诸多话题，很好地运用丰富的词汇知识建构意义，其理解可在句子和句群层面实现。能够理解论证内容，区分主旨和支撑细节，较好地理解态度、观点和隐含意义。能够运用略读和浏览等阅读策略，并能综合信息和进行推断。	在这一级别，重要的是扩大你进一步阅读的文本范围。同时，继续提高根据不同类型文本选用不同阅读方式的意识。某种特定类型的文本通常具有何种特征？该类文本中，信息是如何构成并组织起来的？需要进行推论吗？文本中有无总结性语句？要学会运用上述知识，并以恰当的方式完成阅读任务。而且，应该尽可能高效地识别总论点或分论点。作为练习，可从网上找几篇议论文，然后找出其观点和看法的异同。
30~32	7		

正确题数	对应分数	能力描述	提升建议
27~29	6.5	该分数段的考生通常可以阅读各种事实类和论述类文本，该类文本内容可能相对复杂且信息量相对较大。能就通用类的诸多话题和部分专业性话题，较好地运用词汇知识建构意义，其理解可在句子和句群层面实现。能够理解隐含意义，也能基本理解相对复杂的观点和论点。通常能够运用略读和浏览等策略，并能大体上综合信息和进行推断。	要阅读不同类型的文本，包括通用类和学术类文本，而不是仅仅局限在你的学科领域。在通用类文本中，内容要点出现的位置可能与你的预期不一致；在学术类文本中，有时作者很少表明观点或者观点很难被发现，有时信息量大。要注意这些差异，并根据具体文本调整阅读策略，比如，何时选择仔细阅读，何时快速阅读。建议给自己限制一下阅读的时间，这样，即便你仔细阅读，也会更快、更高效。
23~26	6		
20~22	5.5	该分数段的考生通常能较好地阅读直白型的事实类和论述类文本。能够运用词汇知识建构意义，但其理解大多限于句子层面。能够理解直接表达的信息、观点和论点，以及部分隐含的意义；大体上能够从文本中提取关键词，但综合具体信息和进行推断的能力有限。	要阅读不同类型的文本，包括你所在学科领域的一些学术类文本。阅读时要学会使用不同的策略，例如，确定哪些部分需要仔细阅读，哪些部分可以更快速地读或者根本不读。也可以试着根据标题或已经读过的内容进行预测，或者根据上下文猜测意思。要重新阅读你读过的文本，直到你确信自己理解了文中的观点和论点。你也要识别出构成文章脉络的重点内容、作者的态度以及作者在何处开始论述另一个要点。
16~19	5		
13~15	4.5	该分数段的考生阅读直白型的事实类和论述类文本的能力有限。他们一般仅能运用词汇知识在句子层面进行意义的理解与建构。能够理解直接表达的信息、观点和论证内容的能力十分有限，从文本中提取关键词的能力也十分有限。	要通过阅读涵盖更多话题的有关日常生活的文本提高阅读能力。应该选择那些有生词的文本，必要时可通过猜测词义来理解文本。也要尝试理解相邻的句子是如何关联起来的。然后（通过词典等）查检一下你不懂的地方，以便提高阅读能力。同时，也要阅读那些需要你查找特定信息的文本，如通知、时间表和一览表。要学会把自己母语阅读中所用的快速查找信息的策略用到英语中，尽快地找到重要信息。
10~12	4		
0~9	0~3.5	通常情况下，阅读简单的事实类和论述类文本非常困难。他们仅能理解熟悉话题中的词汇，一般很难找到并理解文本中的关键信息，也很难有效地使用诸如略读和浏览等阅读策略。	要多掌握一些英语单词。你知道的单词越多，就越容易猜到不认识的单词。建议读些简单的文本。要选择那些有生词的文本，认真阅读，努力找出其中的要点和一些细节。同时，也要尝试快速阅读以找到具体的信息，比如通知、时间表和菜单里的具体信息。

（鸭圈雅思根据官方评分细则制表）